2000–2001 Supplement

The Handbook of Insurance Agency Law

MARK S. RHODES
Member of the Illinois and New York Bars

S·P
1865

STANDARD PUBLISHING CORPORATION
BOSTON ◆ DALLAS

This book contains model laws and regulations copyrighted by the National Association of Insurance Commissioners. The author and publisher wish to thank the NAIC for its assistance and cooperation in the preparation of the main volume and this supplement, and for granting permission to reproduce the copyrighted model acts and regulations appearing in this work.

© 2000 by Standard Publishing Corporation
Published 2000.

ISBN # 0-923240-10-1

All rights reserved. No part of this book may be reproduced in any form, by photostat, microfilm, xerography, or any other means, or incorporated into any retrieval system, electronic or mechanical, without the written permission of the publisher.

This publication is designed to provide accurate and authoritative information to professionals with respect to the subject matter covered. It is sold with the understanding that the publisher is not engaged in rendering legal, accounting, or professional advice. If legal advice or other expert assistance is required, the services of a competent professional should be sought.

Printed in the United States of America.

Table of Contents

Part I: The Law of Agents and Brokers

1. The Role of Insurance Agents and Brokers
	1.4 Apparent Authority	1

2. Types of Agents
	2.1 General Agents	11
	2.3 Soliciting Agents	12
	2.4 Subagents	13
	2.6 Dual Agencies	15

3. Ownership and Licensing Requirements in General
	3.2 Agency Acquisitions	17
	3.3 General Licensing Qualifications	18
	3.5 Licensing Statutes and Limitations on Agent Authority	25

4. Contractual Relationship Between Insurer and Agent
	4.1 Agency Contracts in General	29
	4.2 Appointment of Agent	31
	4.4 Agent's Right to Commissions	32
	4.5 Agent's Duties to Insurer	40
	4.6 Termination Rights in General	50
	4.7 Terminations for Cause	57
	4.8 Post-Termination Obligations: Client Lists, Trade Secrets, and Covenants Not to Compete	60
	4.9 Fidelity Bonds and E&O Coverage	65

5. Interactions Between Agents and Insureds

5.1	The Agent as Intermediary	69
5.2	Explaining Coverage and Giving Advice	70
5.3	Filling Out Application for Insurance	87
5.4	Forwarding the Application Without Delay	95
5.5	Obtaining the Coverage That Was Ordered	95
5.6	Placement of Coverage With Solvent Authorized Insurer	110
5.7	Issuing Binders and Certificates of Insurance	115
5.8	Issuing the Policy	118
5.9	Transmitting Premiums	120
5.10	Premium Financing	122
5.11	Waivers of Policy Conditions, Limitations, and Defaults	123
5.12	Claims Handling	125

6. The Role and Duties of Brokers

6.1	Establishing That the Broker Is the Insured's Agent	131
6.2	Duties to Insured in General	134
6.3	Agreements to Procure Insurance	138
6.4	Taking the Application for Insurance	144
6.5	Advising the Insured	146
6.6	Using Care to Obtain and Place Coverage	151
6.7	Collecting and Transmitting Premiums	159
6.8	When May a Broker's Actions Bind the Insurer?	163
6.9	Status of Employer Providing Group Insurance	170

7. Misrepresentation, Fraud, and Unfair Trade Practices

7.1	Misrepresentations in General	177

	7.2	Negligent Misrepresentation	180
	7.3	Intentional Misrepresentation, Fraud, and Bad Faith	185
	7.4	The Role of Unfair Trade Practices and Other Consumer Protection Statutes	196

Part II: State Regulation of Agent and Broker Qualifications

1. NAIC Model Acts

1.1	Agents and Brokers Licensing Act	203
1.1a	Standard Letter of Clearance	203
1.2	Agents Continuing Education Regulation	208
1.4	Producer Licensing Act	208

2. State Guide

2.1	State Insurance Commissioners	233
2.2	Excerpts From Licensing Statutes	235
	Colorado	235
	Connecticut	243
	Georgia	247
	Hawaii	249
	Indiana	251
	Louisiana	255
	Maine	259
	Montana	265
	Nevada	267
	Utah	269

Index   273

Part I: The Law of Agents and Brokers

Chapter 1

The Role of Insurance Agents and Brokers

1.4 Apparent Authority

Page 10, replace first sentence under subheading, "Custom and Practice," with the following:

Apparent authority can be created by the custom and practice of the parties, i.e., the way in which the agent and the insurer conduct their dealings.[1a]

Page 10, add to note 1a (created above):

Apparent authority found: In *Lenox Realty v. Excelsior Ins. Co.*, 679 N.Y.S.2d 749 (1998), the plaintiff property owner and manager sought coverage under the snow removal subcontractor's liability insurance coverage, claiming that they were intended to be named as additional insureds under that policy. The insurer brought a third-party claim against the subcontractor's insurance agent, who had added the plaintiffs as additional insureds in excess of his authority. The agent testified that it was routine procedure when adding a party as an additional insured to send the insurer a copy of the certificate and that he acted within his authority when he added the plaintiffs. The court held that the insurer was equitably estopped from denying coverage to the plaintiffs and that whether the agent acted in excess of his authority was to be decided in arbitration, at which time the terms of the agency agreement would be construed. The issue would only be relevant with respect to the insurer's claim against the agent.

Apparent authority question of fact: In *Mann v. Interstate Fire & Cas. Co.*, 705 A.2d 360 (N.J. Super. App. Div. 1998), the broker had a written brokerage agreement with the nonadmitted insurer, authorizing the broker to act as an independent contractor with authority to bind the insurer. The broker allegedly agreed to add a lessor as an additional insured on the policy but failed to effect the change. The written contract was ambiguous as to the extent of the broker's apparent authority to bind the insurer. The court held that the status of the broker was a question of fact precluding the grant of a summary judgment in favor of the insurer. The court noted that a broker can be placed in the position of a dual agent with respect to the procurement of the insurance and the naming of the lessor as an additional insured.

No apparent authority found: In *Standard Funding Corp. v. Lewitt*, 678 N.E.2d 874 (N.Y. 1997), a premium financing company entered into a number of financing agreements with the insurance agency to finance premiums on various policies. The premium financing company supplied the agent with financing agreement forms, which the agent and the insureds were required to complete and sign. The financing company initially contacted the agent's principal insurer to verify that the agent was in good standing and was licensed to sell all lines of business. The agent ultimately submitted various fraudulent premium financing agreements, whereupon the financing company sued the agent and the insurer to recover its loss. The court reversed the judgment for the financing company against the insurer, holding that the agent had no actual or apparent authority to enter into such premium financing agreement on the insurer's behalf; therefore, the insurer could not be held liable for the agent's fraudulent conduct.

No apparent authority found: In *McKillip v. Employers Fire Ins. Co.,* 932 S.W.2d 268 (Tex. Ct. App. 1996), the insured sued the insurer for breach of contract arising out of the assigned risk policy issued by the insurer. The insured contacted the agent after she was told that another insurer was canceling her husband's auto policy. On April 3, she met with the agent and completed an application and gave a down payment. The agent told her that she was then insured and issued a card designed to serve as temporary proof of insurance. The agent submitted the payment and the application to the assigned risk plan, and the defendant insurer issued a policy with an effective date of April 14. However, she had been seriously injured in an accident on April 11, for which she sought coverage under the policy's uninsured and underinsured motorist sections. The court held that the agent completing the application was not acting as the insurer's agent, and thus, his actions could not bind the insurer who issued the policy pursuant to the assigned risk plan.

Apparent authority found: In *Rickborn v. Liberty Life Ins. Co.,* 468 S.E.2d 292 (S.C. 1996), the decedent applicant's personal representative, seeking policy proceeds, brought suit against the life insurer. During a family gathering, the applicant (19 years old) asked the agent for advice on insurance. The agent recommended that he apply for universal life insurance, ultimately presented him with an application and a conditional receipt, and informed him that the policy would provide the discussed coverage. The agent did not review the application or conditions with the applicant but merely instructed him to sign the form. The applicant did so, but never received a copy of the documents. Also, since the applicant did not have his checkbook with him, the agent said he would take care of the payment and the applicant should simply give a check to his mother. The agent's actions led the applicant to believe that he had immediate coverage, which was consistent with the applicant's mother's testimony.

The agent wrote a personal check in the amount of the premium and submitted it along with an incomplete application to the insurer. The insurer rejected the check because the agent did not have an insurable interest in the applicant's life. The insurer returned the materials to the agent, who neither informed the applicant that coverage was not bound nor resubmitted a proper application and payment prior to the applicant's death in an auto accident.

The court held that the insurer invested the agent with apparent authority and, therefore, was liable for the agent's negligence. The insurer could also be held liable for negligently supervising the agent in view of prior problems with mishandling applications. The applicant was not required to have paid the first month's premium to trigger coverage under the facts of the case.

No apparent authority found: In *Hall v. Modern Woodmen of America*, 68 F.3d 1120 (8th Cir. 1995), applying Arkansas law, the life insurance beneficiary sued the life insurer that refused to pay based on misstatements in the insured's application for insurance. The plaintiff argued that the insurer could not raise the defense where its agent was aware of the insured's true medical history. The court held that such knowledge could not be imputed to the insurer where the agent was only a soliciting agency (and not a general agent) in connection with which it lacked any apparent authority to bind the insurer.

Apparent authority found: In *Capitol Funds, Inc. v. Royal Indem. Co.*, 458 S.E.2d 741 (N.C. App. Ct., 1995), the insured warehouse owner sued both its insurer and agent when it was denied coverage under its property policy after the warehouse was destroyed by fire. When the insured initially determined that the warehouse in question was omitted from the list of properties to be insured, it called the agent to obtain coverage. The insured requested coverage in the amount of $330,000 and was told that the property was covered by the insurer. The insured understood that the property would be added to the existing policy which already covered substantially all of its properties. The agent's view was that the coverage was effective when the insured was told that the building was covered.

The agent gave the information to another agent in the office and instructed her to complete a change request form. She understood that the coverage was bound pursuant to an oral binder. She completed the document, mailed the change to the general agent, and sent a copy by hand delivery to the insured. This was consistent with the way other changes on this policy had been handled. The agent believed that the other agency was a general agent based on its past relations when in fact that other agency was not an authorized agent. The change was not properly handled, and no coverage was ever placed in force before the warehouse was destroyed by fire.

The court affirmed the judgment on the jury verdict for the insured, holding that there had been sufficient evidence on the agent's actual and apparent authority to add the property to the policy for the issue to go to the jury.

Apparent authority found: In *Tassin v. Golden Rule Ins. Co.*, 649 So. 2d 1050 (La. Ct. App. 1994), the insured sought coverage under his health insurance policy for treatment of appendicitis. The insured's employer had changed group insurers following a rate increase. The broker assisted the employer in the search for new coverage and helped the insured complete his application under the new policy. The application disclosed that the insured was being treated for diabetes and was taking medication.

The insurer informed the broker that it would not cover the group with the insured as a member. The insured signed a waiver of coverage, and the insurer issued a policy covering all employees except the insured.

The broker then obtained other coverage for the insured. On the broker's advice, the insured's application did not disclose his diabetes. The new insurer discovered the diabetes while investigating the appendicitis claim and denied coverage for the cost of treating the appendicitis — $19,210.

The court held that the broker was the insurer's agent, where the insurer supplied the broker with application forms and issued the policy following direct transmission of the application by the broker. Therefore, the insurer was responsible for paying the treatment bills subject to its rights to be indemnified by the broker.

Page 12, add to note 6:

Apparent authority found: In *Almerico v. RLI Ins. Co.*, 716 So. 2d 774 (Fla. 1998), the insurer filed this declaratory judgment action alleging that the insured misrepresented the presence of youthful drivers in the household and the presence of high-performance cars on the application for an umbrella policy. One of the youthful drivers was involved in an accident in which one person was killed and two others were seriously injured. The policy was procured by a broker who obtained applications for insurance from an agent authorized by the insurer to market its policies in the state. The insurer knew that the agent would use subproducers to take applications and the insurer relied on the agent to process applications. The insurer had no direct dealings with subproducers such as the broker. However, the broker had been assigned an agent number by the insurer and was required to procure a certain number of policies for the insurer annually to remain in the producer network. The court held that the insurer could be held liable under its policy where it accorded the broker with evidence of an agency relationship, such as the provision of supplies and applications, that would lead a consumer to believe that there was an actual agency relationship. This was found to have created a dual agency.

Apparent authority question of fact: In *Johnson v. Nationwide Gen. Ins. Co.*, 937 F. Supp. 186 (N.D.N.Y. 1996), the plaintiff gave funds to the agent to invest. The plaintiff believed that the agent was still acting as an agent of the defendant insurer even though he had been terminated for financial improprieties. The plaintiff sued the insurer for the loss sustained from the agent's misappropriation of the funds designated to be invested. The agent had been an employee of the insurer for 15 years in various capacities. Upon termination, the insurer allegedly notified all the agent's customers that the agent was no longer acting on behalf of the insurer. There was substantial evidence that various customers never received such notice. The plaintiff in this case, however, admitted that she was aware that the agent did not work exclusively for the insurer.

Nevertheless, she believed that the agent still acted on the insurer's behalf in selling the insurer's investment products, particularly after the agent provided her with a prospectus, other information about the product, and an application. Also, the insurer ultimately issued an official receipt along with a note on the insurer's letterhead, acknowledging her investment. The court held that there were fact questions whether the plaintiff's reliance on the agent acting on behalf of the insurer was reasonable and whether the insurer took all reasonable steps to relieve the agent of his apparent authority.

Apparent authority found: In *Columbia Mut. Cas. Ins. Co. v. Ingraham*, 883 S.W.2d 868 (Ark. Ct. App. 1994), the insured sued the insurer to recover for fire damage to his house. The insured had applied for fire insurance through the agency. An agency employee completed the application from information supplied by the insured. The agency gave the insured a binder, stating:

> The Company binds insurance as above applied for in accordance with all terms and conditions of the policy regularly issued by the Company in the state in which the property is located. It is a condition of this binder that it shall be void if a policy of the Company is issued or coverage shall cease if it is otherwise terminated. In no event shall this binder continue in force beyond 30 days from its inception date unless signed by the duly authorized agent of the Company.

The insured had misrepresented the number of fire losses he had sustained and stated that no member of the household had ever been convicted of a crime. In fact, the insured had previously been convicted of a number of felonies, including arson. The insurer did not know this, but allegedly sent a notice of rejection to the agency based on the form that was used, stating that the insured should have submitted a farm application. The agency denied ever receiving such a notice and never communicated the rejection to the insured.

The insured's home was destroyed by fire nearly six weeks after the date of the notice and more than seven weeks from the date of the binder. The court affirmed a jury verdict for the insured, holding that there was sufficient evidence of an oral modification to extend the contract of insurance beyond the 30-day binder and that the agent had actual or apparent authority to extend such coverage.

No apparent authority found: In *Double K, Inc. v. Scottsdale Ins. Co.*, 515 N.W.2d 416 (Neb. 1994), the insured claimed that its policy was in full force and effect on the date a fire destroyed the insured property. The insurer disclaimed coverage, arguing that the broker had no authority to issue a binder on the insurer's behalf.

The insurer was nonadmitted, and the insured alleged that it did business through its general agent, who advised the insured that the broker had binding authority. The insured paid the renewal premium through the broker and directed all communications through the broker. The insurer failed to notify the insured that the broker was not its agent and also failed to personally advise the insured of the cancellation of the policy. The court nevertheless affirmed summary judgment for the insurer, holding that the insured failed to raise any facts that would create an agency relationship between the broker and the insurer; therefore, the policy lapsed when it was not renewed by the insured.

Apparent authority question of fact: In *Hermann Forwarding Co. v. Pappas Ins. Co.*, 640 A.2d 1200 (N.J. Super. App. Div. 1994), the insured sued the broker and the insurer (which was the servicing carrier for the New Jersey Commercial Auto Insurance Plan) in an attempt to recover an alleged overpayment of premiums to the broker. The plaintiffs made a $166,838 down payment on the total advance premium of $556,128, and financed the balance. The finance agreement was signed by the plaintiffs and their broker. The plaintiffs sent the payments to the broker, and the checks were made payable to the broker.

The policy was ultimately canceled for nonpayment of premiums. The insurer gave the plaintiffs a statement of account, which the plaintiffs disputed as failing to reflect all payments made to the broker. The plaintiffs claimed they had overpaid the broker by $78,740, while the financing company claimed that they had overpaid by $38,840.

The court held that it would be premature to enter summary judgment on the issue of who was responsible for the failure to pay premiums, since there were still questions as to whether the policy had been delivered to the broker. Under N.J. Stat. Ann. § 17:22-6.2a, where the broker is entrusted to deliver the policy, the insured can reasonably believe that the broker is authorized to receive premium payments consistent with the doctrine of apparent authority.

Page 12, add to note 7:

Apparent authority found: In *Fireman's Fund Ins. Co. v. National Bank for Cooperatives*, 849 F. Supp. 1347 (N.D. Cal. 1994), the servicer's insurer sued to determine whether it was liable for an arbitration award in favor of a bank with respect to certificates covering inventory financed by the bank. The insurer claimed that it had not received timely notice. The court held that even though a broker is generally the agent of the insured and not the insurer, notice to the broker would be deemed notice to the insurer due to the ambiguous notice provisions in the servicer's excess liability policy.

No apparent authority found: In *Kirby v. Northwestern Nat'l. Cas. Co.*, 445 S.E.2d 791 (Ga. Ct. App. 1994), the insurer brought suit to determine if there was coverage for a claim made against its insured, an adult entertainment business. The insured was sued after it served alcohol to a driver who was then involved in a fatal accident.

The policy contained the typical liquor liability exclusion. The insured claimed that the policy was supposed to include liquor liability coverage, that the agent had agreed to procure such coverage, and that the presence of the exclusion in the policy was a mistake.

The policy had been issued through an independent agent who qualified as a broker, represented several insurers, and had contacted those insurers to find the coverage sought by the insured.

The court affirmed summary judgment for the insurer, holding that the independent agent was the agent of the insured, not the insurer. The insurer was not bound by the agent's alleged representation as to liquor liability coverage, as he had no apparent authority to bind the insurer to provide such coverage.

Chapter 2

Types of Agents

2.1 General Agents

Page 27, add to note 1:

In *Maville v. Peerless Ins. Co.,* 686 A.2d 1165 (N.H. 1996), the plaintiffs were passengers in a vehicle operated by the insured. They sought a declaration that the insured's earlier request to reduce policy limits was ineffective to reduce the limits for the accident. The insured had called his agent and requested the reduction on September 10. The agent agreed to make the change, but asked that the insured stop by the office and sign a letter confirming the intent to reduce the coverage. The insured signed the letter on the same day. That day the agent forwarded by fax a change request form to the insurer. One week later, the accident occurred. The revised endorsement was not issued until four days later, which was the day after the insured gave notice of the accident to the agent. The endorsement stated that the reduction in coverage was effective on September 10. The court held that the agent was a general agent who had authority to reduce the limits upon the insured's request and that the reduction was effective upon the insured's signing the confirmatory letter on September 10.

2.3 Soliciting Agents

Page 30, add to note 8:

See *Hall v. Modern Woodmen of America*, 68 F.3d 1120 (8th Cir. 1995), applying Arkansas law, discussed in § 1.4.

Page 34, add at end of section:

In *Philadelphia Indemnity Ins. Co. v. Carco Rentals Inc.*, 923 F. Supp. 1143 (W.D. Ark. 1996), the rental customer's excess carrier sued the rental company and others seeking a declaration that it had no duty to defend or indemnify the customer for an accident. The car rental company maintained the minimum statutorily required coverage and made additional coverage available to customers upon an additional payment. The renter involved in this case purchased that excess coverage. The excess coverage was provided through the plaintiff.

The question was raised as to whether the car rental agent showed the customer the pamphlet describing excess policy exclusions, including an exclusion of coverage for the renter while driving while intoxicated. The court held that the rental agent was a soliciting agent of the excess carrier; her knowledge that the customer was intoxicated at the time she rented the car to the customer was not binding or imputed to the insurer. Thus, the insurer could assert the exclusion to bar the extension of coverage in this case.

In *Ginocchio v. American Bankers Life Assur. Co.*, 889 F. Supp. 1079 (N.D. Ill. 1995), the insureds sued the credit disability insurer to recover policy benefits. The plaintiffs entered into a mortgage and promissory note on their home. In connection with the loan, the plaintiffs purchased a credit disability policy covering loan payments in the event the husband became disabled. The plaintiffs signed a one-page, double-sided insurance statement naming the husband as the primary borrower. The term of the loan was listed as 180 months, but the term of the insurance was shown as being for only 36 months. This statement explicitly stated that the coverage would terminate on the scheduled expiration date or the prepayment of the indebtedness.

Ten months after they took the loan, the husband was diagnosed with acute angina and became permanently disabled. The insurer started paying monthly loan obligations. During the period when it made payments, the insurer sent the plaintiffs a claim renewal notice which showed that the coverage was expiring 36 months after its inception as per the initial statement.

The court held that the policy was ambiguous as to whether the insurer was liable for more than 36 months, which raised a question of fact precluding a summary judgment for the insurer.

However, with respect to the agent's duty to the insureds, the court noted that the agent was clearly a soliciting agent, making him an agent of the insurer, and not an agent of the insureds. Therefore, he was not required to look out for the insureds' interests. No liability could be imposed on the agent or the insurer for the failure to give the insureds advice on the property policy term or other incidents of coverage.

2.4 Subagents

Page 40, replace last sentence under subheading, "Subagents," with the following:

Although the unlicensed subagent has no actual authority, he or she may be acting with apparent authority to bind the insurer.[21]

Page 40, add to note 21:

In *Booker v. United American Ins. Co.*, 700 So. 2d 1333 (Ala. 1997), the insureds sued the subagent and the insurer for fraud. They also sued the insurer for negligent supervision of the agent. The insureds claimed that they purchased the policies based on the agent's misrepresentations. The subagent was not authorized to act on the insurer's behalf but was hired by an authorized agent against the insurer's express instructions.

In determining the insurer's responsibilities, the court reviewed the law applicable to subagents and affirmed summary judgment for the insurer. The court held that the insurer could not be held liable for the actions of the subagent who was appointed contrary to express instructions. There was no evidence that the insurer ever ratified the appointment of the subagent or vested the subagent with apparent authority. Clearly, the agent and subagent could potentially be held liable.

In *Rapp v. Lorch*, 667 A.2d 240 (1995), the plaintiffs had an agreement with the insurance agent to refer customers to the agent in exchange for a share of commissions. The parties originally proceeded under an oral agreement. However, after the plaintiffs failed to receive any share of the commissions, the agreement was reduced to writing. The plaintiffs had their wives licensed with the defendant's agency so that the commissions could be paid directly to them. The defendant started selling variable life insurance, which required a special license not held by the wives, and subsequently one wife's license was terminated. At that time, one plaintiff husband discovered that the agent had been writing whole life and variable life policies on persons he had referred to the agent without paying any commissions.

The court held that the agreement was enforceable even though public policy normally prohibits the unlicensed sale of insurance products. The court ordered that the defendant agent account for the commissions derived from the referrals.

Part I □ **Chapter 2** □ **2000 Supplement**
Types of Agents

2.6 Dual Agencies

Page 45, add to note 29:

In *Ballard v. Lee*, 671 So. 2d 1368 (Ala. 1995), the insured sued the broker and the surplus lines insurer for alleged fraud. The insured went to the broker to obtain property insurance coverage on a restaurant. The broker's initial attempts to locate an authorized insurance agency that would supply the coverage were unsuccessful. As a result, the broker went to a surplus lines broker.

The original broker, who worked to procure surplus lines insurance on the insured's request, was a dual agent so that any misrepresentation on the broker's part as to the nature of the coverage obtained could be imputed to the insurer. Similarly, where the insurer suppressed facts that the insured had a right to know with respect to the amount potentially recoverable under "actual cash value" (ACV) coverage, this presented a question of fact for the jury to determine, whether the term ACV was a tool of the insurance trade not normally understood by the public.

Page 46, add to end of main text:

The question of dual agencies often arises in connection with group life and health insurance programs provided as a benefit of employment. The insurer issues a master policy to the employer. There is no direct relationship between the employee and the insurer, and the typical aspects of servicing the policy are handled by the employer or someone hired by the employer. This raises the question of whether the employer is an agent for the purpose of administering the group insurance program, and if so, the effect of such an agency relationship. For cases on this topic, see this supplement, § 6.9, Status of Employer Providing Group Insurance.

In addition to standard employment group insurance relationships, various other arrangements are possible pursuant to the terms of the Employee Retirement Income Security Act (ERISA 29 U.S.C. § 1113 et seq.). Under ERISA, the employer may hire an agent or administrator to handle the details of the plan in addition to handling various other forms of benefits such as pension and cafeteria plans. In this case, especially where the plan is self-funded, the employer may be aware that the administrator is acting as a dual agent. As such, any embezzlement of premiums by the agent may mean that the employer has no viable claim against the insurer for the wrongful actions of the agent.[34] For further cases on ERISA liability, see § 6.9 of this supplement.

Page 46, add to note 34 (created above):

Continental Assurance Co. v. Cedar Rapids Pediatric Clinic, 957 F.2d 58 (8th Cir. 1992), applying Iowa law.

Chapter 3

Ownership and Licensing Requirements in General

3.2 Agency Acquisitions

Page 53, add to note 5:

But in *Parker v. Western Dakota Insurors*, 605 N.W.2d 181 (S.D. 2000), the plaintiff was a salaried sales agent working for the agency when the agency's ownership changed hands. In an attempt to induce the plaintiff to stay with the agency, the original agency owner had agreed to give the agent a percentage of the commissions the agency received after her employment ended in exchange for her signing a noncompetition clause. The owner then sold the agency and the new owners told the agents that their commissions would be substantially reduced and new commission agreements would need to be signed. Instead of accepting the new deal for the reduced commissions, the plaintiff chose to resign. The plaintiff then contacted the defendant's owner, advising him of the contract governing her right to a percentage of commissions after her employment ended. The new owner said he didn't care about his predecessor's obligations and was only buying the book of business and selected assets. This purchase included the right to renewal commissions.

The court held that the defendant was not obligated to abide by the original contract where the defendant's purchase of the renewal commission rights did not constitute an assumption of the original promise to share a portion of those commissions with the plaintiff. This result was proper under the terms of the defendant's asset purchase agreement, which specifically excluded the agency's liabilities.

3.3 General Licensing Qualifications

Page 58, add to note 7:

In *Dona v. Levin*, 693 N.Y.S.2d 677 (N.Y. App. Div. 1999), the agent's licenses were revoked by the Insurance Department and he sought review of that decision. The agent pleaded guilty in federal court to making a false statement in an ERISA document. The statement related to the value of the group annuity contracts in which customer funds were invested. The agent knew that the letter overstated the balances for the contracts, was false and misleading, and related to a scheme to defraud the insurer for the purpose of collecting undeserved commissions.

The plea agreement and the guilty plea were sufficient by themselves to support the revocation of the agent's licenses, even though the agent later claimed that his only wrongful conduct was the failure to supervise his employees properly. The plea was substantial evidence of incompetence and untrustworthiness, either of which are grounds for revocation.

In *Pou v. Department of Insurance*, 707 So. 2d 941 (Fla. Dist. Ct. App. 1998), the agent appealed the temporary suspension of her license. The Department alleged that she willfully misrepresented the amount of the insurance premium to a customer and allegedly misappropriated a premium payment. All funds remained in the agency's escrow account and were not withdrawn or applied improperly. The court held that there was insufficient evidence that the agent willfully misappropriated the premium. The Department failed to sustain its burden of proving its allegations by clear and convincing evidence. Therefore, the suspension was improperly imposed.

In *Werner v. State Department of Insurance*, 689 So. 2d 1211 (Fla. Dist. Ct. App. 1997), the insurance department suspended the insurance representative's license for one year as a result of a single act of misconduct. The misconduct related to the failure of the representative to disclose the possible imposition of interest penalties for early removal of annuity principal. The court reversed the suspension because the misconduct did not constitute "[f]raudulent or dishonest practices in the conduct of business," as required for suspension under the applicable statute. The court determined that the penalty imposed on the representative was inappropriate since it was predicated on a recommendation that was based on violations that were not found to have occurred.

In *Butler v. Insurance Commissioner*, 686 A.2d 1017 (Del. Super. Ct. 1997), the agent's license was revoked after he failed to comply with the terms of a consent order that reinstated his license after a one-year suspension. The license was reinstated after he submitted a new application and passed the examination. The reinstatement was conditioned on the agent's completing three ethics courses. The agent was not told when he submitted the application that there would be additional conditions for reinstatement, and he agreed to complete the required course work. He was ultimately granted three extensions but never successfully completed the courses. As a result, the insurance department held a hearing and ultimately revoked the reinstated license for violation of the consent order. The court held that the agent's consent to the department's letter imposing the course work as a condition of reinstatement did not constitute a consent order. The court held that the written agreement imposing the course work condition was not enforceable where the agreement was not in conformity with insurance code or regulatory requirements.

In *Robinson v. Treasurer of State of Florida Dept. of Ins.*, 676 So. 2d 1378 (Fla. Dist. Ct. App. 1996), the license holder appealed the order revoking his insurance license. The department claimed that he waived his right to a hearing by failing to respond to the administrative complaint. The court held that even though his suspension complied with the rules and regulations, there were still due process problems that required that a hearing be held.

In *John Paterno Inc. v. Curiale*, 668 N.E.2d 395 (N.Y. 1996), the broker was fined for using an excess lines broker to obtain claims-made liquor liability policies from an unauthorized insurer for his bar and restaurant customers. The broker resorted to excess lines brokers after the market for such insurance contracted. There was an insurance department regulation providing that claims-made coverage was not to be provided for liquor liability policies issued or renewed in New York. In addition to the use of the unauthorized insurer and regulatory violation, the insurance department also charged the broker with being untrustworthy or incompetent. The court held that his actions constituted repeated violations of regulations (1,497 violations) and upheld the fine of $45 for each such violation.

In *Kent v. Lyon*, 555 N.W.2d 106 (S.D. 1996), the agent challenged the revocation of his license for alleged violations arising out of his administration and sale of group health insurance plans. The agent agreed to obtain group insurance for an association of banks and obtained fully-insured group health plans for several years. The insurer notified him that the policy would be canceled due to the insurer's business decision to leave the group health insurance business. The agent convinced the insurer to extend coverage for two months and sought a new carrier.

In *Hernandez v. Texas Dept. of Ins.*, 923 S.W.2d 192 (Tex. Ct. App. 1996), the agent sought judicial review of the revocation of her local recording agent's license, which she had held for 12 years.

In response to customer complaints about her, the Department of Insurance held hearings and then sent her an order of revocation, upon which she timely filed a motion for a rehearing. The order of revocation became final after 45 days passed from her receipt of the order. She then had 30 days to file her petition for judicial review, but the filing was not made for more than two weeks following that date. Due to the untimely filing, her petition for judicial review was dismissed for lack of jurisdiction.

Page 58, add to note 8:

In *Pasternack v. Muhl*, 670 N.Y.S.2d 187 (N.Y.A.D. 1998), the Department of Insurance revoked the petitioner's broker and public adjuster licenses after finding that he was untrustworthy and incompetent. The appellate court upheld the revocation where it determined that there was substantial evidence that the petitioner violated insurance regulations by permitting another person to conduct insurance brokerage business under the petitioner's license. The third person had previously had his own license revoked. The petitioner had also permitted the third person access to his temporary insurance identification cards. The petitioner was given monthly payments by the third person. Such conduct clearly violates the applicable statutes and regulations.

In *Department of Insurance v. Universal Brokerage Corp.*, 697 A.2d 142 (N.J. Super. App. Div. 1997), the agency and its president were found to have misappropriated premiums for various insurers. The Department of Insurance ordered that the agency perform restitution. The court recognized that the agent was not entitled to a reduction in the amount of the restitution to account for the commissions that would have been earned. The court held that the commissions would have been forfeited due to the agent's misconduct.

In *Monia v. Melahn,* 876 S.W.2d 709 (Mo. Ct. App. 1994), the agent and broker sought a review of the Administrative Hearing Commission's determination that they were subject to discipline. The individuals were husband and wife and they owned an agency. For part of the time in question, the husband was a captive agent for an insurer. The wife was always an independent agent and was a general agent for a second insurer. When the first insurer terminated the husband's agency, the wife appointed him a subagent for the second insurer.

The department sought disciplinary action against the husband for telling an applicant that he represented various insurers while he was still a captive agent, for rebating premiums, and for taking an application for the first insurer but subsequently forging the applicant's signature on an application for coverage from the second insurer. The husband also made misrepresentations to another insured when he tried to switch her coverage from the first insurer to the second. His wife submitted that application to the insurer and certified that the information was correct despite the fact that she never spoke to the insured.

The court affirmed the imposition of discipline, holding that the Hearing Commission decision was supported by the evidence. The agent's misconduct in rebating premiums and forging the applicant's signature showed a lack of trustworthiness or competence.

Page 58, add to note 9:

In *Stone & Edwards Ins. Agency v. Commonwealth Dept. of Insurance*, 648 A.2d 304 (Pa. 1994), the agents allegedly committed serious insurance law violations, triggering an investigation by the Department of Insurance. During the investigation, the department placed holds on any new license applications from the agents pending the outcome of the enforcement proceedings. The agents appealed the denial of license applications and this was consolidated with the hearing on the enforcement action.

The agents argued that there was an unconstitutional commingling of the prosecutorial and adjudicative functions of the insurance department. The agents did not point to any particular actions taken in their case but rather claimed that there was a potential for commingling the functions. The court held that there was no impermissible commingling and that the agents were not entitled to a hearing prior to the denial of their new license applications. The court further found that the department had the authority to hold new license applications pending the outcome of the violation investigation, despite the fact that the agents' current licenses evidenced their "worthiness" for additional licenses. The court noted that once the department completed its initial investigation into the agents' "worthiness," the department would be required to act on the new license applications by granting or denying them and would not be able to continue to hold the applications until full disciplinary proceedings were completed.

Page 58, add to note 11:

In *Cosby v. Commonwealth ex. rel. State Corp. Commission*, 450 S.E.2d 121 (Va. 1994), the agent purchased the assets and liabilities of an agency doing business as a corporation and continued the business as a sole proprietorship, trading under basically the same name. The proprietor directed the employees to deposit all insurance premium payments into a new business account and make daily transfers from that account to an account the proprietor maintained at another bank. The proprietor was the only person who could draw on the latter account. A premium financing company complained to the State Corporate Commission after the proprietor failed to remit down payments given to the agency by five insureds for transmittal to the financing company. Another financing company subsequently made similar complaints.

The commission revoked the agent's license and fined him for violation of regulatory statutes. The court held that there was sufficient evidence to support a finding that the agent violated the code by failing to remit the premium down payments and by permitting a secretary to solicit and negotiate the issuance of an auto liability policy to a friend.

Page 59, add to note 16:

In *Missouri Dept. of Insurance v. Kenser*, 883 S.W.2d 127 (Mo.

Ct. App. 1994), the department filed a disciplinary action against the agent, but the Administrative Hearing Commission rejected the department's assertion that it had cause to discipline the agent.

The department claimed that the agent was selling insurance for a company not authorized to do business in Missouri. The agent had been a licensee in good standing for 21 years. The agent had asked the department whether the insurer was licensed and was told that the company held a license in good standing, whereupon the agent started soliciting and selling the medical insurance product. In fact, the named insurer never underwrote the plan and the actual underwriter had no certificate of authority to transact insurance in the state.

When the agent was first advised that there was a problem with the plan, he stopped selling it. The Director of the Department wrote a letter to subscribers of the plan, advising them to seek other coverage, but no such letter was sent to the agent. When a subscriber showed the letter to the agent, he told as many clients as he could to cancel the plan and seek other coverage. (The clients had been obtained through a telemarketing company which sold leads about such persons to the agent.)

The court reversed the Hearing Commission decision and found that the agent could be held liable for transacting business with a nonadmitted company, for which he could potentially be subject to discipline; however, the department had not established that he had a duty to do more than he actually did to verify the underwriter and its status.

Page 60, add to note 20:

In *Cleveland v. Department of Insurance*, 614 N.Y.S.2d 620 (N.Y. App. Div. 1994), the excess line broker sought review of a Department of Insurance determination that he violated state insurance law. The broker was licensed to do business in New York and was asked by an out-of-state broker to obtain and deliver a policy of patent infringement abatement insurance for a New York insured. The policy was to be issued by a company not licensed to do business in New York. The broker determined that this kind of insurance was not available from New York insurers and agreed to act as an excess line broker. When the broker filed the appropriate affidavits with the Excess Line Association, the Association determined that this was expense-only coverage and was not considered insurance in New York, and therefore refused to stamp the affidavit. The state Insurance Department informed the broker that he did not have authority to place the insurance because it was not included among those lines that may be procured by excess line brokers and because it was written on a claims-made basis in violation of existing regulations.

The broker refunded the fee he received for his services and requested cancellation, but the insurer did not cancel the policy. The department then cited the broker for various insurance law violations. The court confirmed the department's finding of a violation, holding that the coverage is not the type which excess line brokers in New York are permitted to place.

3.5 Licensing Statutes and Limitations on Agent Authority

Page 63, add to note 3:

In *Massachusetts Ass'n of Insurance Agents v. Commissioner of Insurance*, 682 N.E.2d 836 (Mass. 1997), the insurance agents' trade association sought a review of the insurance department's calculation of commission rates for policies for certain classes of motor vehicles. The court held that the insurance commissioner had discretion to determine that the agent's commissions would be established on a net and not a gross basis where sufficient findings supported the selection of the methodology. The court noted that the commissioner has wide discretion in determining the method used to set such rates.

He found a replacement, and that insurer agreed to provide coverage if the agent would provide administrative work. The group policy was issued. The first insurer had paid the association a 1 percent marketing fee for its promotional efforts to increase enrollment. The second insurer did not make such a payment, and the agent paid the association the same fee from the 8 percent administrative fee he received from the insurer. The insurer then changed the plan from fully insured to a self-insured plan with stop loss insurance. The insurer provided services under an administrative services only agreement for which it received a fee. Neither the insurer nor the agent informed the association that the fully insured plan was canceled.

The agent then notified the association of new premium rates and that another of his companies would act as a clearinghouse for claims. He said this change would mean that checks would bear the agent's name as well as the insurer's. He also informed the association that the insurer would no longer pay the 1 percent marketing fee. In the meantime, the agent continued to negotiate with the insurer to restore the fully insured plan. Finally, they reached an agreement whereby the plan would retroactively be made fully insured. Also, there were provisions requiring that the association indemnify the insurer should an action be brought against the insurer for ERISA violations.

The agent signed the agreements representing that he had authority to bind the association when in fact he had no such authority. Ultimately, the insurance department sought an explanation of the cancellation of the original policy since the proper forms had not been filed. After the association terminated the agent for the refusal to pay the marketing fee, the insurance department conducted hearings on various acts of misconduct and illegal transactions. The insurance commissioner ultimately revoked his license.

The court held that the marketing fee was an illegal rebate, and the agent was acting as the agent of an unauthorized insurer when he funneled the business through his associated company. There was also sufficient evidence that he made repeated fraudulent concealments of material facts and failed to remit returned premiums. The court upheld the revocation action.

Ownership and Licensing Requirements in General

In *Russell v. State Dept. of Insurance*, 668 So. 2d 276 (Fla. Dist. Ct. App. 1996), the department started disciplinary proceedings against an agent to suspend his license for violations of the insurance code.

The agent had received money from the insurer in excess of the commissions that were owed to him. The agent characterized the money as advances or loans, to be repaid from future commissions earned. However, the contract between the parties specified that the insurer would not make such advances.

A new commission technician working for the insurance company took over his commission accounts and brought this situation to the department's notice. The technician was unaware that the prior course of dealing was approved by the insurer's officers.

In taking action against the agent, the hearing officer found that he had, in fact, received such amounts, even when he had no positive balance in his commission accounts. The hearing officer did acknowledge that this occurred with the express and repeated approval of the insurer and that the advances were repaid from future commissions.

The court held that the license was not subject for suspension where the agent was not aware that the amounts he had been receiving were illegally diverted from the insurer. This was particularly appropriate where the insurance company had two pending lawsuits dealing with the advances.

Chapter 4

Contractual Relationship Between Insurer and Agent

4.1 Agency Contracts in General

Page 76, add to end of section:

Frequently, disputes arise over where to draw the line between an insurer's underwriting prerogatives and its obligations under an agency contract. This can become particularly complicated when societal issues such as discrimination are brought into play.

In *Hemmans v. State Farm Ins. Co.*, 653 So. 2d 69 (La. Ct. App. 1995), the agent sued the insurer challenging the insurer's "loss control program," which prevented the agent from writing automobile insurance unless it was for an existing policyholder. The agent was a captive agent of State Farm and worked pursuant to an agency agreement. In 1990, the regional vice president adopted underwriting rules in response to severe automobile underwriting losses. The insurer would not accept new customer auto policies from agents who were identified as high loss agents. Eight hundred agents in the region were so classified. This program did not prevent the agent from writing new policies for life, health, and fire insurance.

The plaintiff alleged that the program violated the agent's agreement and the rights of the plaintiff as an independent contractor. Being black, the plaintiff also claimed that the program was racially discriminatory in that business he was unable to write was sent to State Farm agents who were not among the 800 agents in the program.

The court held that the agent's placement on the program did not violate the agency contract, and there were no viable claims against the insurer. The court reversed the judgment entered on the jury verdict for the agent.

Interestingly, in a separate case involving the same loss control program, another Louisiana appellate court held that there was sufficient evidence to support a jury determination that the insurer discriminated against the agent and the court upheld that award of $350,000 in general damages. *See Guillory v. State Farm Ins. Co.*, 662 So. 2d 104 (La. Ct. App. 1995).

Normally, agency agreements must be in writing to be enforceable. In *Aubrey Rogers Agency v. AIG Life Ins. Co.*, 55 F. Supp. 2d 309 (D. Del. 1999), the plaintiff was a managing general agent for the insurer's credit life and disability insurance business and sued the insurer for breach of the agency agreement. The agency had an oral contract to act for the insurer in three states. Later, the insurer attempted to reduce this contract to writing, sending the agency a written contract. The agency offered revisions to the contract, but the insurer's account manager suggested that the agency sign the original agreement, as it was unlikely that the insurer would sign the revised agreement.

There was subsequently a dispute as to whether the agency or insurer ever signed the agreement. The insurer was unable to find an executed copy of the agreement; the agency had a copy of the agreement bearing only its signature. The business grew dramatically for several years, but ultimately the insurer determined that the credit life insurance business was unprofitable and sought to decrease the commission rate from 57 to 35 percent. This was not acceptable to the agency, which realized that it would be impossible to retain its agents at the new commission rate because other credit insurers were offering higher commissions. The agency tried to move its business to other carriers but was not entirely successful, and the insurer ultimately terminated the relationship. The court held that the agency agreement was unenforceable where it was not in writing, even though it was partly performed.

4.2 Appointment of Agent

Page 78, add at end of section:

Insurers have wide discretion in determining who they will name as agents. In *Ewing v. State Farm Mut. Auto. Ins. Co.*, 6 F. Supp. 2d 1281 (D.N.M. 1998), the plaintiff applied to be an insurance agent and was rejected, whereupon she brought a Title VII gender discrimination claim as well as claims for breach of contract, bad faith, and the intentional infliction of emotional distress. She wanted to be appointed as an agent to succeed her father who, prior to his death, had been an agent of the insurer for approximately 40 years. She had worked for her father for many years and her father had made numerous requests that she be appointed an agent so she could succeed him.

Before the father's death, the insurer restructured its selection process, and at that point an agent was required to have been employed by the insurer full-time for three continuous years before he or she could be appointed an independent contractor agent. When the restructuring occurred, the father's supervising manager's position was eliminated and the father and the manager agreed that the manager would take over the father's accounts. The court granted the insurer's motion for summary judgment, holding that the insurer had a reasonable nondiscriminatory reason for failing to appoint the plaintiff an agent. The court rejected the argument that the plaintiff was a third-party beneficiary of the insurer's contract with her father which would have entitled her to be so appointed upon the retirement of her father.

4.4 Agent's Right to Commissions

Page 82, add new note 9a after first sentence of first full paragraph:

In *ITT Hartford Group v. Virginia Financial Associates*, 520 S.E.2d 355 (Va. 1999), the independent agent sought to recover commissions generated from the sale of a package product created by a joint venture to be sold to dentists. The agent acted as the liaison between the two joint venture insurers. However, the agent had an agency agreement with only one insurer. The agent alleged that it spent considerable time and effort on the venture and had an express or implied assurance that it would be compensated for its work. The agent sought to recover substantial commissions on the premiums generated by the product, claiming that it was defrauded of its right to such compensation.

The court reversed the judgment for the agent, holding that the insurer's representations that the agent would receive fair compensation did not constitute fraud since the representations related to future events. The agent failed to prove the required elements of its fraud claim.

In *Massachusetts Ass'n of Insurance Agents v. Commissioner of Insurance*, 682 N.E.2d 836 (Mass. 1997), the insurance agents' trade association sought a review of the insurance department's calculation of commission rates for policies for certain classes of motor vehicles. The court held that the insurance commissioner had discretion to determine that agent's commissions would be established on a net and not a gross basis where sufficient findings supported the selection of the methodology. The court noted that the commissioner has wide discretion in determining the method used to set such rates.

In *Davidson & Schaaf v. Liberty Nat'l Fire Ins. Co.*, 69 F.3d 868 (8th Cir. 1995), applying Missouri law, the plaintiff insurance agent entered into a brokerage agreement with another agent (the defendant) to sell the latter's insurance products. The defendant agent was a wholly-owned subsidiary of the insurer. The plaintiff placed insurance for a client with the defendant, asking that the quotation not include a commission. The client had agreed to pay a $75,000 fee for placing the insurance, and the plaintiff did not receive any commission from the defendant. The defendant subsequently terminated the plaintiff as a broker and renewed the policies directly with the insured, leaving the plaintiff without a commission for the renewals. The defendant claimed that it did not solicit the renewals but was approached by the insured. The court held that the plaintiff was not protected against the insured's acts; any other decision would defeat the insured's interests and control of expirations. The court affirmed the summary judgment for the defendants.

In *Georgia Farm Bur. Mut. Ins. Co. v. Bishop*, 464 S.E.2d 9 (Ga. Ct. App. 1995), the agent sued the insurer to recover unpaid wages. The agent worked under a series of written contracts under which the agent was to be paid based on the net premiums paid for the previous year and the loss ratio of the accounts. The contracts did not specify the amount of premiums to be generated by the policies or the loss ratio of those accounts.

During the agent's initial period of employment, he was paid less because no adjustment was made to his salary for the loss ratio of assigned accounts. He was transferred to another location and was promised that he would be paid based on the assignment of accounts producing premiums in excess of $300,000 per year. In fact, his compensation after the transfer was based on accounts which had generated less than $255,000. The defendant then started paying the loss ratio adjustment and did so for the remainder of the agent's employment.

The court affirmed the judgment for the agent, holding that there was sufficient evidence for the jury to find that he did not accept a revision of his contract with respect to the level of accounts and that the employer willfully failed to pay him according to the contracts. This supported the award of attorneys' fees to the agent.

See also *Rapp v. Lorch*, 667 A.2d 240 (1995), discussed in § 2.4.

Page 82, add to note 11:

See *Russell v. State Dept. of Insurance*, 668 So. 2d 276 (Fla. Dist. Ct. App. 1996), discussed in § 3.5.

Page 84, add to note 16:

In *Hebert v. Insurance Center Inc.*, 706 So. 2d 1007 (La. Ct. App. 1998), the sales agent sought to recover commissions collected by his employer on policies placed prior to his resignation. The court held that he was not entitled to the commissions because the employment agreement provided that he could not collect these commissions following his voluntary resignation and this did not create an impermissible wage forfeiture since the commissions in question were additional payments, not wages.

In a case involving similar issues, the employment contract did not provide for the loss of such commissions on renewal business the agent secured before her employment was terminated. She was entitled to commissions on policies that had been consummated prior to her termination. Such a result was proper notwithstanding evidence of contrary industry practices and standards. *Sample v. Kinser*, 700 N.E.2d 802 (Ind. Ct. App. 1998).

In *Charles Maggard Agency v. Missouri Public Entity Risk Management Fund*, 974 S.W.2d 671 (Mo. Ct. App. 1998), the agent sued the insurer to recover commissions on renewal policies. The policies in question were sold directly through the insurer. Where the direct sale was initiated by the insured and not the insurer, the agent was not entitled to commissions. The conduct by the insured evidences that he or she has terminated the agent's employment. The agency does not have a perpetual right to commissions for policies written for a customer once it writes a single policy. Clearly, however, if the insurer had solicited the insured to place the insurance directly, that would violate the agency agreement and subject the insurer to liability.

In *Russo v. New York Life Ins. Co.*, 668 N.Y.S.2d 640 (N.Y. App. Div. 1998), the plaintiff was a retired insurance agent who sued the insurer to recover commissions on policies he had procured, but that the insurer canceled after renewal. The plaintiff's field underwriter's contract provided that the plaintiff was required to repay any commissions received or advanced to him that were derived from policies that were ultimately rescinded, reformed, or canceled by the company for any reason. Thus, the insurer was entitled to limit its payments to the plaintiff where it did so in compliance with its contractual rights, even though it was agreed that the insurer could cancel the policies after renewal simply to avoid paying commissions, whereupon another agent could write the new policies with the insurer or the insurer could act as a direct writer.

In *Lykins v. Nationwide Mut. Ins. Co.*, 448 S.E.2d 716 (Ga. Ct. App. 1994), a former agent sued the insurer for breach of contract and bad faith while bringing suit against other agents for tortious interference with contract. The plaintiff had operated an agency for several years and contracted to sell insurance exclusively for the defendant insurer. Under the contract, she would forfeit her entitlement to extended earnings and deferred compensation if she induced or attempted to induce the insurer's policyholders to switch to another insurer or failed to return all materials and records to the insurer within 10 days of termination.

The agent submitted a letter of resignation indicating that she intended to use other insurers, and she transferred her book of business to another of the insurer's agents. She subsequently retracted her resignation, declared her retirement and requested the payment of deferred compensation and extended earnings pursuant to the agency agreement.

The insurer initially paid these benefits but discontinued them due to violations of the noncompetition provisions of the agency agreement. Specifically, the agent sold her equipment to another agency established by her daughter and the agent's office manager went to work for the daughter.

The court held that the agent's failure to return all the insurer's materials supported the termination of benefit payments. Also, the actions of the regional manager in reporting the agent's post-retirement conduct to the insurer, leading to the termination of benefits, did not constitute tortious interference with contract.

Page 85, add to note 17:

In *Srein v. Soft Drink Workers Union*, 93 F.3d 1088 (2d Cir. 1996), applying New York law, the broker sued the insurer for failing to pay commissions and the group-insured union trust fund for withholding consent to the payment. In a complicated fact situation, the court affirmed the summary judgment for the broker, holding that New York Ins. Law § 2119, which prohibits a broker from receiving certain payments from the insured, did not apply to the insurer's contractual obligation to pay commissions. The insurer was held to have breached the fiduciary duty it owed to the broker, and the court found that it so acted in an attempt to gain an advantage in other pending litigation with the broker.

In *Shipley v. Baillie*, 547 N.W.2d 711 (Neb. 1996), the subagent sought to recover unpaid commissions for selling life insurance policies. The subagent sued the insurer and the general agent, who was authorized by the insurer to recruit subagents. The general agent could request that commissions be paid directly to the subagent who sold the policy, rather than to the general agent. In such situations, the insurer would make the check payable to the subagent but still send it to the general agent. Attached to the subagency agreement was a commission authorization form directing the insurer to pay commissions directly to the subagent. The insurer paid commissions to the general agent, and some of these commissions were paid to the subagent. The subagent sought an accounting of the commissions and damages, alleging that the insurer and the general agent failed to comply with the terms of the subagency and direct-payment agreements. The court affirmed the summary judgment granted to the insurer, holding that the mere fact that the general agent was authorized to hire subagents did not subject the insurer to breach of contract claims brought by the subagent with whom it had no contract.

In *Gutfreund v. DeMian*, 642 N.Y.S.2d 294 (N.Y. App. Div. 1996), the plaintiff sought to collect insurance commissions from the insurer even though he was an unlicensed broker. He allegedly entered into an oral agreement with the insurer for the payment of such commissions. The court held that the lack of a license barred his suit for commissions; the broker failed to qualify as the insurer's employee or otherwise fall within the statutory exceptions to the licensing requirement.

In *Crumpton v. Mike Stevens, MGA*, 936 S.W.2d 473 (Tex. Ct. App. 1996), the agent brought suit to recover unpaid commissions from the MGA with respect to policies that the agent allegedly sold while working for the MGA. The court affirmed the award of commissions to the agent. The court held that the agent was potentially entitled to recover his attorney fees incurred in the collection of the unpaid commissions.

In *Ardrey Insurance Agency v. Insurance Co. of Decatur*, 656 A.2d 936 (Pa. Super. Ct. 1995), various agents brought a class action against the insurer to challenge its recalculation of commissions. The independent insurance agents and insurer had entered into agency agreements which provided:

> As full compensation for services, Company shall pay Agent commissions on premiums written and paid for at the rates specified in schedule(s) attached. Agent shall pay Company return commissions at the same

rates on any return premiums, including return premiums on cancellations ordered or made by Company. Where no commission rate has been specified, but insurance has been submitted and accepted by Company, the rates shall be determined by Company. The schedule(s) of commissions allowable shall be determined by Company. The schedule of commissions shall be subject to change by Company at any time by written notice to Agent respecting insurance written or renewed thereafter. (656 A.2d 937)

The first schedule of commissions took effect in 1975. In November 1983, the insurer notified the agents that a new schedule would be implemented. This schedule altered the categorization of insurance policies by creating new subdivisions with different commission rates. The schedule also looked retrospectively at the premium levels attained by individual agents in the previous year and this would affect commission rates.

In 1990, when the Pennsylvania legislature enacted a statute directing insurers to reduce the costs of automobile insurance, the insurer notified the agents that it was sending a new schedule of commissions. The new schedule required individual agents to assume a limited loss ratio on certain classes of auto insurance policies.

The agents filed this suit alleging that the new schedule of commissions was contrary to the original intent of the parties in drafting the agency agreements. The court affirmed the summary judgment for the insurer, holding that the insurer had the unilateral right to change the commissions and was not required to treat all its agents equally.

In *Pennsylvania Life Ins. Co. v. Pavlick*, 637 N.E.2d 1160 (Ill. App. Ct. 1994), the insurers sued their former branch managers for breach of contract and tortious interference with contractual relations, whereupon the managers sought an accounting of commissions. The management agreements authorized the managers to recruit, appoint, and train sales agents. The contract contained a compensation schedule identifying regions for which a manager would receive commissions. The agreements were amended on several occasions, increasing compensation for different zones and types of policies. The managers voluntarily terminated their relationship with the insurers, whereupon the insurers claimed that the managers violated postemployment restrictive covenants not to compete by soliciting customers and sales agents from the insurers. The managers then counterclaimed for commissions due.

The court affirmed summary judgment in the insurer's favor on the counterclaims, where the management agreements provided that the commissions would be paid on net profits for the various regions and lines of business, and not on the amount of premiums.

Page 87, add at end of section:

In *Donovan v. Bankers Fidelity Life Ins. Co.*, 26 F.3d 854 (8th Cir. 1994, applying Missouri law), the agents sued the insurers for breach of contract. The plaintiffs were general agents selling Medicare supplement insurance. The insurers advised the plaintiffs that they would no longer pay commissions on rate increases on accident and health policies. The agency contract provided:

> 14. *Changes in Insurance.* The Company shall, in its sole discretion, determine the adjustments, if any, to be made in Compensation resulting from a change in plan, amount of insurance, amount of premium, other than by term conversion.
> ...
> 21. *Amendment.* Compensation shall be determined by the current Compensation Schedule. This Company may at any time, upon written notice, change the rates of Compensation. Such change will be effective with respect to applications received in the Home Office of the Company on and after the date fixed in the notice, except as specifically provided.

The court affirmed the summary judgment in favor of the insurers, holding that the contract entitled the insurers to change the commission rates for policies sold prior to the date fixed in the notice that the insurers would no longer pay commissions on rate increases.

4.5 Agent's Duties to Insurer

Page 87, add to note 25a at end of first paragraph:

In *Carolina Cas. Ins. Co. v. Cummings Agency*, 110 F.3d 1 (1st Cir. 1997), applying Maine law, the insurer sued the agent claiming that he failed to report that the insured was involved in the business of hauling crushed scrap cars. The insurer contended that had it known the true nature of the business, it never would have issued the policy. The insurer characterized the agent as a producing agent.

The court held that the agent had no duty to disclose the information to the insurer and therefore could not be held liable. Thus, the court held that the agent was actually a broker who had no special relationship with the insurer that would otherwise impose a duty to disclose.

Page 88, add note 25b at end of last full paragraph:

In *Westchester Fire Insurance Co. v. JHC Insurance Group*, 178 F.3d 973 (8th Cir. 1999), applying Minnesota law, the insurer sued the wholesale insurance broker for failing to clearly transmit a change in coverage to the insured. Because the insurer could not establish that any negligence by the broker caused the insurer to sustain a loss, the insurer wasn't entitled to recover. The insurer could not show what would have happened had the change in coverage been communicated to the insured, such as whether the insured would have refused to accept the change, whereupon the coverage afforded under the policy would have been reduced so as to preclude coverage for the loss in question.

In *Life Investors Insurance Co. v. John R. Young Chevrolet*, 730 So. 2d 519 (La. Ct. App. 1999), the insurer sued the agent to recover amounts paid under a credit life insurance policy that was allegedly negligently written by the agent. The agent allegedly failed to indicate that the insured had preexisting illnesses. Less than a year from the issuance of the policy, the insured died of a preexisting heart condition. The court held that such an action was a suit for damages, not for specific performance of an agency contract. Therefore, the suit was subject to the one-year statute of limitations.

In *Bennacer v. Travelers Insurance Co.*, 695 N.Y.S.2d 846 (N.Y. App. Div. 1999), the insurer's agent issued a binder to the owner of a pizza shop that provided nonowned coverage. The policy, as issued, excluded such coverage. During the 30-day period that the binder was in effect, an auto accident occurred involving a nonowned vehicle driven by one of the insured's employees. Because the agent exceeded the authority it was granted by the insurer in binding the risk, the agent was liable for indemnifying the insurer for the amount due to the insured.

In *Colonial Penn Ins. Co. v. Market Planners Ins. Agency*, 157 F.3d 1032 (5th Cir. 1998), applying Texas law, the insurer sued the agency for failing to remit premiums collected on the sale of the insurer's policies. The question was whether the insurer's claim was barred by the statute of limitations. The court was also required to evaluate the effect of the agent's fraud on the insurer's discovery of the misappropriated premiums and the effect of such actions on the insurer's right to pursue its claim. The court held that the limitations period for filing suit does not start to run until the insurer conducts an internal audit placing it on notice of irregularities. Additionally, the agency president was found to be the insurer's local recording agent so as to render him personally liable for the misappropriation. Clearly, the agency is also liable.

Page 90, add new note 26a to end of second full paragraph under "Liabilities Arising from Agent's Actions":

In *Art Goebel, Inc. v. North Suburban Agencies*, 567 N.W.2d 511 (Minn. 1997), the insured car dealer sued the insurer and the agent claiming that there was coverage under the policy as issued, or alternatively, that the agent was negligent in failing to obtain the ordered coverage. The agent filed a cross claim against the insurer seeking indemnity for the cost of defending the suit. After the insured's claim against the insurer and the agent was dismissed, the court held that the insurer was not required to pay the cost of the agent's defense based on the indemnity provisions of the agency agreement. The indemnity clause provided:

> [The insurer] will defend and indemnify [the agent] against liability, including the cost of defense and settlements, imposed on him by law ... for damages sustained by policyholders and caused by acts or omissions of [the insurer], provided [agent] has not caused or contributed to such liability by its own acts or omissions.

567 N.W.2d at 515. The court held that this provision set forth the agent's exclusive indemnity rights and therefore the agent could not recover under common law indemnity theory. The court held that the insurer was not required to indemnify the agent since there was no evidence that any acts or omissions of the insurer resulted in damage to the insured.

In *U.S.F. & G. Co. v. Sulco, Inc.*, 939 F. Supp. 820 (D. Kan. 1996), the insurer sued the agent to recoup amounts paid after settling with the insured on claims of overpayment of premiums, misrepresentation, and errors in handling the insured's insurance requirements. The agent had presented a proposal for various coverages, which the insured had accepted. The insured claimed that it was misled into purchasing insurance on terms other than it reasonably expected. The court held that the insurer had only a potential right to implied contractual indemnity based on the imposition of vicarious liability on the insurer for the agent's conduct. In order to recover, the insurer would be required to establish that it was without fault with respect to the insured's claim. Such claim was subject to a three-year statute of limitations.

In *Carolina Cas. Ins. Co. v. Cummings Agency, Inc.*, 932 F. Supp. 371 (D. Me. 1996), the insurer paid the claim after an auto accident and then sued the agency, arguing that the application forwarded by the agent failed to show the true nature of the insured's business. The insured was in the business of hauling crushed scrap cars. The insurer claimed that the agent knew or should have known that such risks were unacceptable to the insurer. However, the insurer alleged only that the agent was negligent and did not allege that it engaged in fraud or misrepresentation. The court granted the agent's motion for summary judgment, holding that there was no independent duty to exercise reasonable care running to the insurer under the circumstances and that the insurer failed to establish that the agent was negligent in handling the application.

In *Holt v. Aetna Cas. & Sur. Co.*, 680 So. 2d 117 (La. Ct. App. 1996), the insurer sought to avoid the auto policy due to the insured's failure to report his numerous traffic violations, accidents, and nonrenewals. The insurer also brought a claim against the agent for any amounts it would be required to pay to the insured. The defendant insurance producer handled the insured's family's needs for many years. While the agent was handling the insured's business, one of the nonrenewals occurred. He was aware that the problem was the insured's poor loss history.

The agent left the agency where he was working and took the insured's business with him. He then contacted the insured with an outline of coverage even though he did not have the full details of the account. The loss history submitted to the insurer failed to contain several accidents and violations for certain insureds. The court held that where there was no evidence that the insureds acted to mislead the insurer, the insurer could not avoid the policy. There were fact questions concerning the comparative fault of the insurer and the agent and whether the insurer waived the loss history defense.

In *Ohio Farmers Ins. Co. v. Dakota Agency, Inc.*, 551 N.W.2d 564 (N.D. 1996), the insurer sued the agent to recover amounts paid pursuant to a performance bond issued by agency employees without the insurer's authorization. The insurer and agent had entered into an agency agreement, which incorporated the terms of the underwriting guides and limitations on the agent's authority. With respect to fidelity and surety bonds, prior approval from the insurer was required before such bonds could be issued. The employee executed bonds obligating the insurer. After a loss in excess of $300,000, the insurer was given its first notice of the existence of the bonds. The insurer would not have issued the bonds had approval been sought by the agent as required. The insurer nevertheless paid the loss and ultimately sued the agent for the amount of the loss, alleging that the agent was responsible for the employee's unauthorized conduct. The court affirmed the summary judgment for the insurer, holding that the agent could be held liable for breach of contract under the facts of the case.

In *Steinberg v. Mikkelsen*, 901 F. Supp. 1433 (E.D. Wis. 1995), the insureds sued the agent and the health insurer claiming that the insureds were wrongfully denied benefits due to the agent's knowing failure to disclose one of the insured's past health problems on the application for insurance. This resulted in certain uncovered medical expenses.

The insureds invoked ERISA since the insurance was provided as part of their employment benefits. The agent assisted the insureds in completing the applications. While both insureds had various medical problems including the taking of certain medications, a massive stroke and various other disorders, the application submitted to the first insurer did not disclose these health problems. That insurer rejected the application after discovering one insured's poor health history.

The agent entered into an independent agency relationship with the second insurer with which the coverage was eventually placed. The insureds completed an application for the second insurer with the assistance of the agent. This insurer relied on the representations contained in the application in accepting the risk. Had the truth been disclosed, the insurer would not have issued the policy. Ultimately, the insurer discovered the truth when one insured presented a claim. When that claim was rejected, this action was brought.

The court denied the insurer's motion for summary judgment, holding that traditional agency law principles are applicable in a case brought under ERISA, and therefore the agent's knowledge of the true health history could be imputed to the insurer.

Page 92, add to note 30:

In *Lenox Realty v. Excelsior Ins. Co.*, 679 N.Y.S.2d 749 (N.Y. App. Div. 1998), the plaintiff property owner and manager sought coverage under the snow removal subcontractor's liability insurance coverage, claiming that they were intended to be named as additional insureds under that policy. The insurer brought a third-party claim against the subcontractor's insurance agent, who had added the plaintiffs as additional insureds in excess of his authority. The agent testified that it was routine procedure when adding a party as an additional insured to send the insurer a copy of the certificate and that he acted within his authority when he added the plaintiffs. The court held that the insurer was equitably estopped from denying coverage to the plaintiffs and that whether the agent acted in excess of his authority was to be decided in arbitration, at which time the terms of the agency agreement would be construed. The issue would only be relevant with respect to the insurer's claim against the agent.

In *Alliston v. Omega Ins. Co.*, 983 F. Supp. 675 (S.D. Miss. 1997), the insureds sued the agent for fraudulently misrepresenting their coverage under a property insurance policy. The agent allegedly told the plaintiffs that they would be covered for burglary losses, but when one such loss occurred, the insurer denied coverage. The insurer finally admitted that there was coverage but refused to pay the entire amount of the insureds' loss.

The court held that when the insurer admitted that there was coverage for the loss, any misrepresentation made by the agent was rendered irrelevant and therefore the agent could not be held liable. The court further noted that the agent is not obligated to the insureds with respect to the settlement of claims that would support the imposition of liability for the insurer's conduct in handling the claim.

High Country Arts and Craft v. Hartford Fire Ins. Co., 126 F.3d 629 (4th Cir. 1997), applying North Carolina law. Clearly, an agent has no authority, either actual or apparent, to modify the policy provisions following the issuance of the policy in the absence of compelling equities.

See also Rickborn v. Liberty Life Ins. Co., 468 S.E.2d 292 (S.C. 1996), discussed in § 1.4.

In *Southland Lloyd's Ins. Co. v. Tomberlain*, 919 S.W.2d 822 (Tex. Ct. App. 1996), the agent owned property and sued the insurer and an employee for the bad faith of the defendants in failing to investigate and pay a fire claim arising out of damage to the property.

The plaintiff was an independent agent and owned and managed various properties. After making improvements, the plaintiff executed a contract for the sale of a house, with the purchaser paying installments over time. The plaintiff, as agent, issued a policy on the house. The plaintiff did not renew the policy upon expiration because the agency stopped writing policies with that insurer. The agent, acting on his own behalf, executed an application for coverage with the defendant. The defendant approved the policy but reduced the coverage amount.

Prior to the fire in question, the purchaser vacated the premises without notifying the plaintiff. When the plaintiff learned of the situation, he cleaned and made repairs to the house and arranged to rent it out. Ten days before the tenant was to take possession, the fire occurred. There was evidence that the fire was of incendiary origin. The plaintiff filed a completed claim form. The defendant insurer denied the claim and immediately cancelled its contract with the agency, alleging that it was duped by misrepresentations contained in the application for insurance.

The court reversed the judgment on the jury verdict for the defendant, holding that the trial court committed various reversible evidentiary errors and found that it was for the jury to ultimately determine whether the plaintiff agent breached the fiduciary duties owed to the insurer, committed fraud, or otherwise breached the agency contract. It was also for the jury to determine whether the insurer properly investigated the claim.

In *American Nat'l Fire Ins. Co. v. Howland La Clair Assocs., Inc.*, 624 N.Y.S.2d 320 (N.Y. App. Div. 1995), the excess insurer sued the agent for indemnification. It claimed that the agent was negligent in failing to notify it of changes in the underlying coverage, and in failing to cancel the excess policy upon becoming aware of those changes. The court held that agency law principles did not provide the excess insurer with a claim for implied indemnity, since the insurer failed to allege that the agent breached a duty owed to a third party.

In *Plumlee v. Monroe Guaranty Ins. Co.*, 655 N.E.2d 350 (Ind. Ct. App. 1995), the plaintiff was injured while a pedestrian. He sued the tortfeasor insured. The insured then assigned his claims against the insurer and the agent to the plaintiff, who brought this action.

The insured and agent discussed the insured's insurance needs. The agent completed the application for auto liability and umbrella coverage and submitted the application for a quotation. The application listed two vehicles. The insurer twice provided quotations to the agent. When no action was taken within 60 days to procure policies, the quotations expired.

A second application was then completed and forwarded to the insurer. However, even though the insured owned two trucks, only one was listed on the application. When the plaintiff attempted to recover from the insurer, the claim was denied.

The insurer advised that the truck involved in the accident was not listed under the policies.

The court held that the insurer was not entitled to summary judgment due to ambiguities in the policy description of covered vehicles. The agent's alleged negligence in completing the final application could not be imputed to the insurer under the respondeat superior theory, but the agent was required to indemnify the insurer for any liability owing to the agent's negligence by virtue of the agency contract.

In *Southeastern Insurance Agency v. Lumbermens Mut. Ins. Co.*, 650 N.E.2d 1285 (Mass. App. Ct. 1995), the insured oil company was sued by a customer for property damage caused by oil spilling from one of the insured's trucks. Thereupon, the insured sued the agent for negligence in failing to provide sufficient coverage under the primary liability policy. The agent was responsible for purchasing and maintaining two policies for the insured. One policy was an umbrella policy which required that the insured maintain $300,000 in primary coverage. The agent obtained a primary commercial auto policy in that amount.

When the umbrella policy was renewed, the insurer required that the insured maintain $500,000 in underlying coverage for property damage or $1 million combined single limit coverage. The insurer did not notify the insured of the change in terms. Moreover, the agent did not detect the change and never increased the primary coverage. When the loss occurred, there was a $200,000 gap between the primary coverage maintained and that required. The insured was required to fill that gap, and this was the basis of the claim against the agent.

The court held that the reformation of the policy to express the true intent of the insured and the agent as to the proper policy limits was appropriate. The insurer, however, was not entitled to indemnification from the agent for the amounts paid in excess of the $300,000 limit in the policy as issued where the insurer admitted that it would have increased the amount of coverage had it been requested.

In *Maryland Ins. Co. v. Head Industrial Coatings & Services, Inc.*, 906 S.W.2d 218 (Tex. Ct. App. 1995), the insured sued the CGL insurer after it refused to pay a claim brought against the insured. The insurer, in turn, "third-partied" the local agent, claiming that the agent was required to indemnify the insurer for any potential liability.

As a prerequisite to working for a utility, the insured was required to agree to indemnify the utility for any claims arising out of the services performed and to purchase liability insurance to protect the utility against claims arising out of that work.

The insured contacted its local agent and purchased a policy. The insured intended to purchase the required contractual liability insurance coverage and advised the agent accordingly. There was even evidence that the insured was charged for the coverage. The agent allegedly committed a clerical error, and the policy actually issued did not contain the proper coverage.

When a worker on the project was injured and filed suit, the utility sought indemnification and/or insurance coverage from the insured. At this point, the absence of the endorsement was discovered, and the insurer refused to provide coverage. The court held that the insurer could potentially be liable in bad faith for the product of the agent's negligence. The court found that the agent breached its fiduciary duties owed to the insurer.

Page 93, add to note 38:

In *Colonial Penn Ins. Co. v. Market Planners Ins. Agency*, 157 F.3d 1032 (5th Cir. 1998), applying Texas law, the insurer sued the agency for failing to remit premiums collected on the sale of the insurer's policies. The question raised was whether the insurer's claim was barred by the statute of limitations. The court was also required to evaluate the effect of the agent's fraud on the insurer's discovery of the misappropriated premiums and the effect of such actions on the insurer's right to pursue its claim. The court held that the limitations period for filing suit does not start to run until the insurer conducts an internal audit placing it on notice of irregularities. Additionally, the agency president was found to be the insurer's local recording agent so as to render him personally liable for the misappropriation. Clearly, the agency is also liable.

See also Standard Funding Corp. v. Lewitt, 678 N.E.2d 874 (N.Y. 1997), discussed in § 1.4.

In *Central Benefits Mut. Ins. Co. v. RIS Administrators Agency, Inc.*, 638 N.E.2d 1049 (Ohio Ct. App. 1994), the insurers sued the insurance agency and its officers for breach of contract, conversion, and breach of fiduciary duties. The cause of action arose out of the defendants' actions as third-party administrator for the insurers' health and life insurance programs. There were various problems with the defendants' collection and timely transmission of premiums to the plaintiffs. There was evidence that the defendants treated the collected premium funds as their own and delayed transmission while using the funds for unauthorized purposes. In response to a request for summary judgment, the court held that the allegations raised a question of fact for the jury as to whether the defendants' conduct constituted conversion and breach of fiduciary duties.

4.6 Termination Rights in General

Page 98, add to note 45:

In *Vikco Insurance Services v. Ohio Indemnity Co.*, 82 Cal. Rptr. 2d 442 (Cal. Ct. App. 1999), the agent sued the insurer for failing to give it 120 days' notice before terminating the agency agreement. The length of the notice was required by California Insurance Code § 769. The written agency agreement stated that either party could terminate the agency relationship with only 45 days' written notice. The court held that the statutory provision could be modified by the agreement of both parties as evidenced by their contract. The plaintiff agent was entitled to waive the protection afforded him by the statute since the statute was enacted for his benefit. The court refused to write the statutory provisions into the agency agreement, which could have extended the notice period to the full 120 days. The court further noted that the plaintiff agent could not enforce a statutory violation in the court, but rather any statutory violation could be raised in administrative proceedings against the insurer in front of the insurance department.

In *Lange v. TIG Insurance Co.*, 81 Cal. Rptr. 2d 39 (Cal. Ct. App. 1998), a contractors' association started a pooling program to permit its members to purchase liability insurance at competitive rates. The association appointed an agent to administer the program and work with the members. The insurer entered into a written agency agreement with the agent and started selling liability insurance under the program. The agent was authorized to issue and deliver policies to independent brokers who would, in turn, sell the policies to their clients. The agent encouraged the brokers to sell the insurer's policy. The insurer audited the agent's operations and discovered that the agent had not kept premiums in a segregated account, as required, and over $400,000 in premium payments were missing. The agent had also issued policies in violation of underwriting guidelines. The insurer terminated the agency relationship, whereupon the agent falsely notified the brokers that the insurer was having financial problems. The insurer wrote to the brokers directly when it learned of the deception. The question raised was whether the termination letter included a binding promise by the insurer to permit the agent to continue selling policies until a specified date that would comport with the industry custom of providing agents with 90 days' notice of the termination of a program. The brokers continued to solicit as much new business with the insurer as they could during this period. The insurer refused to honor the new policies. The court held that the insurer had not agreed to accept new business from the brokers during the 90-day period, as the brokers could not obtain greater rights than the terminated agent. The custom did not apply to the brokers who had no contractual relationship with the insurer and there was no breach by the insurer of any duty not to interfere with the brokers' relationship with their clients and the association.

In *Martin v. American Fam. Mut. Ins. Co.*, 157 F.3d 580 (8th Cir. 1998), applying Missouri law, the plaintiffs were independent insurance agents for the defendant company. They filed suit after the insurer terminated their agency agreements. The plaintiffs alleged that the insurer committed fraud by canceling the agreements after telling them that they would have "life-long employment." The court held that such statements did not bar the insurer's right to terminate the agreements according to their terms, where the statements in question were not knowingly false when made. In addition, the plaintiffs could not have reasonably relied on the statements since they participated in drafting the agency agreement that permitted the terminations.

In *Barnhart v. New York Life Ins. Co.*, 141 F.3d 1310 (9th Cir. 1998), applying Washington law, ERISA, and the Age Discrimination in Employment Act (ADEA), the plaintiff agent sued the insurer for violations of state and federal law arising out of the termination of his agency contract. The parties entered into a field underwriter's contract authorizing the plaintiff to sell insurance policies on behalf of the insurer. The contract had no termination date, but permitted either, party to terminate the agreement by giving 30 days' notice, with or without cause. The regional general manager informed the plaintiff of new minimum production standards. The plaintiff failed to meet those standards, and upon recommendation of the general manager, the insurer terminated the agency agreement. The district court held that the plaintiff had no viable ERISA or ADEA claim since he was an independent contractor and not an employee. The ninth circuit affirmed this decision and upheld the termination of the agency agreement.

In *Alexander v. Cigna Corp.*, 991 F. Supp. 427 (D.N.J. 1998), the plaintiffs, independent insurance agents, sued the insurer for fraud, breach of fiduciary duties, misrepresentation, and breach of their exclusive representation agreements. The insurer allegedly assured the plaintiffs that they would have lifetime tenure. The court held that such statements did not create a binding obligation on the insurer to keep the plaintiffs

Part I ◻ **Chapter 4** ◻ **2000 Supplement**
Contractual Relationship Between Insurer and Agent

as agents until they retired or died. This decision was supported by the terms of the agreement, which provided that the written agreement controlled any previous written or oral understandings or statements and permitted the insurer to terminate the relationship in compliance with the terms of the contract.

In *Jean Anderson Hierarchy of Agents v. Allstate Life Insurance Co.*, 2 F. Supp. 3d 688 (E.D. Pa. 1998), the plaintiff entered into an executive sales director contract with the defendant. She was authorized to sell the insurer's products. She was also authorized to staff an agency to sell the products in Pennsylvania and New Jersey. The insurer hired her husband as its regional director for those markets. The plaintiff claimed that, based on her contract with the insurer, she started recruiting agents to market the insurer's products and eventually recruited 428 agents. She was recognized as an outstanding executive sales director and was rewarded. She claimed that despite her performance, the insurer refused to pay her commissions or persistency bonuses she earned, claiming she was only receiving them because her husband was the regional director.

After six years, the insurer terminated the plaintiff and her husband. She contended that the termination was retaliatory due to the husband's informing the insurer of inherent defects in some of its products. The court held that the allegations of her complaint failed to state a claim on behalf of her unincorporated association (the hierarchy of agents) arising out of the failure to make payments where there was no allegation that the suit was being brought in the name of a trustee for the benefit of the association. The court also found that she failed to allege discriminatory conduct to support her claim for the intentional infliction of emotional distress. However, she stated viable claims under various federal acts. Clearly, she also would have a claim for the breach of the terms of the agency agreement.

In *Lawhorn & Assoc's, Inc. v. Patriot Gen. Ins. Co.*, 917 F. Supp. 538 (E.D. Tenn. 1996), the agency sued the insurer for breach of the agency contract. The agency primarily sold "nonstandard" auto insurance policies. One insurer notified the agency that it was reducing the commission percentage rates. The agency objected and ultimately demanded arbitration pursuant to the arbitration terms of the contract.

Prior to the arbitration, however, the defendant terminated the agency agreement, whereupon the agency brought this claim. The plaintiff charged that the defendant wrongfully terminated and breached the contract due to the plaintiff's refusal to willingly accept the attempt to cut the commission rates. The court held that the contracts were terminable at will; the insurer had not breached the duty to act in good faith. The court granted the defendant's motion for summary judgment.

In *Cigna Fire Underwriters Co. v. MacDonald & Johnson, Inc.*, 86 F.3d 1260 (1st Cir. 1996), the insurer sued the agent for breach of contract, whereupon the agent claimed that the insurer intentionally interfered with contractual relations and economic gain. The insurer claimed that the agent failed to transmit insurance premiums due it. The court held that there was sufficient evidence that the jury could find the insurer breached the agency contract by canceling it after the agent refused to sign a promissory note, which included a waiver of all claims that the agent might have against the insurer.

There was also evidence that the insurer refused to honor binders, which had been authorized by appropriate officers of the insurer, issued by the agent. There was sufficient evidence that the agent failed to pay premiums as due, notwithstanding the agent's contention that its execution of promissory notes providing for the payment of past due premiums modified the duty to make the payments. The court, however, found that the insurer did not intentionally interfere with the agent's contractual relations with insureds and affirmed the judgment for the insurer.

In *Morgan Assoc. v. Midwest Mut. Ins. Co.*, 519 N.W.2d 499 (Minn. Ct. App. 1994), the agent alleged that the insurer constructively terminated the agency contract without complying with the requirements of Minn. Stat. § 60A.171(1)(a). In 1992, the agent was restricted from writing new business due to its loss ratio for the preceding 12 months. The insurer noted that the goal was to rehabilitate the agency by restricting new business while continuing to issue renewal policies to accumulate earned premium to offset the incurred loss. The court affirmed summary judgment for the insurer, holding that its restriction on new business did not constitute a termination of the agency contracts.

Page 99, add to note 49:

In *Salmons v. Prudential Insurance Co.*, 48 F. Supp. 2d 620 (S.D. W.Va. 1999), the agent claimed that he was unlawfully terminated by the insurer. The agent was employed by Prudential and was covered by a union-negotiated agent's agreement between the agents and the insurer. The agreement specifically stated that it could be terminated by the insurer at any time. The insurer imposed a minimum annual quota. The failure to meet the quota would result in termination. The agent failed to meet the quota and the insurer terminated the agent's agreement. The agent claimed that the agreement provided that agents employed for more than five years under a written contract could not be terminated for other than specified reasons. The insurer argued that the claim was preempted by the federal Labor Management Relations Act. The court held that the Act did not preempt the state-based breach of contract claims.

In *Noack v. Blue Cross and Blue Shield*, 742 So. 2d 433 (Fla. Dist. Ct. App. 1999), the agent sued the insurer for claims arising out of the cancellation of its agency contract. The agent alleged fraud in the inducement to enter into the contract, claiming that the insurer represented that if the agent signed a release promising not sue the insurer, the agent would immediately become the insurer's general agent. The agent alleged that the representation was false. The agent executed the release but was not made a general agent. The court held that the agent stated a viable fraud claim, notwithstanding the fact that the only damages sustained were economic in nature.

In *Hamilton Insurance Services v. Nationwide Insurance Companies*, 714 N.E.2d 898 (Ohio 1999), the insurer terminated the agency agreement, whereupon the agent sued the insurer for wrongful termination. Nationwide sought to have the plaintiff take over an existing agency. The process required that the plaintiff serve the first three years as a Nationwide employee, after which the plaintiff was to become an independent agent with respect to Nationwide. After the initial three-year period, the plaintiff became an independent agent and executed an agent's agreement, providing that agreement could be cancelled by either party at any time, with or without cause. The agreement also contained a noncompetition clause, the breach of which forfeited any post-termination benefits. The plaintiff was ultimately advised that he was not meeting the necessary performance levels and, two years later, the insurer terminated the agency agreement. The plaintiff contended that the termination was wrongful and in bad faith and that the termination clause was unconscionable. He contended that a termination could only be for cause. The court upheld the termination-at-will feature of the agency agreement. The fact that the agency handbook listed various grounds for termination did not mean that termination only could be made for one of those reasons.

In *Iglesias v. Mutual Life Ins. Co.*, 156 F.3d 237 (1st Cir. 1998), applying Puerto Rico law, the agent signed an agency agreement with the insurer authorizing the agent to solicit applications on behalf of the insurer on lines of business the company was writing within the geographic area. Such an authorization did not limit the insurer's ability to withdraw certain insurance products from the agent's geographic area. Thus, the agent had no viable claim against the insurer for totally withdrawing from the locality, thereby terminating his agency relationship. The agency agreement did not give the agent the power to control what lines of business the insurer would write in the area.

In *Bennett v. Farmers Ins. Co. of Ore.*, 945 P.2d 595 (Or. Ct. App. 1997), the agent sued the insurer following the termination of the agency agreement. The insurer initially solicited the plaintiff to terminate his then-existing agency business and enter into a new agreement whereby he would recruit and train insurance agents to sell the insurer's policies.

The insurer signed a district manager's agreement with the plaintiff in which the plaintiff was called an independent contractor. The agreement provided that the insurer would exercise no control over the way in which the plaintiff carried out the terms of the agreement. The agreement also provided that it could be terminated by the insurer without cause. After the plaintiff had built a successful business, the insurer terminated the agreement. The plaintiff alleged that the insurer told him that it was not going to enforce the provision allowing it to terminate without cause and that any termination would only be for cause.

The existence and effect of the alleged statement created a fact question for the jury to resolve. However, the court found that the agreement had been modified by letters signed by the parties in which the insurer agreed to maintain the agency relationship provided the agent met stated production goals. The court affirmed the judgment, in part, on the jury verdict awarding the plaintiff damages for the breach of contract.

4.7 Terminations for Cause

Page 100, add to note 53:

In *Kaniff v. Allstate Ins. Co.*, 121 F.3d 258 (7th Cir. 1997), the agent sued the insurer that employed him, claiming that his employment was terminated in violation of the Age Discrimination in Employment Act. The employment contract provided that either party could terminate the agreement upon the mailing of written notice of termination.

The plaintiff alleged that the insurer agreed that it would not terminate the plaintiff's employment "because of unsatisfactory work unless you have been notified that your work is unsatisfactory and that your job is in jeopardy and unless you have been given a reasonable opportunity to bring your performance up to satisfactory standards." (121 F.3d at 259).

The court, applying Illinois law, held that the plaintiff agent's falsification of applications was an act of dishonesty that entitled the insurer to terminate the agent's employment without notice or opportunity. The mere fact that the insurer suggested that the agent retire did not permit an inference of age discrimination in violation of the statute.

In *G.M. Abodeely Ins. Agency v. Commerce Ins. Co.*, 669 N.E.2d 787 (Mass. App. Ct. 1996), the agent sued the insurer after the insurer canceled the agency contract. The reason given for the insurer's action was that the agent purportedly failed to report coverages bound in accordance with the agency agreement. The agent also allegedly accepted business that did not conform to the insurer's underwriting criteria. The agent claimed that this was a pretext for the insurer's desire to eliminate the agent as a competitor for the insurer's wholly owned subsidiary that also sold insurance. The court affirmed the judgment for the agency, where the contract was not held to be terminable at will and specifically provided for the resolution of objectively reasonable and honest differences.

In *McNeill v. Security Benefit Life Ins. Co.*, 28 F.3d 891 (8th Cir. 1994, applying Arkansas law), an independent insurance agent brought suit for wrongful termination of the contract and tortious interference with client relationships. The insurer had acquired a financially weak insurer and sought state permission to sell its block of policies to the weaker insurer. The agent objected and the proposed sale was disapproved. The insurer's subsequent efforts to service the weaker insurer's policies resulted in numerous complaints from policyholders and the agent. The insurer ultimately terminated the agent, and the agent brought suit.

The contract gave the insurer the right to terminate the agency without cause upon 15 days' notice, which was in fact given. However, the agent claimed that the insurer acted in bad faith by terminating the contract in retaliation for the agent's attempts to protect policyholders.

The court affirmed summary judgment for the insurer, holding that the termination was not wrongful; also, the insurer's failure to service the policies properly did not constitute tortious interference with the agency's relationship with the policyholders. While the insurer's actions may have constituted breach of contract, there was no evidence that the insurer intended to interfere with the agency-policyholder relationship.

In *Strange v. Nationwide Mut. Ins. Co.*, 867 F. Supp. 1209 (E.D. Pa. 1994), the former agents sued the insurer for violations of the Fair Housing Act, Age Discrimination in Employment Act, wrongful discharge, and defamation. The court held that the former agents stated viable claims. The age discrimination claims were only viable where certain plaintiffs could show that they were employees of the insurer and not independent contractors. There was a viable Fair Housing Act claim where the plaintiffs alleged that there was discrimination in insurance related to housing. The court also found viable claims for wrongful discharge arising from the plaintiffs' refusal to participate in illegal redlining practices employed by the insurer.

In *Eastway & Blevins Agency v. Citizens Ins. Co.*, 520 N.W.2d 640 (Mich. Ct. App. 1994), an independent agency sued the insurer for wrongful termination. The plaintiff and all of the defendant's other agents were required to sign an addendum to the agency agreements restricting them from selling or servicing the insurer's products in branch offices without the insurer's express consent. The plaintiff opened a branch office despite the fact that the insurer reiterated the restriction on using and advertising its products in the branch office. (The insurer reasoned that it already had adequate representation in the area.) Nevertheless, the agent permitted at least one of the insurer's policyholders to make payments and ask questions at the branch office. The parties executed a new agency agreement restating that the agent would not sell the insurer's products through branch offices and restating the insurer's right to terminate the agency relationship.

The agency agreement was terminated, and the agent brought suit. The court affirmed the insurer's motion for a summary judgment, holding that the termination was not wrongful where the agency admittedly breached the agreement. Thus, the motives of the insurer in terminating the agent were irrelevant.

See also *Morgan Assocs. v. Midwest Mut. Ins. Co.,* 519 N.W.2d 499 (Minn. Ct. App. 1994), discussed in § 4.6 above (restriction on writing new business, imposed in order to improve agent's loss ratio, did not constitute constructive termination).

4.8 Post-Termination Obligations: Client Lists, Trade Secrets, and Covenants Not to Compete

Page 106, add to note 68:

In *James L. Miniter Ins. Agency v. Ohio Indem. Co.,* 112 F.3d 1240 (1st Cir. 1997), the agent sued the insurer for breach of contract and bad faith. The agent had a nonexclusive contract which did not require the agent to issue insurance exclusively through the insurer.

Conversely, the insurer had no obligation to accept only policies procured by the agent. The claim arose when the insured canceled a policy it obtained through the agent and negotiated a new policy directly with the insurer. The court, applying Massachusetts law, held that there was no breach of contract or bad faith and the agent was not entitled to receive commissions from the new policy.

In *Keith v. Alexander Underwriters Gen. Agency,* 487 S.E.2d 673 (Ga. Ct. App. 1997), the agent sued the insurer and a premium finance company for breach of contract and tortious interference with contractual relationships. The claims sounded in negligence in the handling of customer accounts and the agent's termination of its agency agreement with the general agent.

The general agent solicited the plaintiff's business, and the plaintiff agreed to write certain business through the general agent. After the plaintiff informed the general agent that it would no longer write business with the general agent due to problems with the general agent's handling of client accounts, the general agent demanded additional amounts on a commercial account for premiums due. The plaintiff refused to pay, whereupon the general agent filed suit against the plaintiff. The general agent also canceled policies issued to the plaintiff's clients and applied unearned premiums paid on those policies to the balance allegedly owed by the plaintiff.

The court affirmed the summary judgment for the general agent, holding that there could be no viable claim for breach of contract against the general agent after the plaintiff canceled the contract. The improper cancellation of policyholder contracts raised claims residing in the policyholders that could not be brought by the plaintiff. The court also affirmed the dismissal of the other claims.

Page 107, add to note 73:

In *Winfree v. Educators Credit Union*, 900 S.W.2d 285 (Tenn. Ct. App. 1995), the insurance salesman sued the credit union and a subsidiary after his right to market cancer insurance to the credit union members was terminated and the defendants then solicited his credit union insurance customers. The parties entered into an agreement whereby the salesman would act as an unpaid marketing representative for the credit union in consideration for the opportunity to sell the insurance to its members. At all times, the salesman was an employee of the insurer and not the credit union. The salesman was required to undergo training by the credit union and contact new employees for membership. The credit union agreed to have insurance premiums deducted from purchasers' salaries.

One year after the initial agreement was executed, it was modified to give the credit union the right to cancel the entire agreement upon 30 days' notice. In such event, the credit union would no longer promote the insurance plan. The salesman was permitted to market another insurer's cancer insurance, and the credit union sent its members a letter advising them of this new plan. When a new credit union president took over, she formed a subsidiary to offer insurance to credit union members. This would allow the credit union to retain the commissions that would have been paid to the plaintiff salesman.

The subsidiary entered into an agent's contract with another insurer and then notified the salesman and the insurers for which he placed business of the termination of payroll deductions. The plaintiff claimed that a substantial number of policyholders converted coverage to the credit union's plan and away from the plaintiff's companies. The plaintiff argued that this deprived him of present and future commissions from his customers.

The court held that the credit union breached its duty of good faith and fair dealing when it notified the plaintiff salesman of the cancellation of the agreement. The court, however, stated that the plaintiff had no claim for tortious interference with contract, interference with his right to collect commissions or interferrence with his relationship with his customers.

In *Phoenix Home Life Mut. Ins. Co. v. Brown*, 857 F. Supp. 7 (W.D.N.Y. 1994), the insurer sued the former agents for RICO violations in addition to breach of contract and fiduciary duties, and interference with contractual relations. At the time suit was filed, the defendants were agents of a competing insurer. They allegedly engaged in a campaign to convince the plaintiff's insureds to surrender their policies, then replacing those policies with others issued by the latter insurer. The court held that the policyholder records and files were subject to the remedy of *replevin,* entitling the plaintiff insurer to recover all premium and other such records.

In *Lykins v. Nationwide Mut. Ins. Co.*, 448 S.E.2d 716 (Ga. Ct. App. 1994), a former agent sued the insurer for breach of contract and bad faith while bringing suit against other agents for tortious interference with contract. The plaintiff had operated an agency for several years and contracted to sell insurance exclusively for the defendant insurer. Under the contract, she would forfeit her entitlement to extended earnings and deferred compensation if she induced or attempted to induce the insurer's policyholders to switch to another insurer or failed to return all materials and records to the insurer within ten days of termination.

The agent submitted a letter of resignation indicating that she intended to use other insurers, and she transferred her book of business to another of the insurer's agents. She subsequently retracted her resignation, declared her retirement and requested the payment of deferred compensation and extended earnings pursuant to the agency agreement.

The insurer initially paid these benefits but discontinued them due to violations of the noncompetition provisions of the agency agreement. Specifically, the agent sold her equipment to another agency established by her daughter and the agent's office manager went to work for the daughter.

The court held that the agent's failure to return all the insurer's materials supported the termination of benefit payments. Also, the actions of the regional manager in reporting the agent's postretirement conduct to the insurer, leading to the termination of benefits, did not constitute tortious interference with contract.

In *Pennsylvania Life Ins. Co. v. Pavlick*, 637 N.E.2d 1160 (Ill. App. Ct. 1994), the insurers sued their former branch managers for breach of contract and tortious interference with contractual relations, whereupon the managers sought an accounting of commissions. The management agreements authorized the managers to recruit, appoint and train sales agents. The contract contained a compensation schedule identifying regions for which a manager would receive commissions. The agreements were amended on several occasions, increasing compensation for different zones and types of policies. The managers voluntarily terminated their relationship with the insurers, whereupon the insurers claimed that the managers violated post-employment restrictive covenants not to compete by soliciting customers and sales agents from the insurers. The managers then counter-claimed for commissions due.

The court affirmed summary judgment in the insurer's favor on the counterclaims, where the management agreements provided that the commissions would be paid on net profits for the various regions and lines of business, and not on the amount of premiums.

Page 109, add to note 75:

In *Volunteer Firemen's Ins. Services v. Cigna Prop. & Cas. Ins. Agency*, 693 A.2d 1330 (Pa. Super. Ct. 1997), an independent agent sued the insurer in an attempt to enforce a covenant not to compete clause contained in the agency agreement. The agreement stated that the insurer was prohibited from selling insurance to emergency service organizations nationwide for three years following the termination of the agreement. The noncompetition provision stated:

> Acknowledging the long-standing relationship between you and us, we together agree as follows. For a period of three (3) years following any termination of this Addendum, except termination for [specified grounds], we agree that we will not directly or indirectly solicit, sell or issue a voluntary Property/Casualty policy to any Volunteer Fire Business, except for Volunteer Fire Business which is part of a municipality account.

693 A.2d at 1338-1339. The court held that the noncompetition agreement was valid and enforceable and was triggered by the agent's nonrenewal of the agreement. The fact that even during the tenure of the agreement, the agent was exploring alternative sources to provide the same coverage to its customers did not render the agreement unenforceable. The court

affirmed the injunction issued to prevent the insurer from competing.

Page 116, add at end of section:

Although an agent may have a duty of loyalty to the insurer *vis-à-vis* its clients, this duty isn't necessarily reciprocal. Specifically, the agent has no right to limit the insurer from directly writing business with insureds that formerly dealt with the insurer through the agent. In *Insurance & Consulting Associates v. ITT Hartford Insurance Group*, 48 F. Supp. 2d 1181 (W.D. Mo. 1999), the independent agent sued the insurer for breach of the agency agreement after a client stopped doing business with the agency and purchased its insurance directly from the insurer. The court held that there was no custom or practice preventing an insurer from directly dealing with insureds. The court held that the agent had no viable claim against the insurer where the agency agreement did not prohibit the insurer from bypassing the agency and selling insurance directly to the insured.

4.9 Fidelity Bonds and E&O Coverage

Page 120, add at end of section:

In a case involving the insolvency of an insurer, the claimant sued the insured insurance agency for failing to properly perform its duties. The claimant alleged that he relied on the insured's recommendations in changing medical insurance carriers. He underwent heart surgeries, but his medical and hospital expenses were not paid because the insurer became insolvent. The insurer with which the agent placed the coverage was not licensed to do business in the state. The court held that there was no coverage under the agent's E&O policy where the claim arose from the medical insurer's inability to pay its debts, thereby clearly falling within the policy exclusion.[89]

---

89 *St. Paul Fire & Marine Ins. Co. v. Cohen-Walker, Inc.*, 320 S.E.2d 385 (Ga. Ct. App. 1984).

E&O policies also exclude claims arising out of the insured agent's transmission or failure to transmit premiums from the client to the appropriate insurer, or involving the return of premiums. In *Utica Mut. Ins. Co. v. Impallaria,* the insurance agent sold a policy stating that there was a guaranteed cost premium when the policy actually included an experience rating endorsement. At the end of the policy period, the insurer sought additional premiums, whereupon the client sued the insurance agent. The court held that the agent's E&O insurance provided coverage, where the endorsement seeking the additional premium for experience ratings did not constitute a "premium" within the scope of the policy exclusion.[90]

Policies typically exclude claims involving the agent's dishonesty. In one such case, the client was injured in an uninsured motorist accident and sued the agency after she determined that her signature had been forged on the form choosing lower uninsured motorist coverage limits. The auto insurer paid the client and then sued the agent. The court held that the agent's E&O policy was not required to respond to the claim where the auto insurer could not establish who forged the signature and had not required that the agent verify the signature on the application form.[91] And in a case involving embezzlement by an adjuster's employee, the court held that the exclusion for claims arising out of dishonest, fraudulent, and illegal acts was applicable regardless of the theory raised in the claimant's complaint, where the crux of the action was for the employee's dishonesty.[92]

Even without the dishonesty exclusion, it should be clear that the policy will not cover an agent's intentional acts. In one

---

[90] *Utica Mut. Ins. Co. v. Impallaria,* 892 F.2d 1107 (1st Cir. 1989), applying Massachusetts law.

[91] *Gardiner v. Commercial Union Ins. Cos.,* 488 So. 2d 1331 (La. Ct. App. 1986).

[92] *Huey T. Littleton Claims, Inc. v. Employers Reins. Corp.,* 933 F.2d 337 (5th Cir. 1991), applying Louisiana law.

Contractual Relationship Between Insurer and Agent

case, the insured agency was sued for defamation, tortious interference with prospective business relations and violation of deceptive trade practice statutes. The claimant alleged that the insured intentionally and willfully perpetrated a scheme to coerce the claimant into employing the insured agent as its exclusive agent. The court held that E&O coverage is only intended to cover negligence and not intentional conduct, regardless of the absence or presence of a specific intentional acts exclusion.[93]

Clearly, the insured agent must give the E&O insurer timely notice of a claim potentially falling under the policy. In one such case, the workers compensation underwriter for an agency client canceled the policy and notified the agency's officer. The officer was not able to obtain replacement coverage for eight months, and during that period, the client had no coverage. Claims occurred during the gap; the officer started paying the claims out of unused premiums but ultimately was presented with a claim he could not pay. When that injured worker sued the client, the agency discovered the problem and notified its E&O carrier. The court held that the agency did not have constructive notice of the officer's errors and omissions prior to the actual notice and thus found that coverage existed for the negligent failure to obtain replacement coverage for the eight-month period.[94]

In another case involving the agent's failure to obtain coverage while accepting the payment of premiums, the agent was sued when a client discovered that he had no liability coverage in force. Where the agent agreed to the entry of judgment against it without advising its E&O carrier, the E&O insurer could raise the agent's noncooperation as a potential defense. However, there were questions of fact as to whether the E&O

---

[93] *U.S.F.&G. v. Fireman's Fund Ins. Co.*, 896 F.2d 200 (6th Cir. 1990), applying Ohio law.

[94] *National Union Fire Ins. Co. v. Lomax Johnson Ins. Agency*, 496 So. 2d 737 (Ala. 1986).

insurer's earlier refusal to defend the agent in the underlying suit excused the noncooperation.[95]

It should be noted that many E&O policies are written on a claims-made basis. Therefore, it is necessary to provide the insurer with notice of claims within the policy period or any extension of the reporting period. The failure to provide notice within the required period will generally relieve the E&O insurer of coverage obligations, even where the insurer is not prejudiced by the delay in reporting the claim.[96]

---

[95] *Holt v. Utica Mut. Ins. Co.*, 759 P.2d 623 (Ariz. 1988).

[96] *Industrial Indem. Co. v. Superior Court (Kaku)*, 275 Cal. Rptr. 218 (Cal. Ct. App. 1990); *Pacific Employers Ins. Co. v. Superior Court (Rausch)*, 270 Cal. Rptr. 779 (Cal. Ct. App. 1990).

Chapter 5

Interactions Between Agents and Insureds

5.1 The Agent as Intermediary

Page 124, add to end of section:

It must be remembered that the agent is not a party to the insurance contract and cannot be held liable for the insurer's breach of contract. In *Minnesota Mutual Life Insurance Co. v. Ensley*, 174 F.3d 977 (9th Cir. 1999), applying California law, the insurer issued a life insurance policy through its agent. Significant disputes arose out of changes in ownership of the policy and various transactions among the insured, his wife, and the agent. The agent was involved in the changes of ownership and, at one point after the wife was unable to pay premiums, the agent was named as a part owner of the policy. The court held that the agent could not be held liable for breach of the insurance contract or for bad faith where the agent was not a party to the contract and was not responsible for the insurer's denial of the claim. Furthermore, liability could not be imposed based on negligence in changing the ownership.

In *Swickey v. Silvey Cos.*, 979 P.2d 266 (Okla. Ct. App. 1999), the insured sued the agent and the insurer after uninsured motorist coverage was denied for a claim arising out of the death of the insured's son. The insured obtained the policy to cover a car she purchased for her husband. The policy listed the insured wife as the named insured and provided uninsured motorist coverage for her, her spouse, and family members living with her in the household. However, the insurer denied coverage because at the time of the accident the husband and son had moved out of the household. The court held that there were fact questions as to whether the agent breached any implied contract to procure coverage for the son. Clearly, the agent could not be held liable for the insurer's alleged breach of contract, but only for the agent's own negligence. To recover, the plaintiff had to establish that the agent agreed to provide coverage for the son, but failed to do so. Furthermore, only the plaintiff wife had standing to sue the agent because of her direct dealings with the agent.

5.2 Explaining Coverage and Giving Advice

Page 124, add to note 1:

In *Charlin v. Allstate Ins. Co.*, 19 F. Supp. 1137 (C.D. Cal. 1998), the insured sued the insurer and the agent in an attempt to obtain uninsured motorist coverage. The insured never signed a waiver of such coverage and was involved in an accident with an uninsured motorist whereupon the insurer denied coverage. With respect to the claim against the agent, the court held that the agent was the insurer's agent, not a dual agent. Thus, it had no duty to advise the insured that she had no uninsured motorist coverage. Where the agent did not act in excess of his capacity as the insurer's agent, he could not be given the title and responsibilities of a dual agent. The agent was not required to obtain a new waiver where the insured merely took over the policy obtained by her deceased husband, which had named her as an insured, and the husband's waiver of UM coverage was automatically binding on her.

In *Weisblatt v. Minnesota Mut. Life Ins. Co.*, 4 F. Supp. 2d 371 (E.D. Pa. 1998), the insurer's agent allegedly misrepresented the terms of the life insurance policy and committed fraud in its conduct prior to the purchase of the policy. The agent met twice with the plaintiff and her husband prior to the purchase. The agent allegedly misrepresented that he had wide experience in the field, and he allegedly recommended that the plaintiffs surrender an existing life insurance policy because it would eventually become essentially worthless. He also recommended that they purchase a policy from the defendant insurer. The agent never recommended an amount of death benefits he thought should be purchased and never mentioned the benefits of purchasing term insurance. The insurer paid the surviving plaintiff the full policy death benefit when the insured husband died and the plaintiff widow determined that the policy was insufficient to meet her needs as expressed to the agent. The court held that the agent had no duty to advise the plaintiff of other policy options, and the plaintiff did not rely on the agent's statements in deciding to surrender the first policy and purchase the second.

In *Frith v. Guardian Life Ins. Co.*, 9 F. Supp. 2d 744 (S.D. Tex. 1998), the insureds sued the life insurer for fraud and misrepresentation and violations of state trade practices law. They claimed that the cost illustrations did not disclose critical information. The court held that the agent, being the insurer's agent, and not the insured's agent, had no duty to explain the terms of the policy. It also held that the insured had ample opportunity to read the policy and cost illustrations which were not ambiguous.

In *Manzella v. Gilbert-Magill Co.*, 965 S.W.2d 221 (Mo. Ct. App. 1998), the insureds opened a delicatessen and needed an estimate of insurance costs to include on their application for a Small Business Administration loan. They contacted their insurance agent, who provided them with insurance in the past. The loan application indicated that they intended to carry contents coverage of $50,000. The insureds then ordered coverage from the agent but never told the agent how much coverage they wanted. The insureds believed that the agent "was supposed to advise on that."

The agent procured a policy with $300,000 in fire liability coverage but only $35,000 in contents coverage. After the original insurer increased the deductible after a theft loss, the agent switched the policy to another carrier which provided $40,000 in contents coverage and $5,000 for spoilage. A fire ensued, and the insureds sustained $160,000 in damage to durable and nondurable goods. Thereupon, the insured sued the agent for failing to advise on the appropriate level of insurance for the business. The court held that the agent had no duty to advise the insureds and could not be held liable even if his conduct contravened the insurer's underwriting guidelines.

In *Blevins v. State Farm Fire & Cas. Co.*, 961 S.W.2d 946 (Mo. Ct. App. 1998), the insureds purchased homeowners insurance through the defendant agent. They were issued a burglary and theft policy and ultimately filed a claim. The insurer denied coverage on certain items used by the insured in his hobby of car racing which were classified as automobile parts even though the parts were in dead storage. The policy defined a *motor vehicle* as excluding a car in dead storage but there was no such term in the exclusion relied upon by the insurer. In the claim against the agent, the court held that the agent had no duty to advise the insured to purchase additional coverage which would have covered the loss of the auto parts. The agent's only duty to the insured was to obtain the coverage ordered, and that duty ended upon delivery of the policy. Thus, the agent could not be held liable for any inability of the insured to recover the entire amount of his loss from the insurer.

In *Fillinger v. Northwestern Agency Inc.*, 938 P.2d 1347 (Mont. 1997), the insured sued the agent to recover losses not covered under the policy obtained by that agent. The insured agreed to provide services to another company, and under that contract, the insured was required to obtain coverage that would also cover the other company. When a claim was made and it was determined that the policy coverage did not extend to the other company's liability, that company canceled the contract with the insured.

A new contract was prepared, whereby the insured received less compensation for its services and reduced the liability insurance requirements. When the insured received the policy in question, it did not read every provision but rather relied on the representations of the agent that coverage was provided as required and requested. The agent argued that the insured never requested special coverage but rather only ordered a standard policy.

The court affirmed the judgment on the jury verdict for the insured on the basis of negligent misrepresentation. The court noted that evidence of the negotiations between the insured and the agent leading to the procurement of the policy was admissible to prove the insured's claim.

See also Ginocchio v. American Bankers Life Assur. Co., 889 F. Supp. 1079 (N.D. Ill. 1995), discussed in § 2.3.

In *Hardy v. Fisher*, 901 F. Supp. 228 (E.D. Tex. 1995), the owner of the trucking company, the plaintiff in this case, purchased an accidental death and dismemberment and medical insurance policy from the agent. The plaintiff alleged that the agent informed him that the policy would satisfy the employer coverage requirements of the Texas comp act.

An employee was injured on the job and received the benefits prescribed in the policy. The employee then brought a tort suit against the employer, the owner of the trucking company, claiming that the policy did not meet the statutory requirements and that the owner was subject to tort liability in his capacity as a fellow employee. The owner then took action against the agent.

The court held that even though the policy was an employee

benefit plan within the scope of ERISA, the federal statute did not preempt state law. The court held that the claim against the insurer and the agent selling the policy under state law should be pursued in state court and not federal court.

In *Southwest Auto Painting and Body Repair v. Binsfeld*, 904 P.2d 1268 (Ariz. Ct. App. 1995), the insured auto body shop sued the insurance agent that obtained its insurance coverage. It claimed that the agency was negligent in failing to offer or recommend that the insured obtain employee dishonesty and theft coverage.

The insured went to the agent because the agent's brother worked for the insured. The insured's existing policy was about to expire, and the insured hoped that the agent would provide body work referrals. The insured was satisfied with the rates quoted. The agent allegedly recommended certain insurance coverage which was accepted by the insured, who was not experienced in insurance coverage issues. The agent did not mention employee dishonesty coverage to the insured, and the policy he recommended did not include such coverage. The insured was unaware that no such coverage was provided, nor, in fact, that it was even available. The insured never sought an explanation of the scope of the coverage provided.

During the policy period, a newly hired bookkeeper embezzled approximately $150,000. The court held that the agent could potentially be held liable for breaching the duty to exercise reasonable care, skill and diligence to meet the insured's insurance needs. Nevertheless, a fact question was presented as to whether the agent actually breached that duty in this case.

Page 125, add to note 4:

In *Zinsel Co. v. J. Everett Eaves, Inc.*, 719 So. 2d 798 (La. Ct. App. 1999), the agent allegedly failed to advise the insured that increased flood coverage was available, thereby leaving the insured with an underinsured loss upon the occurrence of a flood. The defendant agency had been the insured's exclusive agent for decades, but due to problems in placing certain workers compensation coverage, the insured started moving all of its business to another agency. Because the defendant agent never undertook to assure that the insured carried the maximum available coverage, the failure to notify the insured that higher policy limits were available did not constitute a breach of any duties owed to the insured.

Page 125, add to note 5:

In *Ambrosino v. Exchange Ins. Co.*, 695 N.Y.S.2d 767 (N.Y. App. Div. 1999), the roof of the insured's bowling alley collapsed and the insurer denied coverage based on the snow and ice exclusion. The insured sued the insurer and the insurer's agent for failing to procure coverage to cover the loss. The court affirmed summary judgment for the agent, holding that there was no special relationship between the insurer's agent and the insured so as to trigger a duty to advise the insured of the most appropriate coverage. The court found that the agent was not negligent in handling the transaction or in procuring the policy in question where the insured had sought the same coverage that had been provided to the previous owner of the property.

In *Macabio v. TIG Ins. Co.*, 966 P.2d 100 (Haw. 1998), the insureds sued the auto insurer and the agent, claiming that the insurer's offer to stack uninsured motorist and underinsured motorist coverage failed to meet statutory requirements. The insureds also claimed that the agent was negligent in failing to advise them of changes in applicable law. Where the agent never made advisory calls to the plaintiffs and there was no evidence that the insureds relied on the agent to inform them of such changes, no liability could be imposed on the agent since there was no general duty to make such an unsolicited call to give an explanation and advise them of the effect of the change.

In *Phillips v. State Farm Mut. Auto. Ins. Co.*, 497 S.E.2d 325 (1998), the insured was injured in an auto accident as a passenger and sued the insurer and agent after he purchased an auto policy with the statutorily required minimum limits and no underinsured motorist coverage. He claimed that the defendants breached their fiduciary duties and were negligent in failing to explain that the UIM coverage would be available if he increased his liability insurance coverage. The court held that the agent's only duty is to assure that the insured is correctly named in the policy and is properly advised as to the content and nature of the coverage afforded by the policy. There is no duty to advise of the implications of obtaining additional insurance and of the benefits of such a purchase.

In *Thompson v. Nationwide Mut. Ins. Co.*, 971 F. Supp. 242 (N.D. Miss. 1997), the insured sued the insurer and its agent seeking to stack uninsured motorist coverage. The insured claimed that he entered into a contract with the insurer through its agent. The agent allegedly represented that the policy permitted the stacking of coverage for all vehicles and that the coverage was adequate to protect him. The court held that the complaint failed to allege a claim for fraud and the statement that the coverage was adequate was only a nonactionable statement of opinion. The only viable claim was against the insurer for an alleged breach of contract.

In *Fitzpatrick v. Hayes*, 67 Cal. Rptr. 2d 445 (Cal. Ct. App. 1997), the insured sued the insurer and its agent for failing to advise the insured of the availability of personal umbrella coverage that would have provided coverage in addition to the liability insurance coverage provided by an auto policy. The court noted that the agent has no duty to volunteer advice to the insured. An agent cannot be held liable where there is no misrepresentation of coverage provided or the insured only requests particular coverage.

The court held that the insurer did not portray the agent as a specialist or expert in personal liability insurance. If it had, the court may have found the agent had a duty to advise the insureds that umbrella coverage was available. There was no duty to discuss umbrella coverage merely because the agent discussed additional underinsured motorist coverage since such coverage is required by statute. The court affirmed the summary judgment for the defendants.

In *Hecker v. Property Ins. Placement Facility*, 891 S.W.2d 813 (Mo. 1995), the question was raised as to whether the insureds were covered following expiration of the initial policy period. There was no evidence that the facility refused to renew the policies, and no notice of nonrenewal or cancellation was ever sent to the insureds. The court held that the agency relationship between the insureds and the agent concluded upon delivery of the policy, and the agent had no duty to advise the insureds of the imminent lapse of the policy and the requirement that renewal applications be prepared.

Page 126, add to note 6:

In *Marlo v. Farmers Ins. Grp.*, 575 N.W.2d 324 (Mich. Ct. App. 1998), the insured beauty supply company sued the insurer and the agent after the insurer denied coverage for the insured's customers for injuries sustained when acetone, sold by the insured, ignited and injured them. The policy, however, clearly excluded coverage for injuries caused by the insured's products. Thus, the court held that the insured had no reasonable expectation of coverage for such claims. The insurance agent was found to have had no special relationship with the insured that would require the agent to advise the insured about the extent of coverage provided by the policy and whether it was adequate. Therefore, the agent could not be held liable for failing to recommend certain coverage that would have specifically covered the claims.

In *McDonald v. Professional Ins. Corp.*, 946 F. Supp. 943 (M.D. Ala. 1996), the insured sued the accident insurer and its agent after she discovered that her policy terminated upon her reaching age 65 in spite of the fact that they continued to collect premiums beyond that age. She had obtained the coverage through her employer. The employer subsequently chose to terminate the ERISA plan and select another insurer, but the insured decided to individually maintain the initial policy. Under such facts, the court held that ERISA did not preempt her state law claims against the insurer, where the policy in question was terminated by the employer but maintained by the insured. The court further held that ERISA claims could not be made against the agent, which did not qualify as an ERISA agent.

In *Paper Savers Inc. v. Nacsa*, 59 Cal. Rptr. 2d 547 (Cal. Ct. App. 1996), the insured sued the insurer and the agent for alleged misrepresentations about the coverage provided by the replacement cost coverage endorsement. The agent recommended that the insured purchase replacement cost coverage. The agent allegedly explained that the endorsement meant that damaged property may be replaced with either new or used equipment but did point out that the endorsement differed from guaranteed replacement cost coverage. While the latter coverage would have provided for the replacement of lost or damaged property without a specified cost limitation, the endorsement actually issued was subject to the policy limit. As it turned out, coverage under the endorsement was insufficient to cover the insured's loss despite the agent's representation that the endorsement would be sufficient. The court held that an agent can assume additional duties to the insured with respect to the advice and explanation of available coverage, but that there were fact questions as to the duty assumed by the agent in this case and the misrepresentations made.

In *Williams v. Fallaize Ins. Agency, Inc.*, 469 S.E.2d 752 (Ga. Ct. App. 1996), the insured's claim for the theft of jewelry was denied by the insurer due to the unattended vehicle exclusion in the policy, whereupon the insured sued the agent for misrepresenting that coverage was provided for such thefts. The insured claimed that she relied on the agent's misrepresentation and therefore did not attempt to secure other coverage that would have covered the theft. The court affirmed the summary judgment for the defendants, holding that the insured did not exercise due diligence in shopping the market to determine if the allegedly desired coverage was even available. This precluded any recovery on her misrepresentation claim.

In *Stefan v. State Farm Mut. Auto. Ins. Co.*, 672 N.E.2d 1329 (Ill. App. Ct. 1996), the insured sued the insurer and the agent for breach of the duty to offer uninsured and underinsured motorist coverage after the agent undertook the duty to review the insured's coverage. The claim was made after the insured was involved in an accident with an underinsured motorist. The insured had requested that the agent update his coverage on various occasions. The agent initiated the insurer's "Family Insurance Check-Up Program," which was designed "to review the adequacy of the insured's coverage in light of the specific circumstances and needs and to recommend the appropriate changes that better serve the insured." The agent, however, failed to inform the insured of the existence of underinsured motorist coverage and failed to recommend that the insured purchase such coverage. The court held that there were fact questions whether the insured was ever meaningfully offered such coverage and whether the agent breached his voluntary undertaking to review the coverage. These issues precluded the grant of the defendants' motion to dismiss.

Page 126, add to note 8:

In *Featherston v. Allstate Ins. Co.*, 875 P.2d 937 (Idaho 1994), the insured sued the auto insurer for negligence, fraud, and misrepresentation after he found that his underinsured motorist claim was not covered by the policy.

When the insured originally contacted the insurer's agent, he had a policy from another insurer and requested a premium quote for the same coverage. The insured never discussed underinsured motorist coverage. The insured transferred his coverage and renewed the policy for the next six years. Had he read the policy, he would have discovered that he had no underinsured motorist coverage.

Summary judgment was entered for the insurer, but the insured appealed. The court held that there were still questions of fact as to whether the insurer undertook to provide underinsured motorist coverage. The court noted that the insurer could be held liable based on any representation of its agent, despite the fact that such a statement would be contrary to the express terms of the policy.

In *American Family Mut. Ins. Co. v. Dye*, 634 N.E.2d 844 (Ind. Ct. App. 1994), the insured motorist sued his insurer and the insurance agent after his claim for underinsured motorist coverage was denied. In addition to bad faith claims, the insured alleged that the agent breached fiduciary duties by failing to inform him that such coverage was available.

The court held that the insured was not entitled to such advice. Although state law required that underinsured motorist coverage be specifically offered, the policy was initially issued before the effective date of the statute. Also, the agent had no fiduciary relationship with the insured; there was no intimate long-term relationship that included the giving of advice. The insured bears the burden of proving the existence of such a special relationship.

In *Wied v. N.Y. Central Mut. Fire Ins. Co.*, 618 N.Y.S.2d 467 (N.Y.A.D. 1994), the insured's auto policy provided liability limits of $300,000 but only $25,000 in underinsured motorist benefits. Following an accident involving an underinsured motorist, the insured sued his insurer and agent, alleging that the agent was negligent in failing to advise him that supplementary underinsured motorist coverage was available. The court held that the agent could not be liable for failing to give such advice where there was no special relationship (such as a fiduciary relationship) between the insured and the agent.

Page 127, add to note 12:

In *Dahlke v. John F. Zimmer Ins. Agency*, 515 N.W.2d 767 (Neb. 1994), the insured sued the agent for negligence. The insured owned and operated a business providing roofing, construction and waterproofing services. One hazard of such work is "overspray," where some roofing coating drifts away from the roof and settles onto other objects, resulting in property damage. The insured suffered an overspray incident damaging four to six cars, and coverage was extended after the insured paid a single deductible. A similar incident occurred four years later involving 25 claims, and the insurer sought to have the insured pay 25 separate deductibles.

The negligence claim against the agent sounded in the failure to disclose material information regarding the deductible. The court held that the agent had a duty to explain the per-claim deductible even though the insured never specifically requested a per-occurrence deductible. However, the court also held that the insured's failure to read the policy could provide the agent with a defense if it were determined that the deductible provisions were clear and unambiguous.

Page 128, add to note 17:

In *MGA Ins. Co. v. Fisher-Roundtree*, 159 F.3d 1293 (10th Cir. 1998), applying Oklahoma law, the insurer filed a declaratory judgment action to clarify coverage for personal injury claims brought against its insured, a liquefied petroleum seller, arising after a propane bottle exploded. The policy excluded coverage for completed operations, but the insured argued that the insurance agent told him that the policy provided all the coverage required by law, and he assumed that this included completed operations coverage. The court held that even if the insurance agent was found to be the insurer's agent, any representations could not create coverage contrary to the clear and unambiguous terms of the liability policy. Thus, no coverage existed for the claims.

In *Moore v. Whitney-Vaky Insurance Agency*, 966 S.W.2d 690 (Tex. Ct. App. 1998), the insured owned an apartment complex and asked the agent to obtain insurance, but they never discussed any types of coverage to be provided. The insured allegedly thought that he was covered for any liability that he might incur, even though the agent never specifically stated that the policy would cover all lawsuits against him. The insured was sued by a former employee for a retaliatory discharge which was not covered by the policy. The court affirmed the summary judgment for the agent, holding that the agent owned no duty to disclose any limitations in the coverage where the agent was diligent in placing the coverage in light of the fact that the insured never specifically requested coverage for such a liability. The court also noted that there was no special relationship between the parties that would require the agent to advise the insured on coverage that should be obtained or disclose limitations on the coverage provided by the policy actually procured.

In *Cavallini v. State Farm Mut. Auto. Ins. Co.*, 44 F.3d 256 (5th Cir. 1994), applying Texas law, the insureds sued the hospitalization insurer and the insurance agents for breach of contract and bad faith after coverage was denied for their newborn son's treatment to correct birth defects. The mother was also within coverage provided by her employer. The defendant insurer contended that the employer's policy was primary, even though the insureds had added the child as an additional insured under the defendant's policy one month prior to the birth. The court held that there was no viable claim stated against the agent, who made no misrepresentations to the insureds and had no independent duty of good faith running to them.

Page 129, add to note 20:

In *Benton v. Paul Revere Life Ins. Co.*, 858 F. Supp. 1112 (M.D. Ala. 1994), the insured sued his disability insurer based on an agent's misrepresentation as to the extent of disability required to trigger policy benefits. The insured had extensive discussions with the insurer's agent on this issue when he filed the application. However, the agent allegedly failed to note that a higher level of disability was required under the lifetime rider. The court held that this could constitute an innocent representation which might mislead the insured. Thus, the court found that a fact question was raised, precluding summary judgment as to the liability of the insurer for coverage consistent with the agent's statements.

In *Celtic Life Ins. Co. v. Coats*, 885 S.W.2d 96 (Tex. 1994), the insured sued the insurer and agent for misrepresenting the psychiatric benefits available under his policy. The agent met with the insured employer to discuss health insurance of his employees and their families. The insured stated he wanted psychiatric care benefits equal to or greater than those provided by his then-current policy because his eldest son had previously required such care and his younger son might require similar care. The agent understood the insured's request and proposed the insurer's policy. The insurer's brochure showed a lower limit on such care, but the agent stated that the limit was only for outpatient care. Based on this erroneous representation, the insured purchased the policy. The court held that the insurer was liable for the agent's misrepresentations in explaining the policy coverage. The insured, however, was not entitled to recover treble damages under the Insurance Code or the Deceptive Trade Practices Act, where the jury found that the agent did not knowingly make the misrepresentation.

Page 129, add to note 21:

In *Harts v. Farmers Insurance Exchange*, 597 N.W.2d 47 (Mich. 1999), the insureds contended that the agent was negligent in selling them a no-fault automobile liability policy that did not include uninsured motorist coverage. They sued the agent and sought to hold the insurer liable for the acts of its agent and for its own negligence in supervising the agent. The application for the policy was signed by the insureds less than a month before the accident and they did not select uninsured motorist coverage. The insurer notified them about the availability of such coverage three months before the accident in a renewal notice for a second vehicle of the insureds. The court held that the insurer and its agent had no duty to advise the insureds to obtain the uninsured motorist coverage where there was no special relationship between the agent and the insureds so as to trigger a duty to advise. The agent was the insurer's agent and not the insureds' agent; therefore, the agent owed no specific duty to the insureds.

In *Clifton v. Allstate Insurance Co.*, 995 S.W.2d 38 (Mo. Ct. App. 1999), the insured requested "full coverage," but the resulting automobile insurance policy did not contain underinsured motorist coverage. The agent did not discuss the option of this coverage because it was not offered in the state at the time. Underinsured motorist coverage became available several years later. A renewal notice was created to inform insureds of the availability of this coverage. The insured was sent the notice but chose not to purchase the coverage. She received a declaration of coverage and a renewal every six months, but she continued to choose not to purchase the underinsured motorist coverage.

After her husband was killed in an accident involving an underinsured motorist, the insured sought to recover underinsured motorist benefits by arguing that the insurer, through its agent, was negligent in failing to procure the coverage since the insured had requested "full coverage." The court held that neither the insurer nor the agent had a duty to advise the insured of the availability of underinsured motorist coverage beyond the inserts in the renewal package. The court reaffirmed the principle that agents of the insurer have no duty to advise insureds of the best coverage for their particular needs.

In *Seckinger-Lee Co. v. Allstate Insurance Co.*, 32 F. Supp. 2d 1348 (N.D. Ga. 1998), the insured sued the insurer in a dispute over coverage provided under a "stated amount" endorsement for the loss of a stolen automobile. With respect to the conduct of the agent, the insured claimed that the agent's purported statement that the antique automobile was insured for the stated value scheduled in the policy extended coverage to the stated amount. The court held that the policy clearly and unambiguously limited coverage to the actual cash value, repair, or replacement value, whichever was less, notwithstanding the agent's alleged statements to the contrary. The agent's statement was held not to constitute fraud where the statement amounted to an opinion of law which was incorrect. No liability could be imposed on the agent or derivatively on the insurer for the agent's statements where there was no fiduciary relationship between the parties.

In *Aetna Casualty & Surety Co. v. Berry*, 669 So. 2d 56 (Miss. 1996), the surviving spouse sued the garage liability insurer and the insurance agent following the death of her husband in an auto accident. The spouse was operating a car with the husband riding as a passenger. The car was loaned to them by the auto manufacturer. They were struck head-on by an uninsured drunk driver who pled guilty to manslaughter. The policy covering the car only provided $20,000 in uninsured motorist coverage.

The court held that the agent was required to explain uninsured motorist coverage and could potentially be held liable for the failure to do so. The agent must provide a sufficient explanation to give the insured the option to intelligently reject increased uninsured motorist coverage even though the agent is not required to recommend that the insured obtain increased coverage. The court found that the breach of that duty may subject the agent to liability up to the policy's liability coverage limits.

In *Klimstra v. State Farm Mut. Auto. Ins. Co.*, 891 F. Supp. 1329 (D. Minn. 1995), the insured sued the agent and the automobile insurer to recover uninsured motorist benefits arising out of a "miss-and-run" accident with an unidentified car which allegedly forced the insured off the road. There was no physical contact between the vehicles. The insurer denied the claim due to the lack of contact. The insured claimed that the insurer and the agent were negligent in failing to inform her that such an accident was not within policy coverage after she moved from Minnesota to Wisconsin. This type of accident would be covered under the Minnesota uninsured motorist statute.

When the insured moved to Wisconsin, she was directed to contact another State Farm agent in that state. She told him that she wanted the same coverage as under the Minnesota policy and was only informed that Wisconsin law requires that insureds purchase medical payments coverage rather than Minnesota PIP coverage. The agent advised her of her rights to purchase additional uninsured motorist coverage but did not inform her of any differences in the coverage provided under each state's law. The court held that neither the insurer nor the agent had any duty to inform her of such differences. *See also Klimstra v. Granstrom*, 95 F.3d 686 (8th Cir. 1996), applying Minnesota law.

In *Trupiano v. Cincinnati Ins. Co.*, 654 N.E.2d 886 (Ind. Ct. App. 1995), the insured was a closely held corporation which hired the defendant insurance agent to handle the corporation's insurance requirements. The agent met the insured's needs for more than 15 years, including advice on various types of coverage. The agent conducted an annual review of all policies and detailed the type and amounts of insurance, losses, projected payrolls, and premiums. The insured purchased a fleet policy through the agent. That policy was renewed every year. The policy contained $40,000 in underinsured motorist coverage.

An accident occurred involving one of the insured's vehicles, with two occupants sustaining serious injuries. The driver was specifically listed as an insured driver in the policy. The driver of the other car was at fault and carried $100,000 in liability limits which were paid to the injured victims. Such being the case, the victims were not entitled to any underinsured motorist benefits.

They sued the agent claiming that the $40,000 in underinsured motorist coverage was wholly inadequate and that the agent was negligent in failing to advise them to obtain higher limits. The court affirmed the summary judgment for the agent, holding that there was insufficient evidence of a special relationship such as would impose the duty to advise even though there was a long-standing relationship between the parties.

In *Robinson v. Charles A. Flynn Ins. Agency*, 653 N.E.2d 207 (Mass. App. Ct. 1995), the insured motorist was injured in an auto accident and sued the insurance agency through which he obtained his insurance, claiming that he had not been properly advised of his option to purchase additional underinsured motorist coverage.

The court held that in the absence of special circumstances, the agency had no general duty to inform and advise the insured of such additional coverage. It should be noted, however, that other states impose such a duty on the agent either by statute or regulation.

5.3 Filling Out the Application for Insurance

Page 134, add to note 34:

In *St. Paul Surplus Life Insurance Company v. Feingold & Feingold Insurance Agency, Inc.*, 693 N.E.2d 669 (Mass. 1998), a woman, injured in a motor vehicle accident, sued the insurer claiming that the driver who hit her had been overserved alcohol by their insured. The insurer sued the agent for intentionally misrepresenting material facts on an application for a liquor liability policy issued to a restaurant.

The court affirmed the jury verdict, holding the agency liable even though the insured had signed the application. The court found that the agent was aware of the discrepancies on the application and that this intentional participation in the submission of false information warranted the finding of liability.

In *Ingalls v. Paul Revere Life Ins. Group*, 561 N.W.2d 273 (N.D. 1997), the insurer denied the insured's disability claim and the insured brought this suit for breach of contract, bad faith, and fraud. The insurer sought rescission of the contract because the insured materially misrepresented his income. The court affirmed the judgment on the jury verdict for the insured, holding that there was no material misrepresentation. The court found that the application was ambiguous with respect to certain questions and the insured completed the application with the assistance of the insurer's agent who assisted in the insured's interpretation of the application questions.

See also Steinberg v. Mikkelsen, 901 F. Supp. 1433 (E.D. Wis. 1995), discussed in § 4.5.

The agent entered into an independent agency relationship with the second insurer with which the coverage was eventually placed. The insureds completed an application for the second insurer with the assistance of the agent. This insurer relied on the representations contained in the application in accepting the risk. Had the truth been disclosed, the insurer would not have issued the policy. Ultimately, the insurer discovered the truth when one insured presented a claim. When that claim was rejected, this action was brought.

The court denied the insurer's motion for summary judgment, holding that traditional agency law principles are applicable in a case brought under ERISA, and therefore the agent's knowledge of the true health history could be imputed to the insurer.

In *Sun Life Assur. of Canada v. Barnard*, 652 So. 2d 681 (La. Ct. App. 1995), a dispute arose as to the beneficiary entitled to obtain the proceeds of a life insurance policy. The insured executed a change of beneficiary form naming his wife as beneficiary. This was filed with the insurer. The day after the death, the agent informed the insurer that the insured had executed a new change of beneficiary form naming a friend as his beneficiary. At that time, the agent stated that the form was executed one month before the insured's death but that he inadvertently failed to send it to the insurer. The insurer paid the proceeds into the court, leaving the court to distribute the policy benefits.

The insurance agent had placed the incorrect date on the change form, omitted the date on the three required places on the form, and failed to effect the change. Therefore, he could be held liable to the insured's friend, who was held not entitled to recover the policy proceeds.

In *Marchiori v. American Republic Ins. Co.*, 662 A.2d 932 (Me. 1995), the insured sued the health insurer to recover medical expenses related to surgery after the insured denied coverage. The insured met with the agent to purchase health insurance. During the meeting, the insured informed the agent that she was born with an intestinal ailment known as atresia of the jejunum and that she had undergone surgery when she was an infant to repair the condition. She further divulged to the agent that she had a history of chronic stomach pain and had visited her family doctor two years earlier, but nothing was found.

The insurance application required the disclosure of pre-existing conditions and purported to disclaim coverage for undisclosed conditions. The agent, however, failed to record that information on the application. The insured acknowledged that she had read language in the application which stated that the application was complete and correct to the best of her knowledge and belief. The court rendered the judgment for the insured, holding that the statute permitted the insurer to avoid coverage based on misrepresentation only if the statement was made fraudulently and was material. The agent's knowledge of the applicant's medical history was imputed to the health insurer without regard to the terms of the application.

Page 136, add to note 39:

In *Priesmeyer v. Shelter Mutual Insurance Co.*, 995 S.W.2d 41 (Mo. Ct. App. 1999), the insureds' fire damage claim was denied by the insurer due to material misrepresentations made by the insureds in their application for insurance. There was a dispute as to whether the agent had ever asked the insureds whether there was a mortgage on the property or whether the insureds had sustained any prior losses. The completed application did not disclose the existence of a mortgage or any prior losses. The insureds claimed that they signed the application while the policy's answer boxes and "remarks" section remained as-of-yet uncompleted.

The court reversed summary judgment for the insurer, holding that there were fact questions as to whether the agent completed the application without asking the questions which might have influenced the insurer about whether to accept the risk. The insurer would be bound by any false answers in the application if the application was completed by the agent knowing that the answers were false. If the agent was unaware of the falsity of the statements at the time he recorded the answers, the insurer would not be liable on the policy.

In *Suggs v. Pan American Life Ins. Co.*, 847 F. Supp. 1324 (S.D. Miss. 1994), the employee sued the insurer and agent after his medical claim was denied and his policy canceled for misrepresentation.

The plaintiff was covered under an employee benefit plan covered by ERISA. As a threshold matter, the court held that the statute did not bar such statutory claims even though claims for fraud in the inducement would be preempted by the statute.

The court held that the insurer's cancellation of the policy for misrepresentation in the application was not valid. Even though the insured signed the completed application, he had communicated information to the agent that was not reflected in the application. The agent's knowledge and actions could be imputed to the insurer, despite language in the policy stating that the agent was the insured's agent and not the insurer's, due to the agent's statutory status as accepting the application for the insurer.

Page 136, add to note 40:

In *Meyer v. National Farmers Union Prop. & Cas. Co.*, 957 F. Supp. 1492 (D. Wyo. 1997), the farmer sought to insure his bean crop through the defendant insurer's Multiple Peril Crop Insurance program and applied through the defendant managing agent. The program was federally regulated and subsidized insurance available pursuant to the Federal Crop Ins. Act (7 U.S.C. §§ 1501-1521). After the policy was issued, a dispute arose as to the amount of coverage and who gave the agent the product figures upon which the policy limits were based. The agent determined that the crop records were insufficient and figured production based on county average data. He miscalculated and issued an acreage report, providing a guaranty significantly less than the true figure. However, there was also a question of whether the insured ever questioned the production rate set forth in the policy. The court held that the insured had no viable claim for negligent preparation of the amount of coverage, bad faith, and negligent misrepresentation under the facts of the case.

Interactions Between Agents and Insureds

In *Roe v. Sewell*, 128 F.3d 1098 (7th Cir. 1997), applying Illinois law, the insured obtained a long-term disability policy. The insurer subsequently rescinded the policy due to a misrepresentation in the application that the insured had no other disability insurance. The insured then sued the agent who sold the policy and the agency office manager.

The court held that the office manager could not be held liable because he did not have a duty to the insured. The agent allegedly promised to complete the application for the insured, but failed to use reasonable care to prepare the form accurately. The manager undertook no duty to review, or even look at, the application before it was submitted. Even though the insured failed to review the application when it was returned to her and after she received a reissued policy, this did not preclude her from recovering from the agent. The court held that questions of whether the agent assumed the duty to the insured and whether he breached that duty were questions of fact for a jury to decide.

In *Hartford Life & Acc. Ins. Co. v. Nittolo*, 955 F. Supp. 331 (D.N.J. 1997), the insurer brought this action seeking rescission of a disability insurance policy for material misrepresentations contained in the application. Thereupon, the insured brought a third-party action against the agent for negligent preparation of the application. The insurer claimed that the insured had made material misrepresentations about his income, occupational duties, insurance history, and medical history.

The court held that any negligence on the independent agent's part could not be imputed to the insurer. The court further held that even if the agent had acted improperly, the insured suffered no harm because, had the insurer been advised of the truth, it would not have issued the policy. The court granted summary judgment for the insurer and the agent.

The court held that the insurer could potentially be held liable for breach of contract arising out of the agent's conduct. In addition, the court found that the insurer could not be liable for

RICO violations arising from the agent's conduct where the fraud and misrepresentation was clearly outside the scope of the agent's authority.

In *Massachusetts Cas. Ins. Co. v. Roe*, 93 F.3d 323 (7th Cir. 1996), applying Indiana law, the plaintiff long-term disability insurer filed suit to rescind the policy and for a declaration that the policy did not provide coverage for the insured's injuries. When the insured discussed the insurance with her cousin, who was an agent of the insurer, she mentioned that she had similar insurance through her employer. The agent stated that he would look into the other coverage and would complete that portion of the application. Although the insured signed the application, she told the agent she wanted to think about it and asked him to leave the application blank. Several days later she told him to submit the application. The agent never asked additional questions about her existing coverage, and he did not follow up with the employer. The agent completed the pertinent section of the application with the statement that she had no other insurance.

The policy was issued, and the insured paid the appropriate premiums; however, she never received a copy of the policy. She was asked to make a back-dated statement of her health upon the ultimate delivery of the policy. When she made a claim, the insurer sought to deny coverage because of the alleged misrepresentation that she had no other disability insurance and for her back-dating the statement of health. The court affirmed the judgment for the insurer, holding that she had made actionable misrepresentations. In addition, there were fact questions as to the liability of the agent and whether the agent was actually acting on the insurer's behalf when he completed the application stating that there was no other insurance.

See also McKillip v. Employers Fire Ins. Co., 932 S.W.2d 268 (Tex. Ct. App. 1996), discussed in § 1.4.

See also Plumlee v. Monroe Guaranty Ins. Co., 655 N.E.2d 350 (Ind. Ct. App. 1995), discussed in § 4.5.

Part I □ Chapter 5 □ 2000 Supplement 93
Interactions Between Agents and Insureds

In *Toups v. Equitable Life Assur.*, 657 So. 2d 142 (La. Ct. App. 1995), the insured sought to recover disability income benefits, while the insurer sought the return of benefits already paid. Both the insured and the insurer sued the agent, who had not recorded the insured's medical history accurately on the application. The agent took the information shortly after he was licensed and appointed by the insurer.

The application was not completed on the day of the sales presentation. Several days later, the agent met with the insured and completed the application. Another agent had been assigned to accompany the new agent on this visit but canceled at the last moment. The insured did not sign the application on that day. The agent took the application back to his office to inquire as to some questionable matters and later presented the application to her for signature.

Her claim for disability as a result of chronic fatigue syndrome was initially accepted by the insurer and later denied based on material misrepresentations. The insurer listed various times she consulted with and was treated by physicians which were not disclosed. The court held that the insured had no intent to deceive the insurer. The misrepresentations were the fault of the agent, not the insured. The agent's negligence in completing the application with erroneous information was not binding on the insured. Under agency principles, the court also held that the insurer was entitled to indemnification from the agent for its liability to the insured.

Page 136, add to note 42:

In *Tassin v. Golden Rule Ins. Co.*, 649 So. 2d 1050 (La. Ct. App. 1994), the insured sought coverage under his health insurance policy for treatment of appendicitis. The insured's employer had changed group insurers following a rate increase. The broker assisted the employer in the search for new coverage, and helped the insured complete his application under the new policy. The application disclosed that the insured was being treated for diabetes and was taking medication.

The insurer informed the broker that it would not cover the group with the insured as a member. The insured signed a waiver of coverage and the insurer issued a policy covering all employees except the insured.

The broker then obtained other coverage for the insured. On the broker's advice, the insured's application did not disclose his diabetes. The new insurer discovered the diabetes while investigating the appendicitis claim, and denied coverage for the cost of treating the appendicitis — $19,210.

The court held that the broker was the insurer's agent, where the insurer supplied the broker with application forms and issued the policy following direct transmission of the application by the broker. Therefore, the insurer was responsible for paying the treatment bills subject to its rights to be indemnified by the broker.

Page 137, add to note 45:

In *Crowne Investments, Inc. v. Bryant*, 638 So. 2d 873 (Ala. 1994), the plaintiffs were the beneficiaries of a life insurance policy who sued the insurer after it refused to pay benefits upon the insured's death. The insurer raised a misrepresentation defense based on the statement in the policy application that the insured had not been treated within three years of the application date.

The insured had been treated for cancer and was having difficulty obtaining life insurance. The agent assisted the insured in obtaining coverage, forwarding medical records to the insurer which stated that the insured was free from residual cancer. The insurer's brochure stated it would issue coverage if the insured was actively at work. The insurer did require answers to two medical questions, one of which inquired as to treatment for cancer. The agent testified that he asked the insured the health question and the insured answered "no." (Disclosure of the prior treatment would have resulted in issuance of a policy that provided lesser benefits for death during the first three years.)

Part I ◻ **Chapter 5** ◻ **2000 Supplement** 95
Interactions Between Agents and Insureds

The court affirmed the summary judgment for the agent, holding that the agent's statement to the beneficiary that the life insurance was "guaranteed issue" would not constitute a false representation sufficient to support the plaintiffs' fraud claim. Furthermore, any misrepresentation by the agent on the application was not the ultimate cause of the denial, where the insured signed the application. The court also held that the agent was not negligent for failing to obtain valid coverage.

5.4 Forwarding the Application Without Delay

Page 140, add to note 51:

In *Skyview Film & Video v. Safeco Life Ins. Co.*, 864 F. Supp. 755 (N.D. Ill. 1994), the owner-beneficiary of a life insurance policy sued the insurer to recover policy proceeds after the insured committed suicide. The insured died one year and fifty weeks after the issuance of the policy, placing the death within the policy's two-year suicide exclusion. The policyowner-beneficiary argued that the insurer was negligent in processing the original application, resulting in a delay of six weeks from the submission of the application to the insurer to the date when the policy was issued. The court held that the owner had no claim for negligence in transmitting and processing the application, where 43 days was not an unreasonable length of time.

5.5 Obtaining the Coverage That Was Ordered

Page 141, replace last sentence in first paragraph with the following:

The agent may or may not be liable when requested coverage is not obtained.[54a]

Page 141, add to note 54a (created above):

No liability found: In *Ambrosino v. Exchange Insurance Co.*, 695 N.Y.S.2d 767 (N.Y. App. Div. 1999), the roof of the insured's bowling alley collapsed and the insurer denied coverage based on the snow and ice exclusion. The insured sued the insurer and the insurer's agent for failing to procure coverage to cover the loss. The court affirmed summary judgment for the agent, holding that there was no special relationship between the insurer's agent and the insured so as to trigger a duty to advise the insured about the appropriate coverage. The agent was not negligent in handling the transaction and procuring the policy where the insured sought the same coverage that had been provided to the previous owner of the property.

No liability found: In *Swickey v. Silvey Cos.*, 979 P.2d 266 (Okla. Ct. App. 1999), the insured sued the agent and the insurer after uninsured motorist coverage was denied for a claim arising out of the death of the insured's son. The insured obtained the policy to cover a car she purchased for her husband. The policy listed the insured wife as the named insured and provided uninsured motorist coverage for her, her spouse, and family members living with her in the household. However, the insurer denied coverage because at the time of the accident the husband and son had moved out of the household. The court held that there were fact questions as to whether the agent breached any implied contract to procure coverage for the son. Clearly, the agent could not be held liable for the insurer's alleged breach of contract, but only for the agent's own negligence. To recover, the plaintiff had to establish that the agent agreed to provide coverage for the son, but failed to do so. Furthermore, only the plaintiff wife had standing to sue the agent because of her direct dealings with the agent.

No liability found: In *Napier v. Bertram*, 954 P.2d 1389 (Ariz. 1998), the plaintiff was injured while riding in a taxi cab which was struck by an uninsured motorist. He sued the cab owner and the insurance agent after he discovered that they had failed to procure uninsured motorist coverage. The court held that the agent did not owe the plaintiff passenger any duty for which liability could be imposed, but the plaintiff had a viable claim against the cab owner for the failure to have the required coverage in force. The owner then had a viable claim against the agent for the failure to obtain that coverage. This is consistent with the general rule that the agent owes duties to its client and not unrelated third parties.

No liability found: In *Dahlke v. John F. Zimmer Ins. Agency*, 567 N.W.2d 548 (Neb. 1997), the insured roofer sued the agent after a claim arose and the insured discovered that the agent failed to obtain the proper overspray liability coverage as requested by the insureds. Additionally, the agent failed to alert the insured that such coverage contained per-claim deductibles as opposed to per-occurrence deductibles.

At the time the claims arose, the insured had not yet received a copy of the policy, but would have discovered the problem had he read the two prior policies. As a result, the court affirmed summary judgment for the agent because the two earlier policies also contained a per-claim deductible and the insured should have discussed the problem in those policies and sought the additional coverage.

No liability found: In *Carterosa, Ltd. v. General Star Indem. Co.*, 489 S.E.2d 83 (Ga. Ct. App. 1997), the insured sued the insurer and the agent after a fire loss claim was denied. The fire occurred after the policy expired. The agent allegedly failed to include the building in question in the proposal for renewal after the insured asked that the agent renew the same coverage as provided by the earlier policy.

The insured failed to review the diagram of buildings covered under the prior policy which did not include the building in question. Assuming that the agent was negligent in failing to renew the policy, the insured suffered no loss since the renewal would have been based on the earlier policy, which did not cover the building that burned.

No liability found: In *Clock v. Larson*, 564 N.W.2d 436 (Iowa 1997), after the insured settled a claim brought by an injured party and assigned all rights to pursue the insurer, the claimant-assignee sued the insurer and the agent for failing to obtain greater liability limits. The court held that the claimant had no viable cause of action against the defendants because in settling the underlying claim, the claimant signed a full release as opposed to an agreement not to execute on the judgment. As a result, the insured was not legally obligated to pay the claimant any additional sums, and this provided the agent and the insurer with a viable defense to the claimant's suit.

No liability found: In *Newpark Resources v. Marsh & McLennan*, 691 So. 2d 208 (La. Ct. App. 1997), the insured corporation and its subsidiaries sued the agent for breach of contract. The plaintiffs alleged that the agent failed to procure the ordered insurance, which was to include the named insured's subsidiaries as additional insureds under the policy. The insured and the subsidiaries were unable to recover under the policy due to their failure to give timely notice.

Because of the lack of timely notice, the court held that the failure to include the subsidiaries was of no consequence and the agent could not be held liable. The agent could only be held liable upon a showing that "but for" the agent's negligence, the plaintiff would have recovered under the policy.

In *Auto-Owners Ins. Co. v. Michigan Mut. Ins. Co.*, 565 N.W.2d 907 (Mich. Ct. App. 1997), the automobile insurer was assigned the claim by the assigned claims facility, paid no-fault benefits for injuries sustained by passengers in the car, and then sued the vehicle owner, the driver, and the agent for reimbursement. The claim against the agent was for the negligent failure to procure insurance. The owner approached the agent, who attempted to secure coverage through the Michigan Automobile Insurance Placement Facility.

The owner paid a premium deposit and was issued a certificate of insurance, but the amount of the deposit was only half of what was required. No coverage was in effect on the date of the accident because the owner failed to pay the proper deposit. The court held that the insurer paying the claim was entitled to pursue the agent under equitable subrogation theories. The passengers to whom the claim payments were made were found to be intended beneficiaries of the contract, and therefore upon the payment, the insurer succeeded to their rights against the agent.

Claim for liability supported: In *Desai v. Farmers Ins. Exch.,* 55 Cal. Rptr. 2d 276 (Cal. Ct. App. 1996), the insured sued the agent and the property insurer for failing to provide the insured with full replacement cost coverage as requested. The insured allegedly asked for 100 percent coverage for the cost of repairing or replacing improvements to the property, including increases for inflation. The agent allegedly advised the insured that the insurer offered the type of coverage sought and provided that measure of recovery. The insured agreed to purchase the coverage based on the representation. Two of the three buildings on the property were destroyed by an earthquake; the third building was damaged by earthquake and then destroyed by fire. The insurer paid less than one third of the total loss as claimed by the insured. The court found that the insured's reasonable expectation was that the policy provided full replacement coverage notwithstanding the policy limits, which could support the insured's recovery in the amount sought. Also, the insured stated a claim for vicarious liability against the insurer and arising out of the agent's negligence.

See also Rickborn v. Liberty Life Ins. Co., 468 S.E.2d 292 (S.C. 1996), discussed in § 1.4.

Liability found: In *Kanter v. Deitelbaum*, 648 N.E.2d 1137 (Ill. App. Ct. 1995), the insured sued the agent who represented that he had obtained health insurance when he had not. The plaintiff believed that he had coverage after supplying the agent with various information and the payment of a premium. The agent told him he was insured with a particular insurer. When the insured required proof, the agent provided him with identification cards.

Subsequently, the insured received certain hospital and medical services and informed the agent. The agent requested and received additional money from the insured which he claimed was to cover additional costs. The plaintiff submitted medical bills, but the insurer denied coverage on the basis that there was no health insurance contract. Thereupon, the agent ultimately obtained the coverage from an insurer not licensed to operate in the state. The court held that the insured could recover for economic losses suffered due to the agent's wrongful conduct.

No liability found: In *Cleveland Builders Supply v. Farmers Ins. Group*, 657 N.E.2d 851 (Ohio Ct. App. 1995), the insured sued the insurer and the agent for breach of contract, bad faith, negligence, misrepresentation, and other misconduct in connection with the denial of coverage under an umbrella policy.

The insured sought to renew its existing primary and umbrella liability coverage and met with its agent in order to do so. The agent, a "captive" agent of the defendant insurer, prepared an initial proposal. The insured forwarded information relating its exposure to asbestos lawsuits as requested by the agent.

The insurer authorized the agent to bind the primary policy but did not authorize binding the umbrella. The agent told the insured that, in his experience, the insurer always issued an umbrella policy after it approved the primary policy. The insured signed the application for the primary policy and requested the umbrella. The insurer's reinsurer stated it would not provide umbrella coverage due to the insured's potential asbestos exposure. Thus, the insurer authorized the agent to pursue other sources for the umbrella coverage. The agent contacted 30 other insurers, all of which refused to provide the coverage. The agent presented one proposal, but the insured rejected it due to cost. The insured then notified the agent that it obtained other coverage and asked the agent to cancel its primary policy.

The insured subsequently sought umbrella coverage from the

insurer under a variety of theories for the claims arising during the period before the new policy was obtained and effective. The court held that where the insurer never provided a quotation for umbrella coverage and no umbrella policy was issued, the insurer could not be held liable. It was not bound by the agent's statement that the insurer generally issued umbrella coverage after the primary policy was approved. Moreover, the insured failed to show that any liability for asbestos claims would exceed the primary policy limits so that the disputed umbrella coverage would be reached.

No liability found: In *Isaacson v. DeMartin Agency, Inc.*, 77 Wash. App. 875, 893 P.2d 1123 (1995), the insured contacted the agent about insuring the beauty salon she was about to open. The agent completed the application and delivered a letter issued by the insurer stating that the annual premium was $100 and enclosing an invoice. The insured then ordered additional coverage and an amended declaration was added reflecting a $777 annual policy premium with a notice that $199.25 was due.

The insured stated that she asked for quarterly billings and understood that the insurer would be billing her. She claimed that the agent never told her that she had to pay the premium by a specified date or the policy coverage would end. She wrote a check but did not mail it or otherwise deliver it to the insurer or agent. The insurer sent her a cancellation notice at the business address specifying that the coverage would cease if the premium was not paid by a specified date. She claimed that she had not received the notice. The agent called her before that date, but she claimed that he did not advise her that the policy would lapse if the premium was not paid. His records, however, contained a notation that he advised her that he would let the policy lapse if no payment was made.

She had not made any premium payment when the beauty salon burned down five days after the cancellation date. The agent refused to accept her check dated more than a month earlier, and she brought this suit. The court held that the agent did not breach any contract or violate any duty owed to the insured to procure or maintain coverage. Nor was the agent required to explicitly warn her that the policy would be canceled if she did not pay the premium.

See also *Capitol Funds, Inc. v. Royal Indem. Co.*, 458 S.E.2d 741 (N.C. Ct. App. 1995), discussed in § 1.4.

Page 142, add to note 58:

In *Daniel v. Florida Residential Prop. & Cas. Joint Underwriting*, 718 So. 2d 936 (Fla. Dist. Ct. App. 1998), the named insured sought to reform the homeowners policy to name his son and daughter-in-law as insureds. The named insured obtained mortgage financing for his son and daughter-in-law so that they could purchase the home where they were going to live. The request for insurance listed the named insured as the homeowner but stated that the couple was to live in the home. Following a fire loss, the defendant determined that the named insured did not live on the premises, as required by the policy, and denied the claim since the couple was not named as insureds. The court recognized that there was a question of fact as to whether the agent negligently failed to name the couple as insureds and whether the agent negligently failed to obtain the requested insurance. This precluded any summary judgment. Clearly, if the agent is found to have been negligent while acting in the scope of its agency, the insurer will be held liable.

In *Banes v. Martin*, 965 S.W.2d 383 (Mo. Ct. App. 1998), the insured allegedly requested that the agent obtain full coverage for her new car but never stated what she meant by that term. Thus, she was held not to have requested that the agent obtain greater coverage than was afforded by her earlier policy and the agent could not be held liable for failing to advise her of the availability of underinsured motorist coverage and obtain such coverage.

In *Blevins v. State Farm Fire & Cas. Co.*, 961 S.W.2d 946 (Mo. Ct. App. 1998), the insureds purchased homeowners insurance through the defendant agent. They were issued a burglary and theft policy and ultimately filed a claim. The insurer denied coverage on certain items used by the insured in his hobby of car racing which were classified as automobile parts even though the parts were in dead storage. The policy defined a "motor vehicle" as excluding a car in dead storage, but there was no such term in the exclusion relied upon by the insurer. In the claim against the agent, the court held that the agent had no duty to advise the insured to purchase additional coverage which would have covered the loss of the auto parts. The agent's only duty to the insured was to obtain the coverage ordered, and the duty ceased upon the delivery of the policy. Thus, the agent could not be held liable for any inability of the insured to recover the entire amount of his loss from the insurer.

In *Burns Motors v. Gulf Ins. Co.*, 975 S.W.2d 810 (Tex. Ct. App. 1998), the agent had been held liable for failing to procure the desired liability insurance coverage. The agent then assigned any rights he would have to pursue the insurer under his agency agreement to the insured. The insured then pursued the insurer for breach of the agency contract. The court held that such an assignment is not inconsistent with public policy even though the agent's liability was established in an agreed judgment and not through a true adversarial proceeding. Thus, the insured could maintain its action against the insurer.

In *Moore v. Whitney-Vaky Insurance Agency*, 966 S.W.2d 690 (Tex. Ct. App. 1998), the insured owned an apartment complex and asked the agent to obtain insurance, but they never discussed any types of coverage to be provided. The insured allegedly thought that he was covered for any liability that he might incur even though the agent never specifically stated that the policy would cover all lawsuits against him. The insured was sued by a former employee for a retaliatory discharge which was not covered by the policy. The court affirmed the summary judgment for the agent, holding that the agent had no duty to disclose any limitations in the coverage where the agent was diligent in placing the coverage in light of the fact that the insured never specifically requested coverage for the liability. The court also noted that there was no special relationship between the parties that would require the agent to advise the insured on coverage that should be obtained or disclose the limitations on the coverage provided by the policy actually procured.

In *Red Giant Oil Co. v. Lawlor*, 528 N.W.2d 524 (Iowa 1995), the insured was sued for negligent welding work performed on the claimant's premises. The damage was discovered more than one year after the insured completed the work. The claimant obtained a judgment against the insured.

The insured had notified the insurer through its agent, and relied on the agent's representation that the insurer would not provide coverage or a defense. Ultimately, the tort claimant accepted an assignment of the insured's claim against the insurer for wrongful denial of coverage and the refusal to defend, and against the agent for failing to procure the proper coverage. The court found that the claimant had a viable claim against the agent for failing to obtain coverage which would have covered the claim.

Page 143, add to note 61:

In *Hart v. Berko, Inc.*, 881 S.W.2d 502 (Tex. Ct. App. 1994), the plaintiff policyholder sued the agent for violations of the Deceptive Trade Practices Act and Insurance Code with respect to the insurer's denial of fire insurance coverage. The insured requested that the agent increase the amount of insurance on the building. The agent allegedly stated that the increase was effective. The building was completely destroyed by fire and on the day after the fire, the agent notified the insured that the coverage had not been increased. The court held that the misrepresentation was the cause of the plaintiff's loss but held that the plaintiff was not entitled to recover treble damages under the statute.

Page 144, add to note 66:

In *United Capitol Ins. Co. v. Kapioloff*, 155 F.3d 488 (4th Cir.

1998), applying Maryland law, the surplus lines property insurer brought a declaratory judgment action against the insured and the insured brought a third-party action against its insurance agent and a wholesale broker for negligence. The insured contacted their insurance agent who submitted an application to the surplus lines broker who obtained the policy in question. The insured gave the agent information on the six properties to be covered, and this was passed on to the wholesale broker. When the policy was issued, it required that the insureds use protective safeguards on the properties and not leave the properties vacant.

In truth, portions of one building were vacant, and another building did not have the required safeguards. The insurer denied the claims based on misrepresentations made by the insured and its representatives in the application process. The court held that there were questions of fact as to whether the broker was an agent or subagent of the insureds and whether the broker's negligence was a cause of the unavailability of coverage following the losses. The court noted that an agent who undertakes to obtain insurance for a client must inform that client that insurance is unavailable under the desired terms or that additional conditions are imposed. The fact that one insurer would not write the business on the requested terms does not establish that the desired coverage is unavailable in the marketplace.

In *Hunt v. Greenway Ins. Agency*, 443 S.E.2d 661 (Ga. Ct. App. 1994), the plaintiff sued the agency for failing to procure the requested coverage. The plaintiff sought to purchase liability insurance to comply with the terms of a lease. The agent's employee obtained quotes from various insurers and offered coverage. The plaintiff accepted the offer and signed an application.

The plaintiff was in the business of making bed sheets on a contract basis from cloth supplied by customers. While a driver was delivering finished sheets to a customer, the sheets were destroyed by fire. The plaintiff did not receive the insurance policy until after this loss occurred, and the policy provided that there was no coverage for the loss of the sheets while they were in transit.

The court affirmed summary judgment for the agent, holding that the agency did not hold itself out as an expert and therefore could not be held liable for the plaintiff's failure to verify the information contained in the application. The plaintiff presented no evidence that the agent had any discretion in the type of insurance actually obtained.

Page 145, add to note 69:

In *Johnson & Higgins of Alaska v. Blomfield*, 907 P.2d 1371 (Alaska 1995), the insureds sued the agent for failing to obtain full coverage under an all-risk policy. The insured owned and managed an office building in which tenants became ill due to a contaminant in the ventilation system. The insureds informed their agent that any loss suffered should be covered by the all-risk policy. The insurer rejected the claim, arguing that the loss was outside policy coverage owing to the contamination exclusion. The court held that the agent was liable for the amount of coverage that would have been available had the agent not been negligent. However, that amount would be reduced by the amount the insured actually received from the insurer in settlement of its claim.

In *Appleton Chinese Food Service v. Murken Ins., Inc.*, 519 N.W.2d 674 (Wis. Ct. App. 1994), the insured sued the independent agent for failing to procure the desired coverage. The insured premises were destroyed by fire. In preparing to submit a claim, the insured determined that the policy only provided actual cash value coverage and not replacement cost. The policy also did not provide business interruption coverage. The policy provided $140,000 in actual cash value (ACV) coverage even though the building only had an ACV of $52,200.

The court held that the agent was liable for failing to obtain the requested coverage even though the insured had released the insurer in exchange of the payment under the policy. The court noted that the measure of damages is the amount the insured would have recovered under a policy containing the requested coverage.

Page 145, add to note 71:

In *Aden v. Fortsh*, 743 A.2d 371 (N.J. Super. Ct. App. Div. 2000), the insured purchased a condominium and contacted the insurer's agent to procure insurance. There was a dispute as to whether the insured sought coverage for any losses he might sustain or whether he simply sought coverage for the unit. The agent asked the value of the contents and the price of the unit. The agent alleged that the insured only sought minimum coverage and agreed to the $1,000 coverage limitation on the interior structural damage. The insured failed to read the policy when issued; had he read it, he would have found the low limit. The court held that the failure to read the policy could constitute comparative fault, thus reducing or removing the agent's liability for the alleged negligence.

In *Wynn v. Avemco Ins. Co.*, 963 P.2d 572 (Okla. 1998), the insured sued the aviation insurer for damages incurred when the insured plane was destroyed in a fire after an emergency landing. The policy excluded damage occurring "in flight," which extended to losses occurring until the plane has safely stopped or left the runway under control. The insured requested full coverage. He had previously been covered under a policy without that exclusion. Upon renewal, the new policy contained the exclusion. The court recognized that the insurer could be bound by the representations made by its agents where there is actual or apparent authority and there is a presumption that a renewal contains the same terms as the policy being renewed. The insurer had a duty to alert the insured to any changes in the new policy. However, the insured was not entitled to reformation to include in-flight coverage where the renewal application required that the insured check coverages for accuracy and the application and policy conspicuously excluded the in-flight coverage.

In *Jim Anderson & Co. v. Partraining Corp.*, 454 S.E.2d 210 (Ga. Ct. App. 1995), the insured's business premises were damaged by fire, whereupon he sought to recover for business interruption losses. At that time, he learned that his two policies provided no such coverage despite the fact that he allegedly had ordered the coverage.

The court held that there were fact questions as to whether the insured's failure to read the policies constituted a defense to the claims against the agent. The defense would be viable if the lack of coverage would have been readily apparent from a layman's review of the policy as issued.

Page 147, add to note 76:

In *Quigley v. Bay State Graphics, Inc.*, 693 N.E.2d 1368 (Mass. 1998), the tenant purchased fire insurance. The building owners and the holders of security interests in the tenant's equipment sued the insurance agent hired to procure the policy. They claimed that they should have been named as loss payees, which would have entitled them to coverage, notwithstanding the fact that the fire was intentionally set by the insured. The court affirmed the judgment for the agency, holding that it was not negligent in failing to name the holders of the security interests as insureds where the agent was never advised that there was a security interest.

The building owner could not have relied on the agent's undertaking to obtain the insurance covering its interest as a loss payee since the tenant was not obligated by law to obtain coverage for the owner's benefit outside the commitment contained in the lease that was never submitted to the agent. Thus, the agent was not aware of the tenant's obligation to name the owner. The agent was only required to procure a policy consistent with the tenant's order. The fact that the agent had prepared a certificate of insurance naming the owner did not constitute notice to the agent that the owner was to be named as a loss payee on a subsequent policy. The owner could not recover under the theories advanced where there was no evidence that the agent knew that the owner would rely on the earlier certificate as evidence that its interests were continually protected in light of the fact that the terms of the certificate were clear and unambiguous and did not extend coverage for the owner in perpetuity.

See also Hardy v. Fisher, 901 F. Supp. 228 (E.D. Tex. 1995), discussed in § 5.2.

In *Workman v. McNeal Agency, Inc.*, 458 S.E.2d 707 (Ga. Ct. App. 1995), the landlord sued the tenant's insurance agent after the agent failed to maintain coverage on the property and did not notify the landlord that there was no coverage in force. The tenant was required to obtain the insurance pursuant to the commercial lease. When a loss occurred, the landlord discovered that the property had been deleted from the coverage. The court affirmed the summary judgment for the agent, holding that there was no contractual relationship between the agent and the landlord such as would impose a duty on the agent to procure the insurance required under the terms of the lease.

In *Tu v. Guidry*, 653 So. 2d 1 (La. Ct. App. 1995), the plaintiff was injured in an auto accident caused by the negligence of the insured. He sued the insurance agent who obtained the policy for the insured under a claim that the agent failed to procure a policy with the limits of liability requested by the insured. Had the policy been issued with the requested limits, the plaintiff victim would have received more money. The court held that the plaintiff had no viable claim against the insurance agent as the accident victim was not a party to the insurance transaction. Clearly, however, the insured could have such a claim.

In *Gilbreath v. White,* 903 S.W.2d 851 (Tex. Ct. App. 1995), the mortgagor borrowed $30,000 and agreed to obtain insurance to cover the house for the benefit of the mortgagees. An ice storm damaged part of the property, but the insurer refused to pay for the damage, claiming that the damage was excluded. The mortgagor sued the agent for breach of warranty that the insurance would cover such a loss, breach of contract, negligence and deceptive trade practices. The court held that the settlement with the mortgagor did not affect the rights of the mortgagee who was named on the policy. Thus, the mortgagee had standing to bring claims against both the agent and the insurer.

Page 149, add to note 83:

In *Scott-Huff Ins. Agency v. Sandusky*, 887 S.W.2d 516 (Ark. 1994), the insured sued the agent to recover for damage to its crane. The bank financing the purchase of the crane required that the insured obtain coverage and the plaintiff called the defendant to obtain the coverage. The agent stated that the insured told him he wanted to satisfy the bank's insurance requirement while paying a low premium. The insured contended that he also told the agent that he wanted coverage for the operation of the crane.

A named perils policy was issued and sent to the insured, who read it; the agent subsequently called the insured to review the policy. Several months later, the crane was damaged in an accident with overhead wires. The insured did not submit a claim but discussed policy coverage with the agent.

Later, the crane was heavily damaged during operations, and the insured brought a claim. No coverage was available under the policy and the insured sued the agent. The court held that the insured could not recover, stating that the insured had a duty to know the coverage provided by the policy and to seek a change of coverage, if necessary, to meet his expectations.

5.6 Placement of Coverage With Solvent Authorized Insurer

Page 150, add to note 87:

In *Gordon v. Spectrum, Inc.*, 981 P.2d 488 (Wyo. 1999), the court was required to determine whether agents and brokers are required to inform insureds of the insolvency of an insurer with which coverage has been placed where the insolvency occurred after the expiration of the policy period. In this case, the insured also claimed that the agent and brokers were liable for placing the coverage with the particular surplus lines insurer. The insurer's receiver denied the insured's claim, whereupon the insured filed this action against the agents and brokers. At the time the coverage was purchased, the insurer was solvent, but it became insolvent after the insured chose not to renew its liability insurance with the insurer. The claimant was injured during the policy period, but he did not act on his injury until four years later when he filed suit. By this time, the insurer had become insolvent. The court held that the agents and brokers were not required to alert the insured about the insolvency under the facts of the case and could not be held liable for placing the coverage with the insurer in the first place where there was no evidence they were aware or should have been aware of the insurer's financial condition at the time of the placement.

In *Popich Bros. Water Transport v. Gulf Coast Marine*, 705 So. 2d 1267 (La. Ct. App. 1998), the plaintiff crewboat company obtained liability insurance through the defendant brokers who procured the coverage from an English company. Subsequently, the English company was placed in liquidation and stopped paying claims, thereby depriving the insured of full liability coverage and subjecting the insured to financial losses. The plaintiff argued that the broker knew, or should have known, that the English company was financially unsound, and an investigation should have been undertaken prior to placing the coverage. The court held that the brokers had no duty to investigate the condition of the company which was a nonadmitted insurer. Louisiana Revised Statutes 22:1262.1 removed any duty to investigate such a carrier, provided that the broker checked to make sure that the company was on the Insurance Commissioner's list of approved nonadmitted insurers.

In *Moss v. Appel*, 718 So. 2d 199 (Fla. Dist. Ct. App. 1998), the plaintiff purchased an annuity for a pension plan and sued the consultants who sold the annuity after the insurer issuing that annuity became insolvent. Where the consultants had a fiduciary duty to exercise appropriate care with regard to the plaintiff, the consultants could be held liable. The defendants placed the annuity and subsequently received a letter from the insurer indicating that the insurer was attempting to obtain an infusion of capital so that it would have adequate reserves to meet future benefit claims. At that time, the defendants were continuing their consulting relationship with the plaintiff. The letter was a red flag indicating that the insurer was in trouble. At that point, the defendant should have informed the plaintiff of the problem and advised him that the annuity be surrendered and alternative arrangements made. Because of the insolvency, the plaintiff lost the entire value of the annuity. The defendants had a fiduciary relationship with the plaintiff and could be held liable for the breach of that duty.

In *Evvtex Co. v. Hartley Cooper,* 102 F.3d 1327 (2d Cir. 1996), applying New York law, the insured purchased a jeweler's block policy using a London broker. The insured sued that broker to recover policy proceeds after the broker paid the proceeds to the insured's excess line broker, through whom the London broker conducted business, and not to the insured. The court held that the brokers acted as agents of the insured and therefore owed the insured a fiduciary duty. This duty requires that the broker exercise reasonable care in following the insured's instructions. The insured alleged that the London broker was aware that the excess broker had financial problems but failed to advise the insured. This resulted in the loss of the funds. The court found that the insured was not bound by the excess broker's fraudulent representations regarding the payment of policy proceeds. The court affirmed the judgment against the London broker in favor of the insured.

In *Cherokee Ins. Co. v. E.W. Blanch Co.*, 66 F.3d 117 (6th Cir. 1995), applying Tennessee law, the insurer sued the reinsurance broker claiming that it failed to exercise due care in determining the financial condition of reinsurers that it recommended to the insurer. The insurer was placed in rehabilitation.

The defendant was the insurer's principal reinsurance intermediary and negotiated arrangements under which the insurer ceded some of the risk to various reinsurers. The defendant would typically analyze the company's reinsurance needs for the coming year and would then work out an agreed reinsurance program which would be shopped to potential reinsurers. The defendant typically told the insurer that the proposed reinsurers offered good or acceptable security, but the insurer was invited to contact the defendant with any questions.

While the commissions for placing the business came from the reinsurers, the defendant viewed the insurer as its client. In the defendant's client brochure describing its services, it emphasized that it places reinsurance with strong responsive reinsurance markets which are monitored on a continuous basis. The defendant monitored the financial strength of reinsurers through an internal committee which looked at A.M. Best's ratings, IRIS ratios, the reinsurer's annual reports and their reputations. Each of the reinsurers in question carried an A+ or A Best rating and each passed IRIS tests.

None of the reinsurers had anything less than a favorable reputation. One reinsurer was placed into conservatorship almost two years after the insurer's last purchase of reinsurance from that company. The other two reinsurers went the same route and defaulted on their reinsurance obligations to the insurer. There was substantial expert testimony on the use of various financial ratios and evaluation of the reinsurers' financial strength. The court affirmed the grant of summary judgment for the defendant, holding that the broker complied with customary industry standards and was not negligent in its reinsurance placement even though it might not have performed a more thorough detailed analysis advocated by the plaintiff's expert.

In *Wyrick v. Hartfield*, 654 N.E.2d 913 (Ind. Ct. App. 1995), the plaintiff purchased an annuity from the broker and sued the broker for negligence after the company issuing the annuity (Executive Life) was placed in conservatorship. For six years, the plaintiff received the full monthly annuity benefit from the insurer. As a result of the intervention of the California

Insurance Commissioner, annuitants such as the plaintiff started receiving reduced benefits, and future benefits remained uncertain. The plaintiff alleged that the broker "carelessly, negligently and without due diligence and reasonable care recommended that [the plaintiff] replace the Transamerica Life Insurance and Annuity Company annuity with an annuity purchased from Executive Life Insurance Company."

The court affirmed the summary judgment for the broker, holding that the broker did not have a duty to advise the plaintiff with respect to the annuity and did exercise reasonable care in procuring the annuity. The broker had no special long-term relationship with the plaintiff after it obtained the single premium annuity even though the broker allegedly knew of the plaintiff's investment of his life savings in the annuity. The broker met its duties where Executive Life was rated A+ by A. M. Best Company and AAA by Standard & Poor when the annuity was purchased.

In *Haapanen v. Bogle*, 643 So. 2d 547 (Ala. 1994), the insured sued the insurance agents, marketers, and underwriters of a group policy for negligent placement of insurance coverage, conspiracy to defraud, misrepresentation and bad faith failure to pay the insured's claim.

The insured's father purchased the group policy after paying a $15 fee to join the American Association of Consumer Awareness. He paid the fee when he applied for coverage. The group policies were moved to another insurer, which was not licensed to do business in Alabama. After the coverage was shifted, the insured was in an auto accident and became severely disabled, both physically and mentally. The insurer paid the insured's father $400,000. The insurer then notified the father that it was terminating the coverage, but the coverage would continue for 90 days after notification for persons who were totally disabled. The insurance was extended for another six months, during which time the plan administrator moved the plan again. This third insurer considered the insured's coverage terminated and refused to honor the extension.

The court affirmed summary judgment for the insurance marketers, holding that the insured failed to introduce any evidence that the marketers of the policy breached any duty they owed him, where they merely distributed information on the particular policy chosen by the insured. There was no evidence that the marketers knew or should have known that the policy was being transferred to an insurer which was financially insecure. The mere fact that the insurer was not licensed to do business in the state did not indicate financial instability.

In *Acadiana Shrimpers, Inc. v. Phoenix Fire & Marine Ins. Co.*, 640 So. 2d 800 (La. Ct. App. 1994), the shrimp boat owner-insured sued the insurance agent after the marine insurer became insolvent and was unable to pay the insured's fire damage claim. The court held that the agent did not breach any fiduciary duties in placing the policy through a surplus lines broker, where the president of the surplus lines broker had a long-standing business relationship, the broker had reviewed the insurer's records, and the insurer was meeting its obligations when the policy was issued. The court found that there was a presumption that the broker was diligent in investigating the financial records of the insurer.

5.7 Issuing Binders and Certificates of Insurance

Page 154, add to note 94:

In *Mashburn v. Meeker Sharkey Financial Group*, 5 S.W.3d 469 (Ark. 1999), the insured purchased a boat and then purchased a binder. The insured advised the agent of his itinerary. He planned to truck the boat to Florida and sail around the Florida Keys. The binder showed coverage in the waters along the eastern United States from Georgia to Maine, even though his application for insurance showed his intended route around the Keys. While en route, he was caught in a storm that disabled his steering gear. The boat was blown off course and ended up beached off the coast of Cuba.

After the loss, when the insured called the agent, he was advised that there was no coverage for losses outside the area described in the binder. The insurer ultimately acknowledged that the boat was covered and settled with the insured. However, the insured incurred substantial expenses traveling from the United States to Cuba and had become financially obligated for marine repairs. He missed time at work and incurred additional living expenses in Cuba. He claimed that the agent breached its duty to act properly and in good faith. He alleged that the agent was negligent in issuing the wrong binder and in telling him that he had no coverage following the loss.

The court affirmed summary judgment in favor of the agent. The court held that the insured failed to establish that he sustained any damages resulting from the agent's negligence in issuing the binder where the application sent to the insurer showed the correct coverage area and the insurer honored the binder and paid the policy limits. The court further held that the agent did not owe the insured any duties with regard to payment of the claim since that was a matter of enforcement of the insurance contract, to which the agent was not a party.

In *Michigan Mut. Ins. Co. v. Sports, Inc.*, 698 N.E.2d 834 (Ind. Ct. App. 1998), the claimant was involved in purchasing a bowling alley purchaser that sustained fire damage. The ensuing claim was denied when the insurer contended that there was no binder in place to protect the claimant's interests. The only way to obtain insurance from the insurer was through a special agent like the one involved in this case. Therefore, it was proper to instruct the jury that the agent was effectively a general agent of the insurer vested with the authority normally granted to such agents. The court held that the agent could orally bind the insurer by showing that there was a course of conduct that would lead the plaintiff to believe that the agent had apparent authority to grant oral binders. The court affirmed the verdict for the plaintiff.

In *Bowers v. Merchants Mut. Ins. Co.*, 670 N.Y.S.2d 274 (N.Y. App. Div. 1998), the insured sued the insurer, claiming that there was a valid property insurance contract in force on the date of the fire. The insurer argued that the binder, prepared by the agent, had not been issued before the fire. The court held that the fact that the insurer retained the agent did not establish that the insurer participated in the alleged fraud perpetrated on the insured in leading the insured to believe that there was coverage in force for the fire. The court held that the insurer was not liable for any loss sustained by the insured due to his reliance on the deceitful, unauthorized representation that there was coverage in force for the fire and that the binder would be backdated to provide coverage. The court further noted that the requirements for an oral binder were not met given the facts of the case.

In *Columbia Mut. Cas. Ins. Co. v. Ingraham*, 896 S.W.2d 903 (Ark. 1995), the insured sued the insurer for a loss sustained after the expiration of the binder. The insured applied for homeowners insurance using the defendant agent. The application included a 30-day binder. The insured gave the agent a check for the first year's premium. The insurer rejected the application within the 30-day period and so informed the agent, who did not transmit the decision to the insured. Within another month, the house burned. The court reversed the judgment for the insured, holding that the agent lacked any apparent authority to bind the insurer beyond the 30 days provided for in the application. Any statement made by the agent that the binder was effective during the normal turn-around time for processing the application did not affect this result.

In *Watts v. Westland Farm Mut. Ins. Co.*, 895 P.2d 626 (Mont. 1995), the insured farmer obtained hail insurance through a local independent agent. He dealt directly with the agent who procured the insurance from the insurer. The agent assured him that coverage would start as of the day following the insured's signing the binder. The insured paid his premium in full and made no claims during the year. The next year, the insured signed a binder even though the agent told him that he would have to check the insurability of one particular crop grown by the insured. The binder included the crop. The insured claimed that he received a message from the agent confirming the insurance on the particular crop.

The farm suffered a hail storm, but there was a question whether the crop was damaged at that time. The insurer informed the agent that it would not insure the crop due to a new reinsurer for hail insurance. The insurer issued a policy, covering other crops, which contained the binder as the declaration page. The reference to the crop in question had been crossed out with the word "delete" written in the margin. The premium was reduced to reflect the lesser coverage.

The insured's farm suffered another hail storm, and this time the crop in question was damaged as were covered crops. The insurer paid for covered crop damage but not for the crops in dispute. The court affirmed the summary judgment for the agent and the insurer, holding that the binder expired when the policy was issued, and therefore, no coverage was provided for the crop in question.

5.8   Issuing the Policy

Page 157, add at end of section:

In *Wolfson v. Bernstein*, 955 S.W.2d 814 (Mo. Ct. App. 1997), the plaintiff tried to obtain key man life insurance on the life of its corporate president before he disappeared. The agent offered a policy that was unacceptable to the president, and the agent sought other coverage. The coverage was not effective until the first premium payment was made.

The insurer forwarded the policy to the agent and specified that the requirements for placing the coverage into effect had to be completed by a certain date. The agent called the plaintiff's president several times requesting a check for the premium, but he did not receive a check. The agent obtained an extension to make the payment conditioned on a certificate of continued good health. No premium payment was made before the president disappeared. Shortly thereafter, the president committed suicide.

The court held that the agent was not liable for a negligent misrepresentation that the policy was in effect where it was clear from the application that the initial premium payment was required to secure the effective coverage. The court held that the agent was not negligent in attempting to collect the premium.

In *Liberty Mut. Ins. Co. v. York Hunter, Inc.,* 945 F. Supp. 742 (S.D.N.Y. 1996), the insurers sued the insured to recover unpaid premiums whereupon the insured counterclaimed for breach of contract and for failing to add a joint venture of the insured's as a named insured on the policy. The insured was the construction manager and a joint venturer in a group formed to provide construction management services to the state of New York for the construction of a state psychiatric center. The insured agreed with the agent to include the joint venture in the policy, and the agent confirmed this agreement in writing. However, the policy as issued failed to include the venture.

The agent stated that the policy would be amended to reflect the agreement, but this was never done. Various meetings took place with respect to correcting the situation in subsequent policies, and the agent continued to state that the insurer covered the joint ventures. However, after an accident occurred on a job site, the insurer declined the claim on the basis that the joint venture was not a named insured. The court held that the insurers could deny coverage on the basis of the failure to name the joint venture in the renewal policy; the insured was charged with the agent's knowledge that the joint venture was not added as a joint venture. Nevertheless, the court found that there were fact questions as to whether the insured was entitled to reformation of the policy to include the joint venture as a named insured.

In *Maryland Ins. Co. v. Head Industrial Coatings & Services, Inc.*, 906 S.W.2d 218 (Tex. Ct. App. 1995), the insured sued the CGL insurer after it refused to pay a claim brought against the insured. The insurer, in turn, "third-partied" the local agent, claiming that the agent was required to indemnify the insurer for any potential liability.

As a prerequisite to working for a utility, the insured was required to agree to indemnify the utility for any claims arising out of the services performed and to purchase liability insurance to protect the utility against claims arising out of that work.

The insured contacted its local agent and purchased a policy. The insured intended to purchase the required contractual liability insurance coverage and advised the agent accordingly. There was even evidence that the insured was charged for the coverage. The agent allegedly committed a clerical error, and the policy actually issued did not contain the proper coverage.

When a worker on the project was injured and filed suit, the utility sought indemnification and/or insurance coverage from the insured. At this point, the absence of the endorsement was discovered, and the insurer refused to provide coverage. The court held that the insurer could potentially be liable in bad faith for the product of the agent's negligence. The court found that the agent breached its fiduciary duties owed to the insurer.

5.9 Transmitting Premiums

Page 160, add to note 105:

In *Ezrasons, Inc. v. American Credit Indem. Co.*, 683 N.Y.S.2d 264 (N.Y. App. Div. 1999), the plaintiff purchased a credit insurance policy from the defendant. On the application, the plaintiff represented that it had no outstandings more than 60 days past due under the original terms of sale and no outstandings under general extension. This was not true. One of the plaintiff's customers became insolvent, and the plaintiff sought to recover its loss arising out of credit extended to the customer. The court held that the agent's oral representation that the policy extended coverage for losses occurring prior to the payment of the premium, despite a clear exclusion, had no effect. This was particularly true where the policy itself clearly limited the agent's authority in the situation. The fact that the agent requested the premium after the insured submitted a claim was not evidence of the agent's intent to modify the terms of the policy, where the insurer had a practice of requesting and accepting late premium payments.

Page 161, add to note 110:

In *Landry v. Prime Insurance Syndicate*, 732 So. 2d 1291 (La. Ct. App. 1999), the agent procured commercial general liability policies from the defendant, which was a foreign insurer not licensed to do business in the state other than as a surplus lines insurer. The agent did not have a broker's license but could place the coverage through an intermediate broker. The plaintiff agent used such a broker and claimed that it paid all premiums on the policies in question. Both businesses sustained insured losses. The defendant insurer paid them, but then claimed that it had not received all the premiums due. Such a claim was for a breach of contract. It was determined that the agent did not owe any additional amounts to the defendant where the agent had paid the intermediate broker. By law, such payment constitutes payment to the insurer.

See also Standard Funding Corp. v. Lewitt, 678 N.E.2d 874 (N.Y. 1997), discussed in § 1.4.

In *Andrews v. Schram*, 252 Neb. 298, 562 N.W.2d 50 (1997), the insurer sued the officers of the agency that was authorized to bind the insurer and handled a variety of funds. The defendants and the agency were involved in a scheme to convert premium payments that were to be transmitted to the insurer. The court held that the officers could be held liable as subagents of the authorized agency, and therefore they owed the insurer a variety of fiduciary duties which they breached in this case.

In *Cates v. Cincinnati Life Ins. Co.*, 947 S.W.2d 608 (Tex. Ct. App. 1997), the plaintiffs sued the insurer for numerous claims arising out of the agent's failure to properly use premium payments to maintain the policies, causing the policies to lapse. The insured received lapse notices from the insurer.

The court held that there were questions of fact as to whether the claims were time-barred by the statute of limitations. The issue was whether the time period started to run from the insured's receipt of the lapse notices or from the date when the insured discovered that the problem was due to the agent's failure to transmit the premium payments. There were also questions of fact precluding summary judgment on the issue of whether the agent had apparent authority to accept the premium payments on behalf of the insurer.

In *Central Benefits Mut. Ins. Co. v. RIS Administrators Agency, Inc.*, 638 N.E.2d 1049 (Ohio Ct. App. 1994), the insurers sued the insurance agency and its officers for breach of contract, conversion and breach of fiduciary duties. The cause of action arose out of the defendants' actions as third-party administrator for the insurers' health and life insurance programs. There were various problems with the defendants' collection and timely transmission of premiums to the plaintiffs. There was evidence that the defendants treated the collected premium funds as their own and delayed transmission while using the funds for unauthorized purposes. In response to a request for summary judgment, the court held that the allegations raised a question of fact for the jury to determine whether the defendants' conduct constituted conversion and breach of fiduciary duties.

5.10 Premium Financing

Page 168, add to end of section:

See Standard Funding Corp. v. Lewitt, 89 N.Y.2d 546, 678 N.E.2d 874 (1997), discussed in § 1.4.

In *Afco Credit Corp. v. Rosenthal Agency*, 672 So. 2d 1077 (La. Ct. App. 1996), the premium finance company sued the insurance agent that acquired another agent's assets in exchange for the assumption of liabilities in connection with the latter's bankruptcy proceedings. The bankrupt agent had failed to remit funds to the premium finance company after certain policies had been canceled and the agent received a return of the unearned premiums from the insurers. The amount to be paid to the finance company was listed as a debt on the agent's bankruptcy petition. The court held that the premium finance company failed to establish any basis for recovery under the agreement for the sale of assets.

In *Illinois Insurance Guaranty Fund v. Evanston Paper & Paper Shredding Co.*, 649 N.E.2d 568 (Ill. App. Ct. 1995), the premium finance company allegedly canceled the insurance in violation of its statutory duties. Where the insurer reasonably relied on the finance company's authority to cancel the policy, the insurer could not be held responsible for a loss occurring following the cancellation despite the finance company's statutory violation.

In *Gill Plumbing Co. v. Imperial Premium Finance, Inc.*, 445 S.E.2d 840 (Ga. Ct. App. 1994), the insured sued the premium financing company for breach of contract after it failed to assure that workers comp and general liability/commercial property insurance was in force. The court held that the finance company had no such duty. The fact that the insured had executed a power of attorney, giving the finance company the power to cancel the policies, did not create a fiduciary duty to verify that the insured's coverage was in force.

5.11 Waivers of Policy Conditions, Limitations, and Defaults

Page 172, add at end of section:

In *Aguiar v. Generali Assicurazoni Insurance Co.*, 715 N.E.2d 1046 (Mass. App. Ct. 1999), the insured's unoccupied restaurant was destroyed by fire. The insurer denied coverage based on the vacancy provisions contained in the policy and material misrepresentations made by the insured in the application for coverage. The vacancy/unoccupancy provision was clear and enforceable. The court held that the insurer's managing agent's letter written to the insured's broker advising the broker that security measures would be required if the building was left unused, did not waive the vacancy provisions.

In *Ezrasons, Inc. v. American Credit Indem. Co.*, 683 N.Y.S.2d 264 (N.Y. 1999), the plaintiff purchased a credit insurance policy from the defendant. On the application, the plaintiff represented that it had no outstandings more than 60 days past due under the original terms of sale and no outstandings under general extension. This was not true. One of the plaintiff's customers became insolvent, and the plaintiff sought to recover its loss arising out of credit extended to the customer. The court held that the agent's oral representation that the policy extended coverage for losses occurring prior to the payment of the premium, despite a clear exclusion, had no effect. This was particularly true where the policy itself clearly limited the agent's authority in the situation. The fact that the agent requested the premium after the insured submitted a claim was not evidence of the agent's intent to modify the terms of the policy where the insurer had a practice of requesting and accepting late premium payments.

High Country Arts and Craft v. Hartford Fire Ins. Co., 126 F.3d 629 (4th Cir. 1997), applying North Carolina law. Clearly, an agent has no authority, either actual or apparent, to modify the policy provisions following the issuance of the policy in the absence of compelling equities.

In *Pankow v. Colonial Life Ins. Co.*, 932 S.W.2d 271 (Tex. Ct. App. 1996), the credit life insurer failed to pay the policy proceeds to the mortgagee, claiming that the policy had not been reinstated prior to the death of the insured decedent. The policy was obtained through the mortgagee, and the insureds continued making payments until they ultimately defaulted. Thereupon, the insurer sent them a letter advising that the policy lapsed for nonpayment of premiums. The insureds met with the mortgagee to discuss the default. The bank officer allegedly stated that he could reinstate the loan and the insurance, and both would be reinstated upon payment of a stated amount. The insureds paid that amount and several weeks later received two sets of coupon books for the mortgage payments and for the life insurance premiums.

The insurer notified the insureds that even though the policy had lapsed, it would reinstate the policy upon completion of the reinstatement form even though the insureds were already making payments. The insureds called the insurer and were advised that there was confusion on the insurer's part and that with the receipt of the premium payments the coverage would be reinstated. The insureds returned the executed reinstatement form, but before doing so, the insured wife received a check from the insurer representing six premium payments that had been paid following the lapse. She cashed the check. She was then told that the policy would be reinstated by repaying the amount of that check plus three more monthly premiums.

The contacts with the insurer continued, but ultimately, the husband died. The insured wife had spoken to the insurer on the day before the husband died. In that conversation, she said that the husband was still in good health. The court held that these facts precluded a summary judgment for the insurer and the bank employees. The court also noted that the statements that the policy had been reinstated could not have reasonably been relied upon by the insureds, where they knew that they had not complied with the conditions of reinstatement, which required proof of insurability and the payment of outstanding premiums.

See Holt v. Aetna Cas. & Sur. Co., 680 So. 2d 117 (La. Ct. App. 1996), discussed in § 4.5.

5.12 Claims Handling

Page 172, add note 128a after first sentence of section:

In *Alliston v. Omega Ins. Co.*, 983 F. Supp. 675 (S.D. Miss. 1997), the insureds sued the agent for fraudulently misrepresenting that they were covered under a property insurance policy. The agent allegedly told the plaintiffs that they would be covered for burglary losses, but when one such loss occurred, the insurer denied coverage. The insurer finally admitted that there was coverage but refused to pay the entire amount of the insureds' loss.

The court held that when the insurer admitted that there was coverage for the loss, any misrepresentation made by the agent was rendered irrelevant, and therefore the agent could not be held liable. The court further noted that the agent has no obligation running to the insureds with respect to the settlement of claims. Therefore, he could not be held liable for the insurer's conduct in handling the claim.

Page 174, add to note 130:

In *Dodson v. State Farm Gen. Ins. Co.*, 972 S.W.2d 450 (Mo. Ct. App. 1998), the insured sued to recover uninsured motorist benefits under his policy. The insurer denied the claim based on the insured's untimely notice of the claim. The insured delayed nearly 10 years in giving written notice to the insurer but gave a prompt verbal notice to an employee in the agent's office. The court held that the verbal notice did not trigger any duty to advise the insured that the policy required that written notice be given and therefore did not excuse the delay in giving such notice to the insurer. The court affirmed the summary judgment in favor of the defendants.

In *American Cas. Co. v. Rahn*, 854 F. Supp. 492 (W.D. Mich. 1994), the insurer brought a declaratory judgment to determine coverage under a directors and officers liability policy issued to the insured S&L. The question was raised as to whether the insured complied with notice requirements under the claims-made policy. Where the insured S&L designated an individual as its "agent of record for Officers and Directors Liability Insurance" such a person was an independent agent representing the insured and not the insurer. Therefore, notice of claim given to that agent was not imputed to the insurer so as to meet the policy requirements. The court came to that conclusion after noting that the agent lacked authorization from the insurer to sign the insurance binder and to remove a policy exclusion. The individual agent was also a director of the insured S&L. The court further noted that even if the individual was the insurer's authorized agent, his knowledge of the potential claim would not be imputed to the insurer where the agent obtained the knowledge in his capacity as corporate director and not as an insurance agent.

In *Carlton v. St. Paul Mercury Ins. Co.*, 36 Cal. Rptr. 2d 229 (Cal. Ct. App. 1994), the insured sued the insurer and broker for an unreasonable delay in paying under an antique-auto policy. The court was required to determine whether the broker was the insurer's agent for the purpose of imputing the broker's knowledge of the claim to the insurer. The broker had merely secured the policy and thus acted as the insured's agent. Accordingly, the broker's knowledge of the occurrence of loss was not imputed to the insurer.

In *Taylor Machine Works, Inc. v. Great American Surplus Lines Ins. Co.*, 635 So. 2d 1357 (Miss. 1994), a forklift manufacturer sued the insurer for coverage of a product liability claim. The product allegedly caused a fatal accident in 1986, resulting in a suit against the insured in 1987. There was no coverage under the insured's 1986 policy, and the agent explicitly removed the claim from coverage in a subsequent policy. The court found that there was a fact question precluding a summary judgment as to the agent's negligence in removing the claim from coverage. The court noted that a letter written by the decedent's employer to the insured might be considered a claim which should have been covered.

Page 175, add to note 135:

In *Winburn v. Liberty Mut. Ins. Co.*, 8 F. Supp. 644 (E.D. Ky. 1998), the claimants sued the driver's automobile insurer and the insurance agent. They claimed that the agent attempted to settle their wrongful death claim within hours of the accident, advising them that there was some liability insurance coverage available when there was more than $1.2 million in limits available, and by telling the claimant's attorney that only minimum coverage was available when the claim was ultimately settled for $500,000. At the time the settlement was effected, all parties were aware of the policy limit. The court held that the conduct did not constitute bad faith or a violation of the state Unfair Settlement Act.

In *Maintenance, Inc. v. ITT Hartford Group*, 895 S.W.2d 816 (Tex. Ct. App. 1995), the insured obtained its workers compensation coverage through the assigned risk pool. It sued the insurer for bad faith and deceptive trade practices after the insurer allegedly was lenient in the handling and payment of comp claims. The insurer was the servicing company for the pool and, as such, was not the actual insurer. Thus, the pool could be held liable for the alleged improper claims handling. However, the insurer acting as the pool's agent could not unless the agent's acts caused reasonably foreseeable harm to the insured. It should be noted that with respect to assigned risk plans, there may be special statutes limiting the plan's liability in such situations.

In *Toops v. U.S.F.&G.*, 871 F. Supp. 284 (S.D. Tex. 1994), the plaintiff was riding in a car being towed on the highway when the car was struck in the rear by another vehicle. The jury in the trial of the underlying tort claim found the owner of the latter vehicle liable. The tort defendants submitted a claim for coverage to the defendant insurer in this case; after the insurer declined coverage, the tort defendants assigned their claims against the insurer and the agent to the plaintiff. The court held that the agent, who was hired only to procure coverage, could not be held liable for the wrongful denial. The insurer, who acted as an agent for the underwriters in obtaining excess umbrella coverage, could not be held liable where it did not act outside the scope of its authority or misrepresent its status to the insured.

Page 177, add to note 142:

In *Custard Ins. Adjusters v. Youngblood*, 686 So. 2d 211 (Ala. 1996), the insured trucking company's agent obtained surplus lines insurance from an unauthorized insurer. After the insurer denied the insured's claim, the trucking company sued the agent, broker, the adjuster, and others. The court held that the adjuster could be held liable under Ala. Code § 27-10-2 for investigating and adjusting claims for unauthorized insurers. The court affirmed the partial summary judgment for the insured against the adjuster.

In *Yoakum v. Hartford Fire Ins. Co.*, 923 P.2d 416 (Idaho 1996), the parents of the minor victim killed in an accident involving the insured's golf course maintenance vehicle sued the insurer and its investigator under various theories. The police chief initially requested that the state police perform an accident investigation. After the investigator completed his investigation and filed his report, he was placed on administrative leave for unrelated reasons. He was hired as an expert witness by the law firm hired by the insurer.

The investigator subsequently revised his computations and his original opinion that the vehicle was unsafe to operate at any speed. The insured also complained of other actions undertaken by the insurer in the investigation. The court affirmed the judgment for the insurer, holding that the insurer did not commit racketeering or the intentional interference with the plaintiffs' right in the suit. The court also found that the adjuster did not unreasonably interfere with the plaintiff's wrongful death action, holding that he had not committed spoliation of evidence.

Page 177, add to note 144:

In *French v. State Farm Ins. Co.*, 156 F.R.D. 159 (S.D. Tex. 1994), the insured sued the insurer and the adjuster handling the claim for bad faith and violations of the state's deceptive trade practice statute, arising out of the rejection of his underinsured motorist claim. The court held that the adjuster could not be held liable for negligence in claims handling since Texas law recognizes no such claim. The court further held that the adjuster could not be held liable in his individual capacity for any alleged bad faith or statutory violations. The only potential liability would be imposed on the insurer, either directly or for the acts of the adjuster (its agent).

In *Natividad v. Alexsis, Inc.*, 875 S.W.2d 695 (Tex. 1994), the plaintiff was a workers compensation claimant who sued the adjuster for bad faith arising out of the handling of her claim. She also raised claims for economic duress, negligent infliction of emotional distress, and extreme and outrageous conduct.

The Texas Supreme Court held that the adjusting firm and the individual adjuster did not owe the plaintiff a duty of good faith and fair dealing where there was no contractual or special relationship between the parties. The adjusting company contracted with the comp insurer to provide adjusting services. The court held that the plaintiff's allegations failed to state a claim for infliction of emotional distress or outrageous conduct.

Chapter 6

The Role and Duties of Brokers

6.1 Establishing That the Broker Is the Insured's Agent

Page 184, add to note 3:

See also Ballard v. Lee, 671 So. 2d 1368 (Ala. 1995), discussed in § 2.6.

In *Fireman's Fund Ins. Co. v. National Bank for Cooperatives*, 849 F. Supp. 1347 (N.D. Cal. 1994), the servicer's insurer sued to determine whether it was liable for an arbitration award in favor of a bank with respect to certificates covering inventory financed by the bank. The insurer claimed that it had not received timely notice. The court held that even though a broker is generally the agent of the insured and not the insurer, due to the ambiguous notice provisions in the servicer's excess liability policy, notice to the broker was sufficient even if it was not transmitted to the insurer in a timely and proper manner.

In *Clark-Peterson Co. v. Independent Ins. Assocs.*, 514 N.W.2d 912 (Iowa 1994), the insured sued the insurer for defense and indemnity of a wrongful discharge claim brought against it. The insured also sued the agent for breach of fiduciary duties, misrepresentation, and intentional infliction of emotional distress. The agent had represented to the insured that the policies purchased (a multiperil policy and contractor's umbrella policy) would cover employment discrimination claims.

At trial, the court applied the "reasonable consumer" doctrine, holding that the insured had coverage. Therefore, the court held, the insured could not recover from the agent; the judgment already entered against the insurer provided the coverage the agent had promised. While the insured argued that it should be entitled to recover its attorneys' fees from the agent as damages, the court held that this was not possible without a determination that the agent was the insured's agent, not the insurer's.

In *Paramount Ins. Co. v. Brown*, 613 N.Y.S.2d 910 (N.Y. App. Div. 1994), the insurer sued the insured to obtain additional premiums earned with respect to four consecutive liability policies. The court held that the insurance broker was the insured's agent. The agent's renewal of the policies without objection for consecutive policy periods, with the insured's ratification of the broker's acts, could render the insured liable for the broker's acts or omissions. Since the broker was not the insurer's agent, the insurer was entitled to recover the premiums earned.

Page 183, add to note 4:

In *Wells Fargo & Co. v. Industrial Indemnity Co.*, 980 P.2d 1138 (Or. Ct. App. 1999), after the excess liability insurer denied coverage for an errors and omissions claim arising out of the insured bank's handling of escrow accounts, the insured sued the insurer. With respect to the broker's liability, the court was required to determine the implications of the addition of an endorsement to the policy made at the request of the brokers. The new endorsement was more restrictive than the previous coverage and arguably removed the coverage for the claims in question. With respect to the conduct of the broker, the court found that the broker acted as the insured's agent. Although the broker had an agreement with the insurer permitting the broker to execute certain policy forms on behalf of the insurer, this agreement did not involve the type of policy involved in this case. Thus, any actions undertaken by the broker could not serve as a basis for imposing liability on the insurer.

In *Soanes v. Empire Blue Cross/Blue Shield*, 970 F. Supp. 230 (S.D.N.Y. 1997), the union trust fund sued the group health insurer and other parties including brokers for breach of contract, deceptive acts, and breach of fiduciary duties. The insurer brought a third-party action against the brokers and others who solicited nonunion people to join the health plans as "associated" members.

With respect to the brokers, the court noted that one who procures coverage on behalf of the insured is the insured's agent and any fraud perpetrated by such a broker is binding on the insured. The court held that the insurer failed to establish that it sustained any damages from the scheme because it paid no claims submitted by any associated members.

In *Commercial Union Ins. Co. v. Connors*, 679 N.E.2d 1012 (Mass. App. Ct. 1997), the claimant brought suit seeking payment under the insured's personal umbrella policy that expired the day before the accident in question. The claimant argued that the policy remained in force because the insurer failed to send a notice that it was not going to renew the coverage.

The agent was deemed to be the insured's agent, and therefore, the agent's knowledge that the insurer would only write umbrella coverage if it also wrote the insured's homeowners insurance was imputed to the insured. The agent's notification to the insurer that the insured decided not to renew the homeowners and umbrella policies was likewise imputed to the insured and provided the insurer with a defense to the claim.

6.2 Duties to Insured in General

Page 188, add note 12a at end of first sentence of second paragraph:

In *Lincoln Electric Co. v. St. Paul Fire and Marine Ins. Co.*, 10 F. Supp. 2d 856 (N.D. Ohio 1998), the insured manufactured welding equipment and products that contained asbestos. The insured was sued by various claimants for asbestos exposure injuries and sought coverage under its liability insurance policies. Coverage disputes arose after the coverage was changed from occurrence basis coverage to a claims-made coverage. With respect to the agents' liability, the court recognized the general agency principles that agents and brokers have fiduciary duties and must disclose any conflicts of interest. In this case, the broker, while acting on behalf of the insurer, owed the duty of loyalty to the insured to disclose its profit-sharing deal with the insurer. However, the court found no actionable misrepresentation or breach of duty where the insured knew that the broker was compensated by the insurer and acquiesced in the dual agency employment.

In *Arctic Tug & Barge v. Raleigh, Schwartz & Powell*, 956 P.2d 1199 (Alaska 1998), the shipper of goods sued the carrier after the goods were lost in rough seas. The carrier then sued the shipper's insurance broker for failing to obtain coverage for the shipper, naming the carrier as an additional insured or alternatively waiving subrogation rights against the carrier. The fact that the carrier expected such coverage could not impose liability on the broker where such expectation was not articulated to the broker, who had no duty to explain the actual coverage to the carrier.

In *A.G. Edwards & Sons v. Drew*, 978 S.W.2d 386 (Mo. Ct. App. 1998), the plaintiff self-insured its employee's medical expense claims and sued the broker for failing to procure suitable stop-loss coverage. The plaintiff established that the brokers provided inaccurate information and quotations for the stop-loss coverage. The court held that this supported the breach of contract claim arising out of the failure to obtain coverage for employees who were both actively at work and those who were not actively at work on the first day of the policy period. The court affirmed the judgment for the plaintiff, finding that the broker was the plaintiff's agent and therefore owed it a fiduciary duty to obtain a policy that conformed to the plaintiff's order and that duty was breached in this case.

In *Cogan v. Triad American Energy*, 944 F. Supp. 1325 (S.D. Tex. 1996), the plaintiffs invested in a limited partnership to build windmills for the generation of electricity and later sued the insurer, insurance broker, and various other entities involved in the investment. The project failed, and the general partners filed for bankruptcy. The plaintiffs alleged that the loss of the investment had nothing to do with the economic risk posed by the project. The partnership purchased the turbine manufacturer and obtained insurance policies to secure the warranties on the turbines. The insurance broker could not be held liable under any theory where it delivered the policy as requested and collected the premium. This terminated the broker's duties. Moreover, there was no duty to disclose to the investors that the policy contained standard limitations covering expected downtime for this form of equipment. In the absence of any specific undertaking, the broker has no duty to disclose and explain the terms of the policy.

In *Duignan v. Lincoln Towers Ins. Agency*, 667 N.E.2d 608 (Ill. App. Ct. 1996), the insured sued the broker for breach of fiduciary duties after the broker canceled the auto policy. The insured purchased a car from a dealer and sought insurance coverage from a broker located in the dealer's building. The broker arranged for the financing of the premium. After the insured failed to make a monthly payment, the broker requested that the insurer cancel the policy. When the insured then paid the premium, the broker requested that the policy be reinstated, and this was done.

Several months later, the insured again failed to make the payment, and the broker requested the cancellation. The insurer notified the insured of the cancellation, effective

August 27. The vehicle was destroyed in a fire on September 11. The broker did not seek reinstatement until September 24, when it received a check for the overdue premium. The check was dated August 21. The court held that the broker was acting as an agent of the insured and was found to have breached its fiduciary duties in requesting the cancellation. The court affirmed the grant of summary judgment to the insured but reversed the award of punitive damages.

In *Mark Patterson, Inc. v. R.M. Stephens & Co.*, 647 N.Y.S.2d 760 (N.Y. App. Div. 1996), the insured sued the broker for fraud, fraudulent inducement, and negligence. The court held that the insured stated a viable fraud claim. The insured alleged that the broker knew unfavorable information about the sales representative, that the representative was not insurable, but did not reveal it. The insured's jewelry disappeared while in the representative's possession. A question of fact, however, was raised as to whether the broker's knowledge was superior to that of the insured. There was a question about whether the broker had conflicting information about the representative's alleged involvement in prior criminal activity.

In *JCM Const. Co. v. Orleans Parish School Bd.*, 663 So. 2d 429 (La. Ct. App. 1995), the school board sued the construction contractor and its insurer in connection with damage to the building under construction, which was vandalized shortly before completion. The construction contract required that the contractor obtain builders risk, extended coverage, and other forms of coverage spelled out in the contract. The contractor was to furnish the required certificates to the school board's insurance consultant.

The certificate submitted to the consultant showed general liability, automobile liability, and other coverage, but no builders risk coverage. The certificate was initially rejected by the consultant with the notation that the school board was to be named on the certificate and not the insurance consultant. The consultant reviewed the reissued certificate and approved it.

The court held that the consultant's acceptance of the certificate on behalf of the school board precluded the board's breach of contract action against the contractor for failure to obtain the required coverage. At all times, the consultant was acting within the scope of his authority. The insurer issuing the certificates could not be held liable for the contractor's failure to obtain the correct insurance. Clearly, the school board would have a claim against the consultant for negligence.

Page 188, add to note 14:

In *Benante v. United Pacific Life Ins. Co.*, 639 N.E.2d 375 (Ind. Ct. App. 1994), the applicant sued the insurer and the broker for conversion, alleging that the broker used the funds for its own purposes instead of investing them in the annuity requested. The court held that the broker was not the insurer's agent; the broker never applied for an annuity on the plaintiff's behalf and never collected any checks from the plaintiff payable to the insurer.

Page 189, add to note 16:

In *Frank v. Winter*, 528 N.W.2d 910 (Minn. Ct. App. 1995), the insured sued the insurer and his independent agent for failing to sell or advise him to purchase increased auto liability coverage. The defendant had taken care of the insured's auto insurance needs for 10 years. The insured brought suit after he was in an accident and discovered that his $100,000 policy was insufficient to cover his liability. The agent admitted that he never suggested additional coverage.

The court reviewed the nature of the agency relationship and found that the agent was a broker acting on behalf of the insured and therefore was independently liable for his alleged negligence. No negligence could be imputed to the insurer. The court affirmed the grant of summary judgment to the insurer based on the nature of the parties' contractual relationship.

In *Ramos v. Rodriguez*, 882 P.2d 1047 (N.M. Ct. App. 1994), a tenant sued the landlord for injuries she sustained when she fell through a step on the stairway. The landlord then sued the real estate broker for failing to obtain liability coverage on the premises. The court affirmed the judgment for the tenant and the dismissal of the claim against the broker where the jury found that the negligence of the broker was not the cause of the landlord's damages.

In *Praegitzer Industries, Inc. v. Rollins Burdick Hunter*, 880 P.2d 479 (Or. Ct. App. 1994), the insured sued the broker for allegedly failing to obtain adequate fire insurance. The defendant procured a business interruption policy that was in effect when a fire destroyed the insured's manufacturing plant. The business was closed for nearly a year. The plaintiff suffered large uninsured losses allegedly because it followed the broker's advice to purchase only $9 million in business interruption coverage. The broker alleged that the insured was contributorily negligent in failing to equip the plant with a fire suppression sprinkler system and in violating building code requirements. The court affirmed the judgment for the broker on these facts (also holding that there was no statutory claim for the alleged failure to provide a disclosure statement pursuant to Or. Rev. Stat. § 744.650, and that violation of the statute could not be used as the basis for imposing negligence per se liability on the broker).

See also Distler v. Horace Mann Life Ins. Co., 644 N.E.2d 919 (Ind. Ct. App. 1994), discussed in § 6.9, note 95 (insured's employer, who changed insurers but continued to use enrollment cards from the prior policies, was held to be the insured's agent; thus, the employer's knowledge that the earlier cards would be used to designate beneficiaries — in this case, the decedent's ex-wife — was imputed to the insured).

6.3 Agreements to Procure Insurance

Page 190, add to note 19:

In *Sung v. Hong*, 678 N.Y.S.2d 116 (N.Y. 1998), the insured sued the automobile insurance broker for allegedly breaching his promise to secure greater uninsured/underinsured motorist coverage than the coverage actually obtained. The court held that the plaintiff failed to present sufficient evidence to contradict the terms of the application where he requested the statutory minimum underinsurance coverage of $10,000 and therefore could not recover from the broker.

In *Keeney Mfg. Co. v. Starkweather & Shepley*, 643 A.2d 203 (R.I. 1994), the insured sued the broker and underwriter, alleging negligence. The broker had failed to obtain a rider that would have extended coverage for an otherwise excluded extraterritorial yacht race. Any travel outside the covered territory required that the insured purchase an additional rider.

During an extraterritorial race, the ship sustained considerable damage. The insured filed a claim for the damage and coverage was denied on the basis that no rider had been purchased. The insured contended that he had requested a rider from the broker; specifically, he alleged that he called the broker's office, spoke to an unidentified employee, mentioned the race and requested that a specific agent return his call. The court held that this alleged conversation was not sufficient to impose a duty to procure the rider, as there was no evidence that the broker had agreed to obtain the coverage. In any event, if the broker had accepted the risk, such conduct would constitute an unauthorized act which could not bind the underwriter.

Page 191, add to note 20:

In *Rollins Burdick Hunter v. Ball State*, 665 N.E.2d 914 (Ind. Ct. App. 1996), the plaintiff university sued the broker for breach of contract to obtain insurance covering the potential nonperformance by an athletic event promoter. The plaintiff negotiated with a business about playing a football game in Ireland. The plaintiff informed the business that it would not enter into a contract unless there was an insurance contract in the nature of a performance bond insuring the university in the event that the game was not played. The business contacted the broker to obtain the insurance coverage.

At the business's suggestion, the plaintiff called the broker to discuss the insurance and was told that the broker would procure the required insurance. The broker sent the plaintiff a *telefax* confirming the substance of the call. The deal in connection with the athletic event ultimately fell through; the plaintiff declared the business to be in breach of contract after the business sought additional fees from the plaintiff. The plaintiff then contacted the broker about the policy and was then told that the requested coverage was never obtained. Upon learning that it was not covered against nonperformance by the business, the plaintiff filed this suit.

The court held that there was sufficient evidence that the broker assumed the duty to obtain the coverage and could be held liable in negligence for failing to do so. The fact that the plaintiff failed to read the policy that was issued did not constitute a defense to the claim against the broker.

In *Turner-Bass Assocs. v. Williamson*, 932 S.W.2d 219 (Tex. Ct. App. 1996), the insured sued the agent for breach of contract after the agent failed to obtain workers compensation coverage for one of the insureds work sites. The insured did business in several states. When he worked outside the state of Texas, he took his key employees and hired local employees from the area where the work was to be performed. The insured purchased coverage for a particular job, and the policy indicated that he had Texas-only employees. He started work in New Mexico and told the agent he needed a certificate of insurance showing that he had liability and comp coverage for his employees.

Such a certificate was sent to him and did not purport to limit comp coverage to employees who were Texas residents. The agent knew that the job was in New Mexico, but there was evidence that the insured and the agent never discussed whether the insured would be employing New Mexico residents. The court affirmed the judgment on the jury verdict for the insured, holding that there was sufficient evidence to support the jury finding that the agent agreed to obtain coverage for New Mexico employees and failed to do so, resulting in damages to the insured.

In *Clark, Davis & Easley Insurance Agency v. Tile Technology*, 459 S.E.2d 450 (Ga. Ct. App. 1995), the insured sued the independent agency it used to purchase a workers comp policy alleging that the agency was negligent in failing to advise the insured of the approaching expiration of the policy. The policy expired without being renewed.

The jury found that the insured was 40 percent at fault and the agent was 60 percent at fault. The court reversed the judgment entered on that jury verdict. It held that there was insufficient evidence for the jury to find that the agency owed a duty to assure that the policy would be renewed or, alternatively, that the agency was required to notify the insured that the policy was about to expire.

Page 191, add to note 21:

In *Johnson & Higgins v. Kenneco Energy*, 962 S.W.2d 507 (Tex. 1998), the insured sustained a loss of profits and submitted a claim that was denied by the insurer. The broker brought this declaratory judgment action to determine its liability with respect to the loss. The insured claimed that the broker engaged in unfair and deceptive acts. The court held that such a claim was subject to a two-year limitations period and the period for the filing of suit started to run when the insured's claim was denied by the insurer. Where the court held that any misrepresentation made by the broker with respect to the coverage to be provided by the policy did not amount to fraud, the only viable claim against the broker was for breach of the alleged agreement to procure contingency coverage for the insured.

Page 193, add to note 26:

In *Cincinnati Insurance Co. v. Guccione*, 719 N.E.2d 787 (Ill. App. Ct. 1999), the insurer sued the insured to recover premiums due, whereupon the insured brought a third-party action against the broker for failing to obtain the desired workers compensation coverage at the promised price. The insured paid the deposit premiums of $850 for each of two years, but failed to pay the additional premium as determined by an audit, which added another $23,000 for the two-year policy period. The insured contended that the broker told him that the policy cost would be "modest" and would approximate the initial premium deposit. The estimated premium for each year was the $850 premium deposit. The court held that there were fact questions as to exactly what the broker told the insured about the cost of the policy and whether the representations made were misleading or fraudulent. Furthermore, there was a fact question as to whether the broker breached his duty to exercise reasonable skill and breached his fiduciary duty to disclose the potential for significant costs derived from the audit.

In *City of Cedar Rapids v. INA*, 562 N.W.2d 156 (Iowa 1997), the city was an additional insured under the hotel's policy. After a claim was made against the hotel and the city, the city sued the insurer seeking coverage under the additional insured endorsement. The court granted judgment to the insurer, holding that because the city was not covered because the hotel as named insured failed to obtain the coverage required by its contract with the city, the city's only claim was against the hotel for the failure to obtain the required coverage.

In *Isnardi v. Genovese Drug Stores*, 662 N.Y.S.2d 790 (N.Y. App. Div. 1997), the subcontractor was hired to work on a construction project. By the terms of the subcontract, the subcontractor was required to obtain insurance covering the general contractor. The subcontractor's employee was injured while working on the project and sued the general contractor. The general contractor sued the subcontractor for indemnity.

The court held that the general contractor was entitled to indemnity due to the subcontractor's breach of its contractual obligation to obtain liability insurance naming the general contractor as an additional insured.

See also discussion in *Nitis v. City of New York*, 661 N.Y.S.2d 44 (N.Y. App. Div. 1997) (subcontractor liable for failing to provide liability insurance naming city as additional insured as required by subcontract).

In *In re Estate of Duran*, 692 A.2d 176 (Pa. Super. Ct. 1997), the plaintiff worked for a corporation that was managed and owned by the same individual. The plaintiff worked for the corporation for more than twenty years and for six months after the individual died. The parties had previously executed a document whereby the individual promised to obtain a $50,000 life insurance policy with the plaintiff as a beneficiary until a retirement plan could be established. After the individual died, it was discovered that he never purchased such a policy for the plaintiff's benefit and had not set up a retirement plan. The plaintiff brought suit, claiming that this breached the agreement between the parties to procure the insurance. The court held that the individual undertook the personal obligation to purchase the insurance, and this undertaking could support a recovery against the individual's estate.

In *Champion Billiards Cafe, Inc. v. Hall*, 685 A.2d 901 (Md. Ct. Spec. App. 1996), the employee sued the employer for failing to forward her application for health insurance to the insurer in a timely manner. The employer gave the employee the opportunity to enroll in a group insurance program. Although the employer contributed none of the premiums, it deducted the premium payments from employee paychecks and forwarded the funds to the insurer. The employee completed the application forms and believed that she was covered. Her supervisor, however, did not send her application with those of other employees. She was hit by a car while riding her bicycle and incurred medical expenses. Her claim was denied by the insurer, whereupon she learned that the insurer had never received her application. The supervisor then sent in the application, but the insurer would not cover the accident. The court affirmed the judgment for the employee, holding that the employer had the duty to forward the application after undertaking to do so and therefore was liable for the result of its negligence.

Page 193, add to note 27:

In *Cornielle v. Aetna Cas. & Sur. Co.*, 617 N.Y.S.2d 363 (N.Y. App. Div. 1994), the plaintiffs purchased a two-family residence, which they financed through the defendant mortgagee. When the property was purchased, there was a one-year CGL policy, but that policy had been canceled for nonpayment of premiums. Notice was sent to the plaintiffs.

Two years after the purchase, a tenant was injured in a fall in the building and sued the plaintiffs. The plaintiffs claimed that the mortgagee had the duty to defend and indemnify them. The court disagreed, holding that there was insufficient evidence of an agreement between the mortgagors and the mortgagee to obtain liability coverage for the plaintiffs' benefit.

6.4 Taking the Application for Insurance

Page 194, add to note 30:

In *Ranger Insurance Co. v. Kovach*, 63 F. Supp. 2d 174 (D. Conn. 1999), the aviation insured sought coverage for a newly purchased aircraft and approached the broker. The broker recommended the insurer and conducted all discussions with the insurer. The insured never spoke to the insurer. The insured completed the application and discussed it with the broker. The insured contended that he fully discussed his flying history with the broker and the fact that his medical certification was denied for failure to properly complete an application, resulting in a 30-day suspension of his license. On the insurance application, the insured failed to disclose the suspension based on the broker's advice that the inquiry about any suspensions was actually seeking information about alcohol and drug abuse or other serious infractions. After an accident occurred, the insurer denied coverage. The court held that the policy was void due to the misrepresentation on the application. The court further held that the insurer was not charged with the negligence or other acts of the broker where the broker never acted as the insurer's agent with respect to obtaining the policy.

In *Case v. RGA Insurance Services*, 521 S.E.2d 32 (Ga. Ct. App. 1999), the insured sued the independent agent and the insurer after the insured's boat sank. The insured purchased the boat at a boat show. When she went to complete the transaction at the seller's premises, the seller persuaded her to pay the premium for insurance on the boat. The insured signed a blank insurance application and, later that day, orally completed the application during a telephone interview with the independent agent. The insured received the policy, but never received a copy of the completed application. After the boat sank, the insurer learned that the insured's adult daughter was residing in the household and had a poor driving record. The insurer denied the claim based on these facts, alleging that the insured falsely answered the question on household members' having vehicular accidents and moving violations by checking the "no" box. The court held that the independent agent could potentially be held liable for negligence in completing the application, but such was a question of fact precluding the grant of summary judgment.

In *St. Paul Surplus Lines Ins. Co. v. Feingold & Feingold Ins. Agency*, 693 N.E.2d 669 (Mass. 1998), the plaintiff sued a restaurant and the restaurant's liquor liability insurer for injuries sustained in an auto accident caused by an intoxicated driver who had been drinking in the restaurant. The insurer then brought a claim against the broker who submitted the restaurant's application. The application contained material misrepresentations. The insurer contended that had it been apprised of the true facts, it would not have issued the policy. The court held that the broker could be held liable for negligence or recklessness in submitting the application even though it did not sign the application. There was sufficient evidence to support a finding that the broker committed an intentional misrepresentation and willful conduct that, in addition to normal tort damages, could subject the broker to double damages available for a violation of the unfair trade practices statute. The fact that the broker had not signed the application did not preclude the imposition of liability under the facts of the case.

In *Tassin v. Golden Rule Ins. Co.*, 649 So. 2d 1050 (La. Ct. App. 1994), the insured sought coverage under his health insurance policy for treatment of appendicitis. The insured's employer had changed group insurers following a rate increase. The broker assisted the employer in the search for new coverage and helped the insured complete his application under the new policy. The application disclosed that the insured was being treated for diabetes and was taking medication.

The insurer informed the broker that it would not cover the group with the insured as a member. The insured signed a waiver of coverage and the insurer issued a policy covering all employees except the insured.

The broker then obtained other coverage for the insured. On the broker's advice, the insured's application did not disclose his diabetes. The new insurer discovered the diabetes while investigating the appendicitis claim, and denied coverage for the cost of treating the appendicitis — $19,210.

The court held that the broker was the insurer's agent where the insurer supplied the broker with application forms and issued the policy following direct transmission of the application by the broker. Therefore, the insurer was responsible for paying the treatment bills subject to its rights to be indemnified by the broker.

6.5 Advising the Insured

Page 197, replace first sentence with the following:

Liability for incorrect advice cannot normally be imposed on the insurer's agent for failing to advise the insured on its insurance needs, absent a special relationship between the parties or affirmative duties undertaken by the agent.[38a]

Page 197, add to note 38a (created above):

In *M&E Mfg. Co. v. Frank H. Reis, Inc.*, 692 N.Y.S.2d 191 (N.Y. App. Div. 1999), the insured sued the independent agent for failing to give continuing advice on the adequacy of coverage. The insured sustained a loss far in excess of the amount of business interruption coverage provided and claimed that the agent was negligent in failing to provide the insured "with adequate information with respect to the proper amount of coverage to obtain to adequately protect [the insured]." After coverage had been purchased, the insured's business continued to grow but the agent did not ask the insured to complete another worksheet to determine whether the policy limits should be raised.

The court held that there is no general duty to advise the client under such facts, even if the insured asked that it be fully insured. A request to be "fully insured" is not sufficiently specific to require the agent to initiate inquiries from time to time in order to determine whether additional coverage would be advisable. The fact that the broker gave the insured a worksheet on one occasion for determining the level of coverage did not create a special relationship that would trigger an ongoing duty to give advice about proper policy limits.

In *Wied v. N.Y. Central Mut. Fire Ins. Co.*, 618 N.Y.S.2d 467 (N.Y. App. Div. 1994), the insured's auto policy provided liability limits of $300,000, but only $25,000 in underinsured motorist benefits. Following an accident involving an underinsured motorist, the insured sued his insurer and agent, alleging that the agent was negligent in failing to advise him that supplementary underinsured motorist coverage was available. The court held that the agent could not be liable for failing to give such advice where there was no special relationship (such as a fiduciary relationship) between the insured and the agent.

Page 198, add to note 40:

In *Plumb v. Fluid Pump Service Inc.*, 124 F.3d 849 (7th Cir. 1997), applying ERISA and Illinois law, the employee sued the employer, its insurers, and its brokers after the insurers refused to pay the costs of his son's hospitalization. The employer claimed that the broker failed to advise the employer that the medical insurance coverage would lapse if it did not pay the premiums in a timely manner.

The court held that the employer's allegations did not state a claim for the broker's breach of fiduciary duties because the employer did not contend that the broker failed to obtain the requested coverage. The court also held that the broker could not be held liable for failing to procure certain coverage where there was no evidence that the employer requested a policy without a preexisting coverage restriction. The court further noted that the employer had the duty to examine the policy when issued to determine if it comported to the desired coverage.

In *Society of Roman Catholic Church v. Interstate Fire & Cas. Co.*, 126 F.3d 727 (5th Cir. 1997), applying Louisiana law, the Catholic Diocese settled claims arising out of a number of cases of child molestation perpetrated by some of its priests. They sued the insurance broker for breach of contract and breach of warranty that the insurance would cover losses not retained by the diocese.

The broker indicated that the diocese was fully insured but in fact there was a gap in the excess coverage resulting in $4.5 million in uninsured losses. The broker warranted that there was coverage for all claims above the $400,000 annual retention. The court held that the broker's warranty was an enforceable contract subject to the 10-year statute of limitations.

In *National Union Fire Ins. Co. v. Fidelity Nat'l Title Ins. Co.*, 663 N.Y.S.2d 20 (N.Y. App. Div. 1997), the insured had its own risk manager who reviewed policies and worked with brokers to obtain and place desired coverage. The insured acquired a predecessor company which automatically canceled the policy. The insured claimed that the broker was liable for negligent misrepresentation in failing to inform the insured of the cancellation.

The court held that the broker could not be held liable where the insured and the risk manager never inquired about the impact of the acquisition and therefore could not have relied on anything the broker might have said about the continued existence of policy coverage.

In *Aetna Cas. & Sur. Co. v. Berry*, 669 So. 2d 56 (Miss. 1996), the surviving spouse sued the garage liability insurer and the insurance agent following the death of her husband in an auto accident. The spouse was operating a car with the husband riding as a passenger. The car was loaned to them by the auto manufacturer. They were struck head-on by an uninsured drunk driver, who pled guilty to manslaughter. The policy covering the car only provided $20,000 in uninsured motorist coverage.

The court held that the agent was required to explain uninsured motorist coverage and could potentially be held liable for the failure to do so. The agent must provide a sufficient explanation to give the insured the option to intelligently reject increased uninsured motorist coverage even though the agent is not required to recommend that the insured obtain increased coverage. The court found that the breach of that duty may subject the agent to liability up to the policy's liability coverage limits.

See Cogan v. Triad American Energy, 944 F. Supp. 1325 (S.D. Tex. 1996), discussed in § 6.2.

In *Padeh v. Zagoria*, 900 F. Supp. 442 (S.D. Fla. 1995), the plaintiff physicians sued their insurance representatives for negligent misrepresentation, arising out of the creation and the plaintiff's adoption of certain employer-funded pension plans. The plaintiffs had been receiving pension-related advice from the defendants and informed them of the plaintiffs' financial condition. They alleged that as a result of the defendants' advice, they took higher wages than usual and incurred greater taxes on those wages.

The defendants allegedly represented that the plan would only be funded by annuities, but in truth, the plan actually required that it be funded by life insurance policies sold by the defendants. When the plaintiffs were advised that continued payment of the plans substantial funding requirements meant continued premium payments, the plaintiffs stopped payments, permitting the policies to lapse. The plaintiffs' claims essentially were based on the defendants' initial and continuing misrepresentations designed to induce the plaintiffs into adopting the plans. The court held that these state tort law claims were not preempted by ERISA; therefore, it denied the defendants' motions to dismiss based on the federal statute.

In *Seneca Resources Corp. v. Marsh & McLennan, Inc.*, 911 S.W.2d 144 (Tex. Ct. App. 1995), the insured oil and gas company contracted to move a submersible drilling rig onto an offshore area leased for gas and oil drilling. This was in preparation to drill a well. As the insured was preparing to move the rig, a hurricane passed and a portion of the rig was lost. The insurer refused to pay for the loss, whereupon the insured filed this suit.

The insured obtained the policy by approaching the broker and advising the broker of its insurance requirements. The broker contacted a wholesaler for bids. The broker would eventually contact the insured with its findings, and the insured would have the final decision on the purchase of coverage. Then the broker would bind the coverage by informing the wholesaler.

The insured obtained all-risk platform insurance and operator's extra expense coverage. The insured claimed that the broker misrepresented the benefits provided by the policies and the availability of particular coverages. Even though such a misrepresentation violates the applicable insurance code, the court held that no recovery could be had where the plaintiff failed to establish that the alleged misrepresentation caused the injuries sustained.

In *Trupiano v. Cincinnati Ins. Co.*, 654 N.E.2d 886 (Ind. Ct. App. 1995), the insured was a closely held corporation which hired the defendant insurance agent to handle the corporation's insurance requirements. The agent met the insured's needs for more than 15 years, including advice on various types of coverage. The agent conducted an annual review of all policies and detailed the type and amounts of insurance, losses, projected payrolls and premiums. The insured purchased a fleet policy through the agent. That policy was renewed every year.

The policy contained $40,000 in underinsured motorist coverage.

An accident occurred involving one of the insured's vehicles, with two occupants sustaining serious injuries. The driver was specifically listed as an insured driver in the policy. The driver of the other car was at fault and carried $100,000 in liability limits, which were paid to the injured victims. Such being the case, the victims were not entitled to any underinsured motorist benefits.

They sued the agent, claiming that the $40,000 in underinsured motorist coverage was wholly inadequate and that the agent was negligent in failing to advise them to obtain higher limits. The court affirmed the summary judgment for the agent, holding that there was insufficient evidence of a special relationship such as would impose the duty to advise even though there was a long-standing relationship between the parties.

In *Robinson v. Charles A. Flynn Ins. Agency*, 653 N.E.2d 207 (Mass. App. Ct. 1995), the insured motorist was injured in an auto accident and sued the insurance agency through which he obtained his insurance, claiming that he had not been properly advised of his option to purchase additional underinsured motorist coverage.

The court held that in the absence of special circumstances, the agency had no general duty to inform and advise the insured of such additional coverage. It should be noted, however, that other states impose such a duty on the agent either by statute or regulation.

6.6 Using Care to Obtain and Place Coverage

Page 200, add to note 46:

Liability found: In *Weinlood v. Fisher & Associates*, 975 P.2d

1226 (Kan. Ct. App. 1999), the insured contacted the agency to obtain a less expensive homeowners policy. The independent agent did not procure the policy that was requested and applied for by the insured. The insured never read the policy as issued and, after a loss occurred, the insured learned that the desired coverage was not provided under the terms of the policy. The court held that the independent agent was the insured's agent and could be held liable for failing to exercise reasonable care in obtaining the desired coverage. The fact that the insured failed to read the policy before the loss did not preclude his recovery. The court held that an insured can assume that the independent agent obtained the ordered coverage where the agent failed to alert the insured that different coverage had been issued.

Liability found: In *Cigna Property & Casualty Cos. v. Zeitler*, 730 A.2d 248 (Md. Ct. Spec. App. 1999), the insured's boat was severely damaged by a hurricane in the Caribbean. The insured believed that the yacht was insured at the time, but the policy in question did not provide coverage for losses occurring in the Caribbean during the hurricane season. The insured then sued the insurer and broker. The insured had originally instructed the broker to obtain coverage. The policy was renewed several times, and the agent eventually changed insurers due to the cost of the coverage. In the renewal application, the navigation zone was the Chesapeake Bay and tributaries, but the insured at trial testified that before the renewal he advised the broker that he wanted to sail in the Caribbean. The navigation zone was consequently expanded, but coverage during the Caribbean hurricane season was removed. The broker contended that it mailed a copy of the policy with the restriction prior to the loss, but the insured disputed that claim. The yacht was left in St. Maarten due to engine problems and, therefore, it was in the Caribbean during the season and was damaged in a hurricane.

The court held that it was not necessary to introduce expert testimony on the issue of whether the broker breached its duty to obtain the coverage sought by the insured. The court held that the insured's failure to read the policy and notice the restriction in coverage did not constitute contributory negligence where a reasonable insured would have concluded that the terms of the policy conformed to the request for coverage.

Liability found: In *Gorgone v. Regency Agency, Inc.*, 656 N.Y.S.2d 622 (N.Y. App. Div. 1997), the insured sued the broker for failing to obtain additional underinsured motorist coverage. The plaintiff allegedly requested that the broker increase his underinsurance coverage, effective immediately. The plaintiff completed the necessary paperwork and paid the additional premium. The broker then completed a policy change form which was transmitted to the insurer. The broker informed the insured that the change was effective on November 15, the date of the contact. However, the broker's transmittal to the insurer stated that it was to be effective on December 12. The accident occurred on December 2. The court held that the insured was entitled to judgment against the broker for failing to properly procure the insurance, even though there were unresolved issues on liability between the insurer and the broker.

See also Meyer v. National Farmers Union Prop. & Cas. Co., 957 F. Supp. 1492 (D. Wyo. 1997), discussed in § 5.3 and *Turner-Bass Assocs. v. Williamson*, 932 S.W.2d 219 (Tex. Ct. App. 1996), discussed in § 6.3.

No liability found: In *Westchester Specialty Ins. Services v. U.S. Fire Ins. Co.*, 119 F.3d 1505 (11th Cir. 1997), the manufacturer-insured hired the broker to provide a variety of services with respect to the procurement and servicing of the insured's needs. The insured paid the broker a fee in addition to the commissions it received.

The dispute arose when the insured claimed that it specifically requested that the broker obtain a liability insurance policy which included defense costs coverage for product liability claims that would be the same or better than its prior policy. The broker claimed that the insured only sought the same coverage as the prior policy.

Ultimately, the insurer refused to pay defense costs and the insured sued the insurer, the broker, and others. The court, applying Georgia law, held that the broker could not be held liable where the insured had a copy of the insurance policy but failed to read it and discover the fact that defense costs were not covered.

Claim for liability supported: In *Craddock Int'l Inc. v. W.K.P. Wilson & Son*, 116 F.3d 1095 (5th Cir. 1997), applying Mississippi law, the shipowner and the owner of the cargo on the ship sued the broker after the ship sank. Both alleged that the broker was negligent in obtaining and canceling the protection and indemnity insurance, thereby leaving them uninsured.

The court held that the broker could be held liable for the loss. The court further found that the broker waived any right to argue that the shipowner was responsible for the loss of the cargo, an argument that would arise in a subrogation action after payment of the cargo owner's claim.

Liability claim barred: In *Pittston Co. v. Sedgwick James of N.Y.*, 971 F. Supp. 915 (D.N.J. 1997), applying New York law, the insured sued the broker claiming professional negligence in failing to obtain proper environmental liability insurance coverage. Where the action was brought more than six years after the policy in question was issued, the suit was barred by the statute of limitations. The statute of limitations on a professional liability action against a broker or agent begins to run at the time of delivery of the policy. The fact that the insured did not discover that the policy did not contain the desired coverage for several years thereafter is irrelevant.

Claim for liability supported: In *Commercial Ins. Consultants v. Frenz Enterprises, Inc.*, 696 So. 2d 871 (Fla. Dist. Ct. App. 1997), the plaintiff leased a dredge that sank. It sued the broker for breach of the agreement to procure insurance covering the dredge. The lessor also sued the broker.

The court held that the lessor could not recover from the broker unless and until the lessor prevailed in its action against the lessee. The court noted that the broker could potentially be held liable to third parties like the lessor for negligence in the procurement of coverage where that coverage would have been available to pay the claims of such parties.

No liability found: In *Baldwin Crane & Equipment v. Riley & Rielly Ins. Agency*, 687 N.E.2d 1267 (Mass. App. Ct. 1997), the insured claimed that the broker was negligent and failed to comply with the insured's instructions in procuring replacement coverage. The new policy was written with a minimum premium. The insured claimed that it requested a premium based solely on the amount of sales so that it would be entitled to a return of premiums if the sales failed to reach estimated levels. Under earlier policies, the insured had obtained a return of premiums.

The court affirmed the judgment for the broker, holding that there was no negligence or breach of the broker's agreement with the insured to obtain replacement coverage where it was determined that each of the earlier policies also carried minimum premium provisions even though the insured obtained a return of premiums under those policies. The court recognized the rule that the insured is required to read the policy once it is issued to determine if the policy meets its expectations. The insured failed to do so in this case.

No liability found: In *Production Credit Ass'n v. Gorton Farms*, 573 N.W.2d 549 (Wis. Ct. App. 1997), the insured sued the broker, who was hired to procure crop insurance, and sought a return of premium payments. The court recognized that the broker was required to use due care and skill to follow the insured's instructions in good faith. Crop policies can only be canceled during specified periods, and the insured did not send any notice to the broker before the cancellation date.

Based on the facts in this case, the court held that the insured's oral instructions were ambiguous with respect to the cancellation of the policy. The court reversed the judgment for the insured, finding that the broker acted reasonably under the circumstances.

Liability found: In *Campione v. Wilson*, 422 Mass. 185, 661 N.E.2d 658 (1996), the deceased was killed on the roadside when he was struck by the insured's truck. The deceased's estate released the insured in exchange for policy limits and sued the insurance broker for the alleged failure to procure adequate insurance for the insured's business. The insured had two policies, each providing $500,000, but each policy excluded auto liability. The insured contended that it requested that the broker obtain liability coverage that would include motor vehicle risks.

The court held that the estate's release of the insured did not release the broker. The court found that there was a viable breach of contract based on the oral agreement to procure the insurance even though a written insurance policy was issued to the insured and the insured clearly had the opportunity to review its terms and find that no auto liability coverage was provided.

Liability found: In *Huval v. Offshore Pipelines Inc.*, 86 F.3d 454 (5th Cir. 1996), applying Louisiana law, the insured was engaged in repairing barges and sued the agent for failing to procure certain requested alternate employer endorsements on the insured's workers comp and excess liability insurance policies. These endorsements were required to meet the obligations undertaken under the CGL policy. One of the insured's employees was injured while working on a barge owned by a third party. The employee sued the barge owner, which brought a contractual indemnity claim against the insured. The insured sought coverage under its CGL policy, but this claim was dismissed for the failure of the insured to meet the requirement that the alternate employer endorsement be added to its workers compensation policy. The insured then sued the agent in this action for failing to procure the proper coverage. The court affirmed the judgment against the agent and an insurance consultant, finding that there was sufficient evidence of an agreement on the part of the agent to procure the required insurance and that this breach resulted in the insured's loss of coverage. The insured's consultant could also be held liable for failing to assure that the agent properly obtain the required coverage.

No liability found: In *Calhoun v. Pennsylvania Nat'l Mut. Cas. Ins. Co.*, 686 So. 2d 1332 (Ala. Ct. Civ. App. 1996), the insured brought suit after he was sued in connection with an auto accident. The victim brought a dramshop action against the insured and his grocery store, where alcohol had allegedly been sold to the driver who caused the accident. When the claim was made, the insured learned that he had no dramshop coverage and sued the broker and the insurer. With respect to the claim against the broker, the court affirmed the summary judgment in the broker's favor, finding that the broker exercised no control over the insurance agent and could not be held vicariously liable for the agent's negligence in failing to obtain the appropriate coverage for the insured's business.

See also Clark, Davis & Easley Insurance Agency v. Tile Technology, 459 S.E.2d 450 (Ga. Ct. App. 1995), discussed in § 6.3; *Capitol Funds, Inc. v. Royal Indem. Co.*, 458 S.E.2d 741 (N.C. Ct. App. 1995), discussed in § 1.4; and *Seneca Resources Corp. v. Marsh & McLennan, Inc.*, 911 S.W.2d 144 (Tex. Ct. App. 1995), discussed in § 6.5.

Page 202, add to note 54:

In *West American Ins. Co. v. Meridian Mut. Ins. Co.*, 583 N.W.2d 548 (Mich. Ct. App. 1998), the general contractor required that the subcontractor's insurance policy cover it and was issued a certificate of insurance. The general contractor relied on the certificate in hiring the subcontractor to perform the work. Before the loss occurred, the underlying policy coverage was amended. The court held that the insurer had no duty to inform the certificate holder of such changes and the failure of the independent insurance agent to notify the certificate holder/general contractor of the changes cannot bind the insurer when the agent was the agent of the insured in issuing the certificates on behalf of the insured.

In *American Ref-Fuel v. Resource Recycling*, 671 N.Y.S.2d 93 (N.Y. App. Div. 1998), the property owner filed suit, seeking coverage under the general contractor's and subcontractor's liability insurance. The claims were brought by one of the subcontractor's employees for injuries sustained on the worksite. The construction contracts called for the contractor and subcontractor to obtain coverage. The owner also sued the subcontractor's broker for failing to secure the required coverage naming the owner as an additional insured. The broker issued certificates of insurance showing that the owner had been named even though the owner had not actually been named. The court noted that the certificates, in and of themselves, could not create coverage in the absence of a policy endorsement. The court also found that the owner could not pursue a negligence claim against the broker with whom it had no relationship. The broker owed duties of reasonable care to the subcontractor, its client, but not to the project owner.

Page 203, add to note 58:

In *Trapf v. Commercial Union Ins. Co.,* 886 S.W.2d 144 (Mo. Ct. App. 1994), the insureds sued their auto insurer to recover underinsured motorist benefits, and sued the broker for failing to procure such coverage. The insureds were injured in a collision with an allegedly underinsured motorist whose negligence was the cause of the accident.

While the policy declarations page stated limits for underinsured motorist coverage, there was no indication that a premium was paid for that coverage. Furthermore, it was clear that the tortfeasor was not underinsured. He had $50,000 in limits, and the insureds only sought $25,000 in underinsurance coverage. Thus, the insurer could not be held liable for the payment of underinsured motorist benefits. The court also held that the insureds failed to state a claim against the broker, since even if such coverage had been obtained, no recovery would have been available under the policy.

In *Appleton Chinese Food Service v. Murken Ins., Inc.,* 519 N.W.2d 674 (Wis. Ct. App. 1994), the insured sued the independent agent for failing to procure the desired coverage. The insured premises were destroyed by fire. In preparing to submit a claim, the insured determined that the policy only provided actual cash value coverage and not replacement cost.

The policy also did not provide business interruption coverage. The policy provided $140,000 in actual cash value (ACV) coverage, even though the building only had an ACV of $52,200.

The court held that the agent was liable for failing to obtain the requested coverage even though the insured had released the insurer in exchange of the payment under the policy. The court noted that the measure of damages is the amount the insured would have recovered under a policy containing the requested coverage.

6.7 Collecting and Transmitting Premiums

Page 207, add to note 68:

In *Fidelity & Cas. Co. v. Tillman Corp.*, 112 F.3d 302 (7th Cir. 1997), the insurer sued the insured for premiums due on a workers compensation policy written through the assigned risk pool. The insured made a premium payment to the broker who absconded with the funds and then became insolvent. The court, applying Indiana law, found that the broker was not acting as the insurer's agent when it received the premium payment and therefore the insured bore the risk of loss from the broker's failure to transmit the funds to the insurer.

In *T&R Custom, Inc. v. Liberty Mut. Ins. Co.*, 488 S.E.2d 705 (Ga. Ct. App. 1997), the insurer sued the insured to recover workers compensation coverage premiums. The insured claimed that it paid all amounts to the broker, which it claimed was acting as the insurer's agent. The insured further contended that the insurer sent incorrect premium bills.

The court affirmed the partial summary judgment holding that the agents were brokers and therefore were the agents of the insured and not the insurer. The court held that there was substantial evidence that the agents had neither actual or apparent authority to act on the insurer's behalf in accepting premium payments. The agent's own testimony characterizing himself as a dual agent was not binding on the court where there was no indicia that he was ever authorized to bind or otherwise act for the insurer.

In *18th Avenue Realty Corp. v. Aetna Cas. & Sur. Co.*, 659 N.Y.S.2d 17 (N.Y. App. Div. 1997), the insurer sent the insured a cancellation notice, prior to the loss in question, for nonpayment of premiums. At the time of the cancellation, the broker possessed funds for returned unearned premiums in connection with another policy issued by another insurer. The retention of such funds could not be imputed to the insurer involved in this case so as to bar its right to cancel. Any fiduciary requirement that could be imposed on the broker to use the funds to keep the policy in question in force could not be imputed to the insurer.

In *K. Bell & Assoc. v. Lloyd's Underwriters*, 97 F.3d 632 (2d Cir. 1996), applying New York law, the broker was sued by one of its clients for failing to forward premiums and failing to pay the client reinsurance recoverables obtained by the broker on the client's behalf. The broker made a claim against its errors and omissions liability carrier in an attempt to secure coverage for the underlying claim. The court held that the broker had no coverage for the underlying claim by virtue of the policy exclusion for claims arising out of the loss of funds received by the broker or credited to the insured's account. The exclusion was effective, even though the broker claimed that the failure to pay the funds was due to the loss of records.

In *Ruiz v. Fortune Ins. Co.*, 677 So. 2d 1336 (Fla. Dist. Ct. App. 1996), the insureds filed suit against the homeowners insurer, which denied the claim on the basis that the policy had been canceled prior to the loss. The insureds purchased the coverage through an insurance broker who obtained the policy through the insurer's agent. The insurer subsequently terminated the agency and filed the statutorily required notice. The insurer sent the insureds a cancellation notice advising that the policy would not be renewed. The insurer also indicated that the former agent was still its agent on one part of the notice but elsewhere stated, "Non-renewal agency is no longer doing business with us."

There was no evidence that the broker received a copy of this notice. Shortly before the expiration of the policy, the broker sent the insureds a renewal notice for their homeowners and auto policies with the defendant. The insureds went to the broker's office and agreed to the renewal and did not mention that they had received a cancellation notice. The court held that the insureds were required to take affirmative action and contact the insurer for an explanation if they did not understand the cancellation notice. Since the broker was not the insurer's agent, his acceptance of the insureds' renewal premium check was not binding on the insurer. Moreover, the fact that the broker forwarded the funds to the former agent was also of no consequence to the insurer's liability.

In *Branch v. Alliance Syndicate Inc.*, 469 S.E.2d 807 (Ga. Ct. App. 1996), the insured was required to pay an initial minimum premium with the final premium to be determined at the policy expiration based on the insured's total sales. The agent was to collect the premiums from the insured and transmit the funds (less the commission) to the broker. After the expiration of the policy period, the insured questioned the amount of the audit premium. The broker took steps to collect the audit premium sought, but subsequently reduced the premium after auditors discovered that they had incorrectly included freight charges in the sales figures. The independent agent participated in this review and was informed that the insurer and the insured agreed to installment payments of the audit premium.

The insured made the first three payments in a timely manner. However, the fourth and fifth were late, and the final payment was not made. The independent agent was then sued by the broker to recover the audit premium under its contract. Subsequently, the independent agent collected the remaining audit premium and evidence that the other payments had been made. Ultimately, the insurer filed this suit for conversion against the independent agent and the broker. The court affirmed the judgment holding the independent agent and the broker jointly and severally liable for the funds. It held that the independent agent was not entitled to a jury verdict that would specify which damages were recoverable from which defendant.

See also Evvtex Co. v. Hartley Cooper Assoc's, 102 F.3d 1327 (2d Cir. 1996), applying New York law, discussed in § 5.6.

In *Potamkin Cadillac Corp. v. B.R.I. Coverage Corp.*, 38 F.3d 627 (2d Cir. 1994), applying New York law, the insured sued the commercial insurance broker seeking an accounting of premiums to be returned, unapplied payments, and overpayments. The insured was a group of corporate entities engaged in the sale, leasing and servicing of automobiles. The group retained the defendant insurance broker, but the broker allegedly defrauded the group by charging for insurance coverage that was not provided, charging service fees in lieu of commissions, overstating premiums due and converting payments made. The court affirmed the judgment for the insured and the dismissal of the broker's counterclaims.

In *Benante v. United Pacific Life Ins. Co.*, 639 N.E.2d 375 (Ind. Ct. App. 1994), the applicant sued the insurer and the broker for conversion, alleging that the broker used the funds for its own purposes instead of investing them in the annuity requested. The court held that the broker was not the insurer's agent; the broker never applied for an annuity on the plaintiff's behalf and never collected any checks from the plaintiff payable to the insurer.

In *Hermann Forwarding Co. v. Pappas Ins. Co.*, 640 A.2d 1200 (N.J. Super. App. Div. 1994), the insured sued the broker and the insurer (which was the servicing carrier for the New Jersey Commercial Auto Insurance Plan) in an attempt to recover an alleged overpayment of premiums to the broker. The plaintiffs made a $166,838 down payment on the total advance premium of $556,128, and financed the balance. The finance agreement was signed by the plaintiffs and their broker. The plaintiffs sent the payments to the broker, and the checks were made payable to the broker.

The policy was ultimately canceled for nonpayment of premiums. The insurer gave the plaintiffs a statement of account, which the plaintiffs disputed as failing to reflect all payments made to the broker. The plaintiffs claimed they had overpaid the broker by $78,740, while the financing company claimed that they had overpaid by $38,840.

The court held that it would be premature to enter summary judgment on the issue of who was responsible for the failure to pay premiums, since there were still questions as to whether the policy had been delivered to the broker. Under N.J. Stat. Ann. § 17:22-6.2a, where the broker is entrusted to deliver the policy, the insured can reasonably believe that the broker is authorized to receive premium payments consistent with the doctrine of apparent authority.

In *Paramount Ins. Co. v. Brown*, 613 N.Y.S.2d 910 (N.Y. App. Div. 1994), the insurer sued the insured to obtain additional premiums earned with respect to four consecutive liability policies. The court held that the insurance broker was the insured's agent. The agent's renewal of the policies without objection for consecutive policy periods, with the insured's ratification of the broker's acts, could render the insured liable for the broker's acts or omissions. Since the broker was not the insurer's agent, the insurer was entitled to recover the premiums earned.

6.8 When May a Broker's Actions Bind the Insurer?

Page 207, add to note 69:

In *West American Ins. Co. v. Meridian Mut. Ins. Co.*, 583 N.W.2d 548 (Mich. Ct. App. 1998), the general contractor was required that the subcontractors obtain coverage for it and was issued a certificate of insurance. The general contractor relied on the certificate in hiring the subcontractor to perform the work. Before the loss occurred, the underlying policy coverage was amended. The court held that the insurer had no duty to inform the certificate holder of such changes. The failure of the independent insurance agent to notify the certificate holder/general contractor of the changes cannot bind the insurer where the agent was the agent of the insured in issuing the certificates on behalf of the insured.

Page 207, add to note 70:

In *Dodds v. Hanover Ins. Co.*, 880 S.W.2d 311 (Ark. 1994), the plaintiffs sued their property insurer following the insurer's refusal to pay a claim for preexisting wind damage. The damage was known to the plaintiffs but was not disclosed to the insurer when the policy was issued, and the insurer backdated the policy to cover the date when the damage occurred. The court affirmed summary judgment for the insurer, holding that the broker was not the agent of the insurer and the plaintiffs were not entitled to assume that the broker was the insurer's general agent with the power to bind the insurer to a preexisting loss. Clearly, the situation would be different if the insurer and the insureds were all ignorant of the existence of the loss. (Contrast with *Trefethen v. N.H. Ins. Group*, 645 A.2d 72 [N.H. 1994], discussed in § 4.5 above.)

Page 208, add to note 71:

In *American Cas. Co. v. Rahn*, 854 F. Supp. 492 (W.D. Mich. 1994), the insurer brought a declaratory judgment to determine coverage under a directors and officers liability policy issued to the insured S&L. The question was raised as to whether the insured complied with notice requirements under the claims-made policy. Where the insured S&L designated an individual as its "agent of record for Officers and Directors Liability Insurance" such a person was an independent agent representing the insured and not the insurer. Therefore, notice of claim given to that agent was not imputed to the insurer so as to meet the policy requirements. The court came to that conclusion after noting that the agent lacked authorization from the insurer to sign the insurance binder and to remove a policy exclusion. The individual agent was also a director of the insured S&L. The court further noted that even if the individual was the insurer's authorized agent, his knowledge of the potential claim would not be imputed to the insurer where the agent obtained the knowledge in his capacity as corporate director and not as an insurance agent.

Part I □ **Chapter 6** □ **2000 Supplement**

The Role and Duties of Brokers

Page 208, add to note 72:

In *U.S. Delivery Systems v. National Union Fire Ins. Co.*, 696 N.Y.S.2d 502 (N.Y. App. Div. 1999), the court held that fact questions were presented as to whether the insurer's conduct invested the broker with the powers of an agent so as to make notice of an accident given to the broker, notice to the insurer.

In *Almerico v. RLI Ins. Co.*, 716 So. 2d 774 (Fla. 1998), the insurer filed this declaratory judgment action, alleging that the insured misrepresented the presence of youthful drivers in the household and the presence of high-performance cars on the application for an umbrella policy. One of the youthful drivers was involved in an accident in which one person was killed and two others were seriously injured. The policy was procured by a broker who obtained applications for insurance from an agent authorized by the insurer to market its policies in the state.

The insurer knew that the agent would use subproducers to take applications, and the insurer relied on the agent to process applications. The insurer had no direct dealings with subproducers like the broker. However, the broker had been assigned an agent number by the insurer and was required to procure a certain number of policies for the insurer annually to remain in the producer network. The court held that the insurer could be held liable under its policy where it accorded the broker with indicia of an agency relationship, such as the provision of supplies and applications, which would lead a consumer to believe that there was an actual agency relationship. This created a dual agency.

In *U.S. Underwriters Ins. Co. v. Manhattan Demolition Co.*, 672 N.Y.S.2d 384 (N.Y. App. Div. 1998), the insurer sought a declaration that it had no duty to indemnify or defend its insured under the liability insurance policy. The policy was secured by the insured through the efforts of a broker acting as an agent of the insurer. The question was raised as to the limits of the broker's authority to act on behalf of the insurer. The court followed the general rule that the broker was the insured's agent, and therefore, notice of a subsequent claim given by the insured to the broker was insufficient to constitute timely notice to the insurer. The broker was only used by the insured to comply with a procedure instituted by the insurer for adding worksites to an existing policy.

In *Kinard v. National Indemnity Co.*, 483 S.E.2d 664 (Ga. Ct. App. 1997), the claimants injured in an auto accident sought to recover from the truck driver who allegedly caused the accident and his business auto insurance carrier. The independent agent allegedly made representations that the insured had coverage for the truck in question.

The court held that the insurer was not bound by the independent agent's representations of coverage where the agent had no authority to bind coverage and was considered to be the agent of the insured. The mere fact that the independent agent issued certificates of insurance was insufficient to establish apparent authority to act on the insurer's behalf.

In *Hickey v. Centenary Oyster House*, 690 So. 2d 858 (La. Ct. App. 1997), the claimant was injured in an armed robbery occurring in a parking lot and sued the security firm responsible for security in the lot and the firm's insurer. With respect to the agent, it was alleged that the insurer was bound by the independent insurance agent's representation that the policy provided the coverage required for security firms.

The court held that the agent had no written agency agreement with the insurer and could not bind the insurer or modify the terms of the policy. The subjective belief of the insured was of no consequence. Thus, the insurer was not bound by the alleged misrepresentations. However, the court held that where the policy was designed to satisfy state requirements for security firms, the assault and battery exclusion was void as against public policy and coverage was required to be provided.

Page 208, add to note 73:

In *Briggs & Stratton Corp. v. Royal Globe Insurance Co.*, 64 F. Supp. 2d 1346 (M.D. Ga. 1999), the insured and the excess insurer disputed liability for environmental cleanup costs. The insured was ultimately unable to recover from the insurer where it failed to give notice of the claim within a reasonable period. With respect to agency issues, the court recognized that independent agents are not agents of the insurer where the insurer has not specifically accorded authority to the independent agent to act on its behalf. Thus, any failure on the part of the independent agent to transmit the notice of claim to the insurer could not serve to impose liability on the insurer. The independent agent did not fall within the policy provision that permitted the insured to give notice to the insurer or any of its authorized agents.

In *Guarente-Desantolo v. John Alden Life Insurance Co.*, 744 So. 2d 1123 (Fla. Dist. Ct. App. 1999), the insured sued the health insurer following the denial of coverage for breast cancer treatment. The insurer denied the claim due to material misrepresentations on the application for insurance. At the time of the application's completion, the agent and the insured were both present; the agent had brought with him the insurer's brochures and applications bearing the insurer's name. The agent was the one who read the questions on the application to the insured and then wrote down her answers. After completing the application, the agent gave the application to the insured to sign. She signed it without reading what the agent had written. One month later, she was diagnosed with breast cancer.

The insurer charged that the insured failed to disclose a previous detection of a cancerous lump during a mammogram taken shortly before the application was submitted. The insured claimed that she told the agent about the lump's discovery prior to signing the application and that she correctly responded to the agent's questions, but the agent inaccurately recorded her answers. She claimed that she did not have an opportunity to review the application before she signed it because the agent was in a hurry to get to another appointment.

The court held that there were fact questions as to whether the agent was the insured's agent or the insurer's agent with respect to the application's completion and whether the agent's knowledge of the insured's medical condition could be imputed to the insurer. The fact that the agent had blank forms, applications, brochures, and other materials prepared by the insurer were indicia of at least apparent authority.

Page 209, add to note 76:

In *Fireman's Fund Ins. Co. v. Haslam*, 35 Cal. Rptr. 2d 135 (Cal. Ct. App. 1994), the insured sued the insurer and the broker after the insurer refused to pay his fire loss claim. The insurer argued that the policy had been canceled prior to the loss.

The insurer had conducted a routine loss control inspection of the insured property and determined that the property was not an apartment building (as stated in the insurance application), but rather was a residence and rest home. The insurer treated the difference as a misrepresentation and instructed the broker to cancel the policy. Two months later, this broker contacted the broker who had procured the policy, and the procuring broker obtained the insured's reluctant signature on the cancellation form. The insurer canceled the policy but accepted two more monthly payments, and the insured believed that the coverage was still in force because he continued to receive subsequent billings. The court affirmed the judgment for the insurer against the broker, holding that the insurer could recover extracontractual damages paid to the insured due to the failure of the broker to properly cancel the policy as instructed by the insurer.

Page 209, add to note 77:

In *Fireman's Fund Ins. Co. v. National Bank for Cooperatives*, 849 F. Supp. 1347 (N.D. Cal. 1994), the servicer's insurer sued to determine whether it was liable for an arbitration award in favor of a bank with respect to certificates covering inventory financed by the bank. The insurer claimed that it had not received timely notice. The court held that even though a broker is generally the agent of the insured and not the insurer due to the ambiguous notice provisions in the servicer's excess liability policy, notice to the broker was sufficient even if it was not transmitted to the insurer in a timely and proper manner.

In *Carlton v. St. Paul Mercury Ins. Co.*, 36 Cal. Rptr. 2d 229 (Cal. Ct. App. 1994), the insured sued the insurer and broker for an unreasonable delay in paying under an antique-auto policy. The court was required to determine whether the broker was the insurer's agent for the purpose of imputing the broker's knowledge of the claim to the insurer. The broker had merely secured the policy and thus acted as the insured's agent. Accordingly, the broker's knowledge of the occurrence of loss was not imputed to the insurer.

In *Tassin v. Golden Rule Ins. Co.*, 649 So. 2d 1050 (La. Ct. App. 1994), the insured sought coverage under his health insurance policy for treatment of appendicitis. The insured's employer had changed group insurers following a rate increase. The broker assisted the employer in the search for new coverage, and helped the insured complete his application under the new policy. The application disclosed that the insured was being treated for diabetes and was taking medication.

The insurer informed the broker that it would not cover the group with the insured as a member. The insured signed a waiver of coverage and the insurer issued a policy covering all employees except the insured.

The broker then obtained other coverage for the insured. On the broker's advice, the insured's application did not disclose his diabetes. The new insurer discovered the diabetes while investigating the appendicitis claim, and denied coverage for the cost of treating the appendicitis — $19,210.

The court held that the broker was the insurer's agent, where the insurer supplied the broker with application forms and issued the policy following direct transmission of the application by the broker. Therefore, the insurer was responsible for paying the treatment bills subject to its rights to be indemnified by the broker.

6.9 Status of Employer Providing Group Insurance

Much of the health and life insurance written in this country is provided as an employee benefit. The insurer issues a master policy to the employer; the employer pays the whole premium, generally with the contribution of employees. Each employee who is covered under the plan receives a certificate of insurance showing the coverage afforded and the basic terms of the policy. There is no direct relationship between the employee and the insurer, and the typical aspects of servicing the policy are handled by the employer or someone hired by the employer. This raises the question of whether the employer is an agent for the purpose of administering the group insurance program and, if so, the effect of such an agency relationship.

In addition to standard employment group insurance relationships, various other arrangements are possible pursuant to the terms of the Employee Retirement Income Security Act (ERISA, 29 U.S.C. § 1113 *et seq.*). Under ERISA, the employer may hire an agent or administrator to handle the details of the plan in addition to handling various other forms of benefits such as pension and cafeteria plans. In this case, especially where the plan is self-funded, the employer may be aware that the administrator is acting as a dual agent. As such, any embezzlement of premiums by the agent may mean that the employer has no viable claim against the insurer for the wrongful actions of the agent.[81]

The employer has been held to stand in a fiduciary position with respect to covered employees and is required to advise them of all changes in group insurance coverage.[82] The employer may be considered the insurer's agent with respect to its termination and failure to reinstate the coverage of a

---

[81] *Continental Assurance Co. v. Cedar Rapids Pediatric Clinic*, 957 F.2d 588 (8th Cir. 1992), applying Iowa law.

[82] *Calhoun v. Kut-Kwick Corp.*, 323 S.E.2d 699 (Ga. Ct. App. 1984).

particular employee. Where the employer is the insurer's agent, the insurer can ultimately be held liable for the employer's failure to inform the employee of his lack of insurance coverage.[83]

However, the determination as to whether the employer is acting as the insurer's agent can only be made on a case-by-case basis after looking at the particular circumstances of the relationship and the actions in question. The crux of the examination will be the degree of control and supervision exercised or permitted to be exercised by the insurer over the employer's administration of the group insurance policy.[84] There is no agency relationship between the insurer and the employer where the insurer exclusively administers the plan, but as the degree of employer involvement in administration grows, so does the chance that the employer will be considered the insurer's agent — and with it, the chance of insurer liability for the employer's negligent or improper handling of coverage for the individual employees.[85]

ERISA raises various questions as to whether the employer is liable to provide certain types of health benefits retroactively where the employer simply failed to properly enroll the employee in the plan. If the situation requires that the employer function as a fiduciary, the breach of duty can be determined with reference to the duties of an insurance agent pursuant to state insurance law.[86] But generally speaking, fiduciary status can only be imposed on the employer where it is required under the terms of the statute.[87]

Where the employer collects premiums from the employees for coverage, it is considered the insurer's agent for the transfer

---

83 *Carr v. Port Ship Service*, 406 So. 2d 632 (La. Ct. App. 1981).

84 *Kirkpatrick v. Boston Mut. Life Ins. Co.*, 473 N.E.2d 173 (Mass. 1985).

85 *Paulson v. Western Life Ins. Co.*, 636 P.2d 935 (Or. 1981).

of those funds; thus, the insurer bears the risk that the funds will be lost or converted by the employer. The insurer may only terminate an employee's coverage for failure to pay premiums where it has previously given that employee notice that the employer is improperly handling the premiums and directs the employee to send the premiums directly to the insurer or another of the insurer's agents.[88] If the employer is required to pay premiums under a group medical plan and does not do so, and the insurer therefore refuses to provide coverage to an employee for medical expenses incurred, the employer will be held liable for the payment of the medical expenses to the degree they would have been covered under the policy. The fact that this amount is greatly in excess of the amount of premiums not paid is irrelevant to the employer's liability.[89]

---

[86] *Andre v. Salem Technical Services*, 979 F. Supp. 1416 (N.D. Ill. 1992). See also *Suggs v. Pan American Life Ins. Co.*, 847 F. Supp. 1324 (S.D. Miss. 1994), discussed in § 5.3 (insurer's cancellation for misrepresentation was invalid, where the insured had communicated information to agent that was not reflected in the application. Although the policy purported to make the agent the insured's agent, by statute the agent was deemed to accept the application for the insurer).

In *Lakeview Farms, Inc. v. Patten*, 640 N.E.2d 1092 (Ind. Ct. App. 1994), an injured employee sued the employer for breach of the agreement to procure medical insurance as a condition of employment. The court held that the oral agreement to procure insurance was not sufficiently definite to be enforced by the court where the parties did not discuss the risks insured against, the amount of coverage, and other similar details.

See also *Tourtillott v. Ormson Corp.*, 526 N.W.2d 515 (Wis. Ct. App. 1994), discussed in § 6.3, note 26 (employer was not held liable for failing to enroll an employee who never completed application for life insurance).

[87] *First Nat'l. Life Ins. Co. v. Sunshine-Jr. Food Stores*, 960 F.2d 1546 (11th Cir. 1992), applying Alabama law and ERISA.

[88] *Dearman v. Prudential Ins. Co.*, 727 F.2d 479 (5th Cir. 1984), applying Mississippi law.

[89] *Bushman v. Pure Plant Food Int'l.*, 330 N.W.2d 762 (S.D. 1983).

Part I □ **Chapter 6** □ **2000 Supplement**

The Role and Duties of Brokers

However, where the employer seeks to procure the group insurance coverage for its employees, it is the employees' agent; once the policy is obtained, the agency relationship changes and the employer becomes the insurer's agent.[90] Where the plan administrator or agency places the coverage with an insurer not licensed to do business in the state, such a claim will normally be available under state law without reference to the terms of ERISA.[91]

It should be noted that where the policy qualifies under ERISA but fails to provide statutorily required coverages, the insured may be limited to his or her rights under ERISA and not under state law.[92] The key criterion is whether the

---

90 *Miles v. Great Southern Life Ins. Co.*, 398 S.E.2d 772 (Ga. Ct. App. 1990); *Stewart v. City of Mt. Vernon*, 497 N.E.2d 939 (Ind. Ct. App. 1986).

91 *Ball v. Life Planning Services, Inc.*, 421 S.E.2d 223 (W. Va. 1992).

92 *Walters v. Pan American Life Ins. Co.*, 800 F. Supp. 436 (S.D. Miss. 1990).

In *Mann v. Interstate Fire & Cas. Co.*, 705 A.2d 360 (N.J. Super. App. Div. 1998), the broker had a written brokerage agreement with the non-admitted insurer, whereby the broker was to act as an independent contractor with authority to bind the insurer. The written contract could not resolve the extent of the broker's apparent authority to bind the insurer under the facts of the case where the broker allegedly agreed to add a lessor as an additional insured on the policy but failed effect the change.

The court held that the status of the broker was a question of fact precluding the grant of a summary judgment to the insurer. The court noted that broker can be placed in the position of a dual agent with respect to the procurement of the insurance and the naming of the lessor as an additional insured.

In *Wilson v. Zoellner*, 114 F.3d 713 (8th Cir. 1997), applying ERISA and Missouri law, the worker sought coverage under the employer's group health insurance policy. He sued the agent for misrepresenting to the employer that the worker was covered under the plan. The court held

(continued)

claim directly relates to the ERISA plan or to normal employment duties.[93]

Under the Consolidated Omnibus Budget Reconciliation Act (COBRA), an employee insured under an employer's group health insurance policy has the right to continue coverage even if he or she is no longer employed by the employer. The right is triggered by an election made by the insured. Normally, this right is disclosed in a letter written by the employer describing the reasons for the severance. The employee is entitled to make a COBRA election even if the termination is due to misconduct. Where the agent fails to provide information on the right to continue coverage, the burden falls on the plan sponsor and not the health insurer.[94]

---

92 (continued) that the claim did not relate to the provisions of ERISA and the duties imposed thereunder. Thus, the employee's only viable claim was under state law.

However, in *Massachusetts Cas. Ins. Co. v. Reynolds*, 113 F.3d 1450 (6th Cir. 1997), applying Tennessee and ERISA, the court held that the federal statute preempted the insured's claim that the agent made misrepresentations on postemployment coverage which was similar to continuation coverage and not conversion coverage. The court found that this was an ERISA claim since the insured sought specific performance of the insurance agreement.

In *Camp v. Pacific Financial Group*, 956 F. Supp. 1541 (C.D. Cal. 1997), the plaintiff, an ERISA trustee, sued the insurance agent and others for fraud and the wrongful inducement to enter into the ERISA plan. Where the plaintiff only sought damages from claimed fraud and mismanagement by the defendants, not from any alleged wrongful inducement to enter into the plan, state law was inapplicable and the only potential claims could be for ERISA statutory violations.

In another case, *Alacare Home Health Services v. Prudential Ins. Co.*, 957 F. Supp. 208 (M.D. Ala. 1997), where the claim was based on ERISA violations, the court held that fraud claims brought against the insurer, for the actions of the agent, did not preempt state law where the claim against the insurer was not for any actions undertaken as an ERISA plan administrator, but was for the vicarious liability of a principal arising from the actions of the agent.

Problems also arise when employees decide to switch between available health insurance options afforded by their employer. In such a situation, the plan administrator may not be required to explain the effect of changing plans on coverage for preexisting conditions. In at least one case, it was held that a plan administrator was not required to disclose information on the effect of changing insurance plans if the employee did not affirmatively seek such information or seek to learn of the differences in coverage.[95]

Clearly, if the employer misrepresents the status of an employee to render that person within the plan coverage, or makes other misrepresentations in connection with the administrative functions of the group insurance plan, the employer can be held liable to the insurer for the misrepresentation. In one such case, the employer stated that the employee was eligible for benefits when, in fact, he died on a two-year leave of absence.[96]

---

93 *Greany v. Western Farm Bur. Life Ins. Co.*, 973 F.2d 812 (9th Cir. 1992), applying Montana law and ERISA. *See also Dearth v. Great Republic Life Ins. Co.*, 12 Cal. Rptr. 2d 78 (1992); *Peterman v. Midwestern Nat'l. Ins. Co.*, 503 N.W.2d 312 (Wis. Ct. App. 1993).

94 *Connery v. Bath Assoc.*, 803 F. Supp. 1388 (N.D. Ind. 1992).

95 *Hardy v. Blue Cross and Blue Shield of Ala.*, 585 So. 2d 29 (Ala. 1991). *See also Distler v. Horace Mann Life Ins. Co.*, 644 N.E.2d 919 (Ind. Ct. App. 1994), in which the estate of the insured sued the group life insurer to recover proceeds paid to the insured's former wife, who remained the named beneficiary on the date of the insured's death. The policy was obtained through the insured's employer, who changed insurers but continued to use the enrollment cards from the prior policies. The court held that the employer was the insured's agent, and thus the employer's knowledge that the earlier cards would be used to designate beneficiaries was imputed to the insured. The court affirmed the summary judgment for the insurer.

96 *Pacific Standard Life Ins. Co. v. Tower Industries*, 12 Cal. Rptr. 2d 524 (Cal. Ct. App. 1992).

Chapter 7

Misrepresentation, Fraud, and Unfair Trade Practices

7.1 Misrepresentations in General

Page 213, add to note 1:

In *Kansas Bankers Surety Co. v. Bahr Consultants*, 69 F. Supp. 2d 1004 (E.D. Tenn. 1999), the insurer started writing employment practices liability and D&O policies to banks in Tennessee using salaried employees. Various banks hired the defendant consultant on a fee basis. The consultant represented himself to be a risk management specialist with expertise in bank insurance. He held licenses as an insurance consultant and an insurance agent, but was not the agent of any insurer and did not sell any insurance product. The insurer sued the consultant, alleging that the consultant misrepresented its policies to various client banks. The court granted the consultant's motion for summary judgment, holding that any misrepresentations where not made knowingly and that there were no violations of the state Insurance Trade Practices Act, which by its terms did not apply to such consultants.

In *Cincinnati Insurance Co. v. Guccione*, 719 N.E.2d 787 (Ill. App. Ct. 1999), the insurer sued the insured to recover premiums due, whereupon the insured brought a third-party action against the broker for failing to obtain the desired workers compensation coverage at the promised price. The insured paid the deposit premiums of $850 for each of two years, but failed to pay the additional premium as determined by an audit, which added another $23,000 for the two-year policy period. The insured contended that the broker told him that the policy cost would be "modest" and would approximate the initial premium deposit. The estimated premium for each year was the $850 premium deposit. The court held that there were fact questions as to exactly what the broker told the insured about the cost of the policy and whether the representations made were misleading or fraudulent. Furthermore, there was a fact question as to whether the broker breached his duty to exercise reasonable skill and breached his fiduciary duty to disclose the potential for significant costs derived from the audit.

In *Levy v. T.P. Luss & Co.*, 699 N.Y.S.2d 438 (N.Y. App. Div. 1999), the insured sued the agent for false representations made in a letter. The court held that any such misrepresentations concerning existing policies could not support a breach of contract claim where the plaintiff failed to allege that the misrepresentations were incorporated into the policies or modified the coverage provided by the policies.

In *Lexington Insurance Co. v. Buckingham Gate Ltd.*, 993 S.W.2d 185 (Tex. Ct. App. 1999), the insured sued the insurer for violating the Deceptive Trade Practices Act and for statutory bad faith after the insured denied a claim brought under an all-risk policy because policy exclusions applied. The broker had obtained the insurance and misrepresented to the insured that the all-risk policy would cover anything that could happen to the insured property. With regard to the broker, this misrepresentation could constitute a deceptive act for statutory purposes where the broker knew that the policy included exclusions. But, with regard to the insurer, any such misrepresentation would not be imputed to it where the broker was not a recording agent or soliciting agent for the

Part I □ Chapter 7 □ 2000 Supplement
Misrepresentation, Fraud, and Unfair Trade Practices

insurer and the broker was not granted authority to act on behalf of the insurer.

In *Seckinger-Lee Co. v. Allstate Ins. Co.*, 32 F. Supp. 2d 1348 (N.D. Ga. 1998), the insured sued the insurer in a dispute over coverage provided under a stated amount endorsement for the loss of a stolen automobile. The insured claimed that the agent's purported statement that the antique automobile was insured for the stated value scheduled in the policy extended coverage to the stated amount. The court held that the policy clearly and unambiguously limited coverage to the actual cash value or the repair or replacement value, whichever was less, notwithstanding the agent's alleged statements to the contrary. The agent's statement was held not to constitute fraud where the statement amounted to an opinion of law that was incorrect. No liability could be imposed on the agent or derivatively on the insurer for the agent's statements where there was no fiduciary relationship between the parties.

In *Small v. King*, 915 P.2d 1192 (Wyo. 1996), the insureds sued the agent, who allegedly misrepresented that the insureds had full coverage under the policy. There was a dispute about whether they requested such full coverage. The policy issued excluded coverage for weather-related damage and contained a care, custody, and control exclusion. Based on the exclusions, the insurer refused to provide coverage for damage to a drum set destroyed when a lighting rack blew onto the stage during a concert put on by the insureds. The court affirmed the judgment on the jury verdict for the agent, holding that an insured's knowledge that the policy as issued did not provide full coverage precluded her recovery on the misrepresentation claim.

See also McDonald v. Professional Ins. Corp., 946 F. Supp. 943 (M.D. Ala. 1996), discussed in § 5.2.

See also Cleveland Builders Supply v. Farmers Ins. Group, 657 N.E.2d 851 (Ohio Ct. App. 1995), discussed in § 5.5; and *Padeh v. Zagoria*, 900 F. Supp. 442 (S.D. Fla. 1995), and *Seneca Resources Corp. v. Marsh & McLennan, Inc.*, 911 S.W.2d 144 (Tex. Ct. App. 1995), discussed in § 6.5.

In *Celtic Life Ins. Co. v. Coats*, 885 S.W.2d 96 (Tex. 1994), the insured sued the insurer and agent for misrepresenting the psychiatric benefits available under his policy. The agent met with the insured employer to discuss health insurance of his employees and their families. The insured stated he wanted psychiatric care benefits equal to or greater than those provided by his then-current policy because his eldest son had previously required such care and his younger son might require similar care. The agent understood the insured's request and proposed the insurer's policy. The insurer's brochure showed a lower limit on such care, but the agent stated that the limit was only for outpatient care. Based on this erroneous representation, the insured purchased the policy. The court held that the insurer was liable for the agent's misrepresentations in explaining the policy coverage. The insured, however, was not entitled to recover treble damages under the Insurance Code or the Deceptive Trade Practices Act, where the jury found that the agent did not knowingly make the misrepresentation.

7.2 Negligent Misrepresentation

Page 219, add to note 5:

No liability found: In *Conagra Inc. v. Arkwright Mutual Insurance Co.*, 64 F. Supp. 2d 754 (N.D. Ill. 1999), the insured sustained losses of over $28 million in two warehouse fires and sued the insurer and the broker. Prior to the fires, the insurer discussed the possibility of providing coverage for the insured and ultimately presented a proposal for property coverage. A policy was issued and then modified on several occasions. Sometime later, the fires occurred at nonowned outside warehouses used for the temporary storage and consolidation of the insured's products while they were in the process of distribution.

With respect to the liability of the broker, the court found that there were fact questions as to whether the broker was indeed the insured's broker with respect to the policy in question. The broker admitted that it was the insured's broker for placing the excess coverage, but denied that it was the broker for the property insurance. The court held that even if the defendant was the insured's broker, there was no viable claim for negligent misrepresentation where the insured suffered purely economic loss. Furthermore, the insured did not establish that the broker made any false statements about material facts that the insured then relied on; the insured merely reported that the broker failed to advise the insured that it was not protecting the insured's interest with respect to the policy in question.

No liability found: In *Weisblatt v. Minnesota Mut. Life Insurance Co.*, 4 F. Supp. 2d 371 (E.D. Pa. 1998), the insurer's agent allegedly misrepresented the terms of the life insurance policy and committed fraud prior to the purchase of the policy. The agent met with the plaintiff and her husband twice prior to the purchase. The agent misrepresented his experience in the field and allegedly recommended that the plaintiffs surrender an existing life insurance policy because it would eventually become essentially worthless. He also recommended that they purchase a policy from the defendant insurer. The agent never recommended an amount of death benefits he thought should be purchased and never mentioned the benefits of purchasing term insurance. The insurer paid the surviving plaintiff the full policy death benefit when the insured husband died and the plaintiff widow determined that the policy was insufficient to meet her needs as expressed to the agent. The court held that the agent had no duty to advise the plaintiff of other policy options and the plaintiff did not rely on the agent's statements in deciding to surrender the first policy and purchase the second.

Claim for liability supported: In *Thomas v. Ohio Casualty Grp.*, 3 F. Supp. 2d 764 (S.D. Tex. 1998), the insured sued two insurers and the agent for breach of contract, misrepresentation, negligence, and violations of state statutes. The agent sold the plaintiff the policy and allegedly misrepresented the scope of the homeowners policy coverage. There was no breach of contract claim brought against the agent arising out of the insurers' denial of coverage. Such a claim is normally not viable under state law. Where the agent allegedly made an affirmative misrepresentation of fact and acted outside the scope of his authority to act on behalf of the insurer, the agent could be held liable. The court denied the motion to dismiss the claims against the agent but remanded the case to state court.

Page 219, add to note 8:

In *Vickers v. Progressive Cas. Ins. Co.*, 979 S.W.2d 200 (Mo. Ct. App. 1998), the court held that the injured victims of an automobile accident could maintain a suit against the insurer for negligent misrepresentation arising out of the statements made by its agent that the insurer would settle their claims. The agent further failed to exercise reasonable care in giving them correct information on the coverage provided by the policy, but rather gave them inaccurate information which they relied upon to their detriment.

Page 220, add to note 9:

In *Gonzalez v. Blue Cross/Blue Shield*, 689 So. 2d 812 (Ala. 1997), the insureds sued the insurer and claims administrator for fraud and breach of contract after the insurer refused to pay the insureds' maternity claim. The insurer denied the claim because the baby reached full term prior to the expiration of the policy's waiting period.

With respect to the agency issues, the court held that there was no evidence that the agent was acting on behalf of the insurer when prior to the purchase of the policy he allegedly misrepresented that they would have full coverage immediately upon issuance of the policy.

In *Kinard v. National Indem. Co.*, 483 S.E.2d 664 (Ga. Ct. App. 1997), the claimants injured in an auto accident sought to recover from the truck driver who allegedly caused the accident and his business auto insurance carrier. The independent agent allegedly made representations that the insured had coverage for the truck in question.

The court held that the insurer was not bound by the independent agent's representations of coverage where the agent had no authority to bind coverage and was considered to be the agent of the insured. The mere fact that the independent agent's issuance of certificates of insurance was insufficient to establish apparent authority to act on the insurer's behalf.

In *Hickey v. Centenary Oyster House*, 690 So. 2d 858 (La. Ct. App. 1997), the claimant was injured in an armed robbery occurring in a parking lot and sued the security firm responsible for security in the lot and the firm's insurer. With respect to the agent, it was alleged that the insurer was bound by the independent insurance agent's representation that the policy provided the coverage required for security firms.

The court held that the agent had no written agency agreement with the insurer and could not bind the insurer or modify the terms of the policy. The subjective belief of the insured was of no consequence. Thus, the insurer was not bound by the alleged misrepresentations.

However, the court held that where the policy was designed to satisfy state requirements for security firms, the assault and battery exclusion was void as against public policy and coverage was required to be provided.

In *Wolfson v. Bernstein*, 955 S.W.2d 814 (Mo. Ct. App. 1997), the plaintiff tried to obtain key man life insurance on the life of its corporate president before he disappeared. The agent offered a policy that was unacceptable to the president and the agent sought other coverage. The coverage was not effective until the first premium payment was made. The insurer forwarded the policy to the agent and specified that the requirements for placing the coverage into effect had to be completed by a certain date. The agent called the plaintiff's president several times requesting a check for the premium but did not receive a check. The agent obtained an extension to make the payment conditioned on a certificate of continued good health. No premium payment was made before the president disappeared. Shortly thereafter, the president committed suicide. The court held that the agent was not liable for a negligent misrepresentation that the policy was in effect where it was clear from the application that the initial premium payment was required to secure the effective coverage. The court held that the agent was not negligent in attempting the collect the premium.

In *Fillinger v. Northwestern Agency Inc.*, 938 P.2d 1347 (Mont. 1997), the insured sued the agent to recover losses not covered under the policy obtained by that agent. The insured agreed to provide services to another company, and under that contract, the insured was required to obtain coverage that would also cover the other company.

When a claim was made and it was determined that the policy coverage did not extend to the other company's liability, that company canceled the contract with the insured. A new contract was prepared whereby the insured received less compensation for its services and reduced the liability insurance requirements.

When the insured received the policy in question, it did not read every provision but rather relied on the representations of the agent that coverage was provided as required and requested. The agent argued that the insured never requested special coverage but rather only ordered a standard policy.

The court affirmed the judgment on the jury verdict for the insured on the negligent misrepresentation claim. The court noted that evidence of the negotiations between the insured and the agent leading to the procurement of the policy was admissible to prove the insured's claim.

In *National Union Fire Ins. Co. v. Fidelity Nat'l Title Ins. Co.*, 663 N.Y.S.2d 20 (N.Y. App. Div. 1997), the insured had its own risk manager who reviewed policies and worked with brokers to place desired coverage. The insured acquired a predecessor company which automatically canceled the policy. The insured claimed that the broker was liable for negligent misrepresentation in failing to inform the insured of the cancellation.

The court held that the broker could not be held liable where the insured and the risk manager never inquired about the impact of the acquisition and therefore could not have relied on anything the broker might have said about the continued existence of policy coverage.

In *McDonald v. Houston Brokerage, Inc.*, 928 S.W.2d 653 (Tex. Ct. App. 1996), the broker allegedly committed misrepresentations as to the true cost of a replacement policy used to fund the employer's ERISA plan. The employer obtained a group medical insurance policy for its employees through a multiple employer welfare arrangement pursuant to ERISA. At the time the employer subscribed to the arrangement, the policy was underwritten by one insurer. The arrangement replaced the policy with another; the broker represented to the employer that the replacement policy was substantially the same as the earlier policy, whereas in truth they were not. The major difference was in the method for calculating experience rating, which caused substantial increases in premiums charged. The court held that the employer's claims for misrepresentation under state law did not relate to the employee benefit plan such as would result in the preemption of state law claims by ERISA.

See also U.S.F. & G. Co. v. Sulco, Inc., 939 F. Supp. 820 (D. Kan. 1996), discussed in § 4.5 and *Paper Savers Inc. v. Nacsa*, 59 Cal. Rptr. 2d 547 (Cal. App. Ct. 1996), and *Williams v. Fallaize Ins. Agency, Inc.*, 469 S.E.2d 752 (Ga. Ct. App. 1996), discussed in § 5.2.

7.3 Intentional Misrepresentation, Fraud, and Bad Faith

Page 221, add to note 12:

In *Cartwright v. Equitable Life Assur. Soc.*, 914 P.2d 976 (Mont. 1996), the insureds purchased life insurance but were unaware that the payment of premiums on the policy was financed by the policies' automatic loan features. They brought a fraud action against the insurer and the agent. The court held that there was sufficient evidence that the agent in fact misrepresented the nature of the premium financing. In addition, the damages awarded to the insured would not be reduced by the insured's own comparative negligence.

In *Potamkin Cadillac Corp. v. B.R.I. Coverage Corp.*, 38 F.3d 627 (2d Cir. 1994) applying New York law, the insured sued the commercial insurance broker seeking an accounting of premiums to be returned, unapplied payments, and overpayments. The insured was a group of corporate entities engaged in the sale, leasing, and servicing of automobiles. The group retained the defendant insurance broker, but the broker allegedly defrauded the group by charging for insurance coverage that was not provided, charging service fees in lieu of commissions, overstating premiums due, and converting payments made. The court affirmed the judgment for the insured and the dismissal of the brokers' counterclaims.

In *Parsaie v. United Olympic Life Ins. Co.*, 29 F.3d 219 (5th Cir. 1994), applying Texas law, the insured sued the insurer for wrongful rescission of a health insurance policy, bad faith, and violation of the deceptive trade practice statute. The plaintiff's application falsely stated that she had not been diagnosed or treated for diabetes or for injury to her reproductive system and that she was not taking any medication. The plaintiff claimed that she understood very little English and could not understand the application, but signed the form at the insistence of the soliciting agent. The insurer rescinded the policy based on the misrepresentation after she filed a claim and the insurer investigated her true medical condition. The court vacated the summary judgment for the insurer, holding that there was a fact question whether the insured had the intent to deceive the insurer so as to support the rescission for misrepresentation. The court noted that any wrongful conduct on the part of the soliciting agent could be imputed to the insurer pursuant to Texas law, which makes no distinction between such agents and recording agents.

Page 222, add to note 14:

In *Mehaffey v. Boston Mut. Life Ins. Co.*, 31 F. Supp. 2d 1329 (M.D. Ala. 1998), the plaintiff/employee sued the employer's insurance agency and the insurer, claiming that the agent committed fraud and negligence in failing to obtain insurance for the plaintiff and other employees. The employer had an employee benefits cafeteria plan whereby employees could use the employer's contribution for a variety of purposes. The plaintiff decided to purchase the insurer's health policy, and the agent received the initial premium. The agent subsequently informed the employees that the insurer applied a 20 percent rate up based on additional health information about certain employees, whereupon the employees decided not to accept the policy. The agent had informed them, on several occasions, that the policy became effective on the date of the premium payment, but in fact, it was never issued. The court held that the plaintiff's claims did not relate to an ERISA plan where the policy was never issued and the plaintiff did not seek to recover benefits under the policy and their claim did not relate to any policy provisions. Thus, state law would govern the fraud and negligence claims brought against the agent.

In *Engelhardt v. Paul Revere Life Ins. Co.*, 951 F. Supp. 1003 (M.D. Ala. 1996), the physician was covered under a group disability policy issued to a medical corporation and covering the practice of four physicians. He sued the insurer under state law and ERISA. He claimed that the agent and the insurer fraudulently induced him to sign an amendment to his application after he disclosed that he had previously been diagnosed with glaucoma. The amendment excluded coverage for either or both eyes. More than two years after the policy took effect, he experienced serious vision problems resulting from a detached or torn retina that was unrelated to his glaucoma. This rendered him unable to continue his medical practice. When he made a claim under the policy, that claim was denied based on the policy amendment. The court held that his claim against the agent who sold the policy was not preempted by ERISA. Moreover, under the facts of the case, he did not have standing as an ERISA participant or beneficiary to bring an ERISA claim against the insurer. This meant that his state law claims against the insurer were not preempted by the federal statute.

In *American Buying Ins. Services v. S. Kornreich & Sons*, 944 F. Supp. 240 (S.D.N.Y. 1996), the insurance purchasing group sued the broker and others with whom the group was involved in purchasing agreements under fraud and RICO claims. The plaintiffs contacted the broker in connection with creating the buying group for property owners and recruited the owners. In the first year of operation, the group had 30 customers. The plaintiffs were to receive 10 percent of the premiums paid to the broker by customers who were new to the program and 5 percent for existing customers of the broker who entered the program. The plaintiffs received additional fees. The payment of commissions to the plaintiffs arguably violated state insurance laws since the plaintiffs were not licensed brokers. The broker had problems obtaining renewals for the program, and allegedly problems arose with insurers with respect to the broker's improper actions. The plaintiffs argued that the program members were forced to pay higher premiums due to the lack of timely renewals. Moreover, they claimed that the renewal problem was merely a pretext used by the broker to avoid paying fees to the plaintiffs and that the broker placed some of the customers outside the group to deprive the plaintiffs of their fees. The plaintiffs alleged that there was a continuing plan to defraud them of such fees. The court held that the plaintiffs were still entitled to attempt to prove their RICO claims, even though their contract with the broker violated state insurance laws. The court denied the defendants' motion to dismiss the suit.

In *Randolph v. Mitchell*, 677 So. 2d 976 (Fla. Dist. Ct. App. 1996), the insured sought to purchase medical insurance from the agent. The agent represented that the new policy would provide the same or better coverage as her existing policy, but at a lower premium. The insured accepted this proposal, and the agent had a policy issued. After the insured was injured in the course of her employment, she submitted a claim that was denied based on a policy exclusion. The insured alleged that the agent committed fraud in the inducement to change the

Part I □ **Chapter 7** □ **2000 Supplement**
Misrepresentation, Fraud, and Unfair Trade Practices

policies. The court reversed the dismissal of the suit. Since the agent committed fraud outside the scope of the contractual relationship, the suit was not barred by the economic loss rule.

In *North American Shipbuilding v. Southern Marine & Aviation Underwriting*, 930 S.W.2d 829 (Tex. Ct. App. 1996), the insured sued the insurer and the agent after the builders risk insurer denied coverage for the cost of replacing defective welds on ships built by the insured. The insured went to the agent to obtain insurance, and the agent went to the wholesale broker, who placed the coverage with the insurer. The insured's claim against the wholesale broker was based on bad faith, misrepresentation, fraud, negligence, and violations of the Texas Insurance Code. The court held that the wholesale broker could not be held liable; it did not misrepresent the scope of the coverage provided by the policy when it stated that the policy provided all-risk coverage. It had no duty to inform the insured that the policy did not cover faulty workmanship.

In *Finn v. Nachreiner Boie Art Factory*, 549 N.W.2d 273 (Wis. Ct. App. 1996), the insureds sued the life insurer and its agents for fraud in the inducement to purchase split-dollar life insurance policies sold to the employer. The policies were designed to provide both insurance and retirement benefits. The employer purchased the policy intending that the excess cash value accumulating on the policy would be the source of retirement income for the president of the business, who was also one of its two shareholders. The insurance was designed to meet the requirements of ERISA. The employer agreed to various split-dollar insurance arrangements with various employees. The court held that since the policies were part of employee benefit plans, they were subject to ERISA, which preempted the state law fraud and misrepresentation claims against the insurer and the agent. This was the case even though some of the statements in question were made prior to the issuance of the policies in question.

Page 222, add to note 16:

In *Lambert v. Independent Life & Acc. Ins. Co.*, 994 F. Supp.

1385 (M.D. Ala. 1998), the insured's surviving spouse sued the agent and the medical insurer for misrepresentation after a claim for hospital expenses was denied due to a lapse in coverage. The plaintiff and her husband purchased identical sickness and accident policies issued by the defendant insurer. The agent collected the premium payments. The question arose as to whether a particular monthly premium payment was made by the plaintiff and her spouse but was unaccounted for. The payment was allegedly made in cash and delivered by the plaintiff's son directly to the agent. The plaintiff failed to establish when this cash premium payment was made. The court held that any statement allegedly made to the son could support a misrepresentation claim where it was clear that the agent expected the son to pass the statement to the plaintiff. The statement that the payment would be credited to the policy was not false and was not relied on by the plaintiff as required to support a fraud or misrepresentation claim since the statement was made after the payment was tendered to the agent. Therefore, the plaintiff did not rely on the statement in making that payment.

Page 224, add to note 19:

In *Head v. United Ins. Co. of Am.*, 966 F. Supp. 455 (N.D. Miss. 1997), the insured sued the agent and the insurer for fraud claiming that the multiple policies purchased duplicated coverage and the benefits available to her under Medicaid. The court recognized that the agent could be held personally liable for fraud and concealment with respect to the fact that the policies were worthless and therefore the agent was properly made a defendant in the suit.

In *Booker v. United American Ins. Co.*, 700 So. 2d 1333 (Ala. 1997), the insureds sued the subagent and insurer for fraud. They also sued the insurer for negligent supervision of the agent. The insureds claimed that they purchased the policies based on the agent's misrepresentations. The subagent was not authorized to act on the insurer's behalf but was hired by an authorized agent against the insurer's express instructions.

In determining the insurer's responsibilities, the court reviewed the law applicable to subagents and affirmed the summary judgment for the insurer. The court held that the insurer could not be held liable for the actions of the subagent, who was appointed contrary to express instructions. There was no evidence that the insurer ever ratified the appointment of the subagent or vested the subagent with apparent authority. Clearly, the agent and subagent could be held liable in another action.

In *Modern Woodmen of Amer. v. Crumpton*, 487 S.E.2d 47 (Ga. Ct. App. 1997), the insurer brought this action seeking a determination that it was not liable for the employee agent's fraudulent procurement of loans on the insured's policy.

The court held that the insurer could not be held liable for fraud since the employee agent's actions were outside the scope of his employment and were undertaken for his own personal gain. However, the court also held that such a finding did not preclude the imposition of liability under contract theories for the policy value not reduced by the agent's misconduct.

Page 225, add to note 23:

In *Alliston v. Omega Ins. Co.*, 983 F. Supp. 675 (S.D. Miss. 1997), the insureds sued the agent for fraudulent misrepresentation of coverage under their property insurance policy. The agent allegedly told the plaintiffs that they would be covered for burglary losses, but when one such loss occurred, the insurer denied coverage. The insurer finally admitted that there was coverage but refused to pay the entire amount of the insureds' loss.

The court held that when the insurer admitted that there was coverage for the loss, any misrepresentation made by the agent was rendered irrelevant and therefore the agent could not be held liable. The court further noted that the agent had no obligation to the insureds with respect to the settlement of claims. Therefore, he could not be held liable for the insurer's conduct in handling the claim.

In *Hays v. Jackson Nat'l Life Ins. Co.*, 105 F.3d 583 (10th Cir. 1997), applying Oklahoma law, the life insurance beneficiary sued the insurer after it denied the claim based on misrepresentations and omissions in the insurance application with respect to the insured's medical history. The agent completed the medical information portion of the application based on the insured's responses to the agent's oral questioning. The court held that the insurer could only avoid coverage for misrepresentation where the insured intended to deceive the insurer. The court also held that there were fact questions on the insured's intent, thereby precluding a summary judgment on that issue. In addition, the court held that the beneficiaries were not entitled to reformation of the policy to reflect the policy limits of the coverage that would have been issued had the insurer known the insured's true medical condition. The agent's knowledge of the insured's condition when the application was completed would not be imputed to the insurer for the purposes of determining whether the insurer acted in bad faith in denying the claim based on the purported misrepresentation.

In *Griffin v. Allstate Ins. Co.*, 920 F. Supp. 127 (C.D. Cal. 1996), the plaintiffs sought to recover for earthquake damage to their home. The insurer did not receive the premium payment when due and sent a cancellation notice warning the plaintiffs that the policy would be canceled if the December payment was not received by January 2. The plaintiff husband received the letter, but disregarded it because the plaintiff wife told him that she had mailed the premium payment. The insurer canceled the policy because it did not receive the payment. The plaintiffs claimed that they mailed the payment, even though they could not show any canceled check or even a check register showing that they paid the premium. The court dismissed the suit, holding that the plaintiffs had no viable claim against the insurer or the agent for breach of fiduciary duties in failing to keep the policy in force. The agent cannot be liable for bad faith since it is not a party to the insurance contract.

In *Keiter v. Penn Mut. Ins. Co.,* 900 F. Supp. 1339 (D. Haw.

1995), the insured and the beneficiary sued both the life insurer and the agent who sold the universal life policy. The plaintiffs charged that the insurer and agent were engaged in a plan to deliberately and fraudulently sell the policies during periods of high interest rates. The plaintiffs claimed that the agent told them they needed to change the policy from whole life to universal life. They alleged that the agent sold the insured a universal life policy, and the insured made all premium payments until a dispute arose more than a decade later. The plaintiffs claimed that the agent did not disclose to them that in a universal life policy, a drop in interest rates would erode the insured's equity and greatly increase premium payments.

The premium increased from $529 per month to $2,784 per month while the death benefit remained relatively constant. The insured could not afford the increased premiums, let the policy lapse and obtained a new policy with a death benefit that was $280,000 lower than the universal life policy.

The court held that the plaintiffs did not state a viable tortious bad faith claim under Hawaii law. The court also held that they had no viable claims for the infliction of emotional distress. However, the court did hold that the insured had a viable claim for contractual bad faith, even though the claim was related to marketing and not contractual performance.

In *French v. State Farm Ins. Co.*, 156 F.R.D. 159 (S.D. Tex. 1994), the insured sued the insurer and the adjuster handling the claim for bad faith and violations of the state's deceptive trade practice statute, arising out of the rejection of his underinsured motorist claim. The court held that the adjuster could not be held liable for negligence in claims handling since Texas law recognizes no such claim. The court further held that the adjuster could not be held liable in his individual capacity for any alleged bad faith or statutory violations. The only potential liability would be imposed on the insurer, either directly or for the acts of the adjuster (its agent).

In *Chavez v. American Life and Cas. Ins. Co.*, 872 P.2d 366 (N.M. 1994), the plaintiff beneficiaries sued the decedent's life insurer and the group policyholder. The insured had obtained the life insurance through his membership in the National Guard and authorized a monthly deduction in his drill pay. The insurance certificate specifically stated that the insurance would terminate at the end of the last month for which a premium was paid. The insured did not attend drill for two consecutive months; thus, there was no drill pay and no deductions were made. Shortly thereafter, the insurer canceled the certificate of insurance for nonpayment. The court held that the statutory 10-day notice requirement for cancellations was inapplicable to life insurance, and that there was no bad faith or breach of duty in failing to give the insured notice of the policy cancellation under the facts of the case.

In *Natividad v. Alexsis, Inc.*, 875 S.W.2d 695 (Tex. 1994), the plaintiff was a workers compensation claimant who sued the adjuster for bad faith arising out of the handling of her claim. She also raised claims for economic duress, negligent infliction of emotional distress and extreme and outrageous conduct. The Texas Supreme Court held that the adjusting firm and the individual adjuster did not owe the plaintiff a duty of good faith and fair dealing where there was no contractual or special relationship between the parties. The adjusting company contracted with the comp insurer to provide adjusting services. The court held that the plaintiff's allegations failed to state a claim for intentional infliction of emotional distress or outrageous conduct.

Page 226, add to note 25:

In *Morstein v. National Ins. Services, Inc.*, 93 F.3d 715 (11th Cir. 1996), applying ERISA and Georgia law, the employer sued the independent insurance agent for fraudulent inducement to purchase an insurance plan subject to ERISA. Where the claims referred to the agent's misrepresentations and deceit in procuring the policy, the court held that there was insufficient connection to the insurance itself to trigger the preemption provision of ERISA that would have precluded the plaintiff employer's state law claims.

In *Suggs v. Pan American Life Ins. Co.*, 847 F. Supp. 1324 (S.D. Miss. 1994), the employee sued the insurer and agent after his medical claim was denied and his policy canceled for misrepresentation.

The plaintiff was covered under an employee benefit plan covered by ERISA. As a threshold matter, the court held that the statute did not bar such statutory claims even though claims for fraud in the inducement would be preempted by the statute.

The court held that the insurer's cancellation of the policy for misrepresentation in the application was not valid. Even though the insured signed the completed application, he had communicated information to the agent that was not reflected in the application. The agent's knowledge and actions could be imputed to the insurer, despite language in the policy stating that the agent was the insured's agent and not the insurer's, due to the agent's statutory status as accepting the application for the insurer.

Page 226, add to note 26:

In *Johnson & Higgins v. Kenneco Energy*, 962 S.W.2d 507 (Tex. 1998), the insured sustained a loss of profits and submitted a claim that was denied by the insurer. The broker brought this declaratory judgment action to determine its liability with respect to the loss. The insured claimed that the broker engaged in unfair and deceptive acts. The court held that the claim was subject to a two-year limitations period and the period for the filing of suit started to run when the insured's claim was denied by the insurer. Where the court held that any misrepresentation made by the broker with respect to the coverage to be provided by the policy did not amount to fraud, the only viable claim against the broker was for the breach of the alleged agreement to procure contingency coverage for the insured.

7.4 The Role of Unfair Trade Practices and Other Consumer Protection Statutes

Page 234, add to note 29:

In re The Prudential Ins. Co. Sales Practices Litigation, 962 F. Supp. 450 (D.N.J. 1997) was a class action brought by policyholders against the insurer for deceptive sales practices. The insurer allegedly engaged in churning or twisting designed to sell replacement policies. In connection with the scheme, the insurer and its agents allegedly misrepresented the value of the policies as investments and the problem of vanishing premiums.

The court found that the settlements were fair and appropriate. The case includes an excellent discussion of deceptive trade practice law in the context of the scheme. *See also* subsequent decision in the same case reported at 975 F. Supp. 584 (1997) where the court held that the policyholders stated viable bad faith claims, but did not state any viable claim for breach of fiduciary duties. The insurance code and accompanying regulations preempted any claims alleging state consumer fraud act violations.

In *Treski v. Kemper Nat'l Ins. Cos.*, 674 A.2d 1106 (Pa. Super. 1996), the insureds purchased automobile insurance policies retaining their full tort options and claimed that the auto insurers misrepresented the nature of the coverage by failing to advise them that the tort option would be ineffective in New Jersey accidents. This meant that they would be unable to recover noneconomic losses when injured in New Jersey accidents. The court held that the plaintiffs' allegations were not sufficient to support a class action against the insurer for deceptive trade practices. Such claims could only be brought by individuals who had actually been injured in such accidents. No liability could be imposed where the insurers and their agents complied with the terms of Pennsylvania law, which was the law of the state where the policies were sold.

Misrepresentation, Fraud, and Unfair Trade Practices

In *INA v. Morris*, 923 S.W.2d 133 (Tex. Ct. App. 1996), the guaranty bond surety paid claims arising out of investors defaulting on promissory notes in connection with the purchase of gas and oil partnership interests. The surety sued the investors to recover under the terms of the guaranty, and the investors brought third-party claims against the surety's managing general agent. The investment program had been reviewed by a marketing agent for the surety's bond programs. That agent reviewed and screened syndicator offerings and submitted programs to the surety.

The oil and gas company furnished the agent with a draft format of the program, and the agent notified the company that the program had been turned down for various reasons. The program was changed to meet the surety's requirements, and the bonds were issued and executed by the managing general agent. The investors signed various documents and did not learn until later that the documents contained disclaimers as to the surety's involvement in the program. The investors subsequently discovered that the partnership interests sold to them were based on fraud and misrepresentation.

When they defaulted on their promissory notes, the surety paid the notes and received an assignment of those notes from the lenders. The surety demanded reimbursement pursuant to the indemnification agreements and then sued the investors who claimed fraud and bad faith on the part of the surety and the managing general agent.

The court held that there was sufficient evidence that the managing general agent and the marketing agent were acting with implied or apparent authority from the surety in selling the investments and collecting the surety bond premiums. This could serve to impose liability on the surety for any misrepresentations made by such persons. The court affirmed the judgment holding that the notes, bonds, and indemnification agreements were unenforceable and that the investors were entitled to damages under the Deceptive Trade Practices Act.

In *Choczner v. William Penn Life Ins. Co.*, 623 N.Y.S.2d 597 (N.Y. App. Div. 1995), the life insured allegedly completed an application to replace a policy issued by one insurer with a policy issued by the defendant. The agent failed to provide him with a disclosure statement required by 11 NYCRR Part 51 upon the application for the "replacement" coverage. The regulation is designed to assure that such applicants are aware of the effect of the replacement on incontestability and suicide clauses. The regulation provides that the failure of the agent to make the required disclosure will bar the insurer from relying on the undisclosed policy provisions.

The court held that the regulation did not apply under the facts of the case. The prior policy had lapsed for nonpayment of premiums six months before the application for coverage with the defendant was submitted, neither the insurer nor the agent induced the applicant to terminate the first policy.

See also Seneca Resources Corp. v. Marsh & McLennan, Inc., 911 S.W.2d 144 (Tex. Ct. App. 1995), discussed in § 6.5. The insured oil and gas company contracted to move a submersible drilling rig onto an offshore area leased for gas and oil drilling. This was in preparation to drill a well. As the insured was preparing to move the rig, a hurricane passed and a portion of the rig was lost. The insurer refused to pay for the loss, whereupon the insured filed this suit.

The insured obtained the policy by approaching the broker and advising the broker of its insurance requirements. The broker contacted a wholesaler for bids. The broker would eventually contact the insured with its findings, and the insured would have the final decision on the purchase of coverage. Then the broker would bind the coverage by informing the wholesaler.

The insured obtained all-risk platform insurance and operator's extra expense coverage. The insured claimed that the broker misrepresented the benefits provided by the policies and the availability of particular coverages. Even though such a misrepresentation violates the applicable insurance code, the court held that no recovery could be had where the plaintiff failed to establish that the alleged misrepresentation caused the injuries sustained.

In *Celtic Life Ins. Co. v. Coats*, 885 S.W.2d 96 (Tex. 1994), the insured sued the insurer and agent for misrepresenting the psychiatric benefits available under his policy. The agent met with the insured employer to discuss health insurance of his employees and their families. The insured stated he wanted psychiatric care benefits equal to or greater than those provided by his then-current policy because his eldest son had previously required such care and his younger son might require similar care. The agent understood the insured's request and proposed the insurer's policy. The insurer's brochure showed a lower limit on such care, but the agent stated that the limit was only for outpatient care. Based on this erroneous representation, the insured purchased the policy. The court held that the insurer was liable for the agent's misrepresentations in explaining the policy coverage. The insured, however, was not entitled to recover treble damages under the Insurance Code or the Deceptive Trade Practices Act, where the jury found that the agent did not knowingly make the misrepresentation.

In *Hart v. Berko, Inc.*, 881 S.W.2d 502 (Tex. Ct. App. 1994), the plaintiff policyholder sued the agent for violations of the Deceptive Trade Practices Act and Insurance Code with respect to the insurer's denial of fire insurance coverage. The insured requested that the agent increase the amount of insurance on the building. The agent allegedly stated that the increase was effective. The building was completely destroyed by fire, and on the day after the fire, the agent notified the insured that the coverage had not been increased. The court held that the misrepresentation was the cause of the plaintiff's loss, but held that the plaintiff was not entitled to recover treble damages under the statute.

Page 237, add to note 40:

In *Good v. Prudential Ins. Co.*, 5 F. Supp. 804 (N.D. Cal. 1998), the plaintiff sued the insurer and its agent, alleging that he met with the agent to discuss purchasing additional insurance and the agent made various representations on the benefits of a variable appreciable life insurance policy. The plaintiff alleged that the agent told him he could obtain a $1 million policy of this variety by paying an annual premium of $10,000 for three to six years, after which the premiums would vanish. The plaintiff alleged that the insured never intended to permit the premiums to vanish after the three to six years. The misrepresentations were part of the insurer's nationwide pattern of deceptive conduct. The court held that the agent could not be held liable for acts committed within the scope of the agency for the insurer. The court rejected the contention that the agent was actually a dual agent owing the plaintiff duties where the agent was not an independent broker and had no special relationship with the plaintiff.

In *Grove v. Principal Mut. Life Ins. Co.*, 14 F. Supp. 2d 1101 (S.D. Iowa 1998), the plaintiff policyholders sued the insurer for fraud, negligence, and breach of fiduciary duties. The plaintiffs alleged a fraudulent scheme and course of deceptive sales practices perpetrated by the defendant involving using the insurer's agents to deceive and induce them to purchase insurance policies through false and misleading policy illustrations, marketing materials, and sales presentations with respect to vanishing premiums. There was no mention that even if the out-of-pocket premiums did actually vanish, they might reappear if variables were altered. The court denied the insurer's motion to dismiss, holding that the plaintiffs stated viable fraud claims and the insureds had the right to rely on the statements made by the insurance agents within the scope of their agency. For a similar case, *see Parkhill v. Minnesota Mut. Life Ins. Co.*, 995 F. Supp. 983 (D. Minn. 1998), where the court held that false statements made by an agent in another state could not support a claim under the Minnesota False Statement in Advertising Act, and whether the agent owed the plaintiffs fiduciary duties was a question of fact to be determined on a case-by-case basis.

In *Frith v. Guardian Life Ins. Co.*, 9 F. Supp. 2d 744 (S.D. Tex. 1998), the insureds sued the life insurer for fraud and misrepresentation and violations of state trade practices law. They claimed that the cost illustrations did not disclose critical information. The court held that the agent being the insurer's agent, and not the insured's agent, had no duty to explain the terms of the policy and the insured had ample opportunity to read the policy and cost illustrations that were not ambiguous.

In *Goldberg v. Manufacturers Life Ins. Co.*, 672 N.Y.S.2d 39 (N.Y. App. Div. 1998), the life insureds sued the insurer and the agent. They purchased two policies. Several years later, they agreed to a vanishing premium option. After a dispute arose about the premiums on one policy, the insurer paid the plaintiffs a lump sum in exchange for a receipt and general release, and that policy was rescinded. The release extended protection to the insurer and its representatives and past and present agents. The court held that the release included the agent the insureds were trying to sue, and barred fraud claims, since the release discharged the insurer and the agent from any and all such claims.

Page 239, add to note 44:

In *Winburn v. Liberty Mut. Ins. Co.*, 8 F. Supp. 644 (E.D. Ky. 1998), the claimants sued the tortfeasor driver's automobile insurer and the insurance agent. They claimed that the agent attempted to settle their wrongful death claim within hours of the accident, advising them that there was some liability insurance coverage available when there was more than $1.2 million in limits available, and by telling the claimant's attorney that only minimum coverage was available when the claim was ultimately settled for $500,000. At the time the settlement was effected, all parties were aware of the policy limit. The court held that such conduct does not constitute bad faith or a violation of the state Unfair Settlement Act.

PART II

State Regulation of Agent and Broker Qualifications

Chapter 1

NAIC Model Acts

1.1 Agents and Brokers Licensing Act

Page 262, change citation to D.C. Code Ann. in Table of Enactments and Related State Laws Governing Agent and Broker Licensing to § 35-1321 et seq.

Page 262, add at end of section:

1.1a Standard Letter of Clearance

NAIC has also created the following Standard Letter of Clearance to be used to verify the status of an agent's license in the agent's state of domicile when the agent seeks to be licensed as a registered agent in another state:

Model Regulation Service October 1994

NAIC Editor's Note: The Standard Letter of Clearance is to be used in verifying the status of an agent's license in his or her state of domicile when the agent is seeking to be licensed as a registered agent in a new state.

State of _____   2. Date: 00/00/0000
Department of Insurance   Page: 1
Licensing Unit

1. _____   RE: Certification of
    _____   Licensing Authority for:
    _____

3. To: Whom It May Concern   4. _____
    1 Main Street   _____
    Anywhere, U.S.A.   _____

5. The above names have qualified by A. _____ for the following lines of insurance:

	DATE ISSUED	EXPIRATION DATE
B. Life	00/00/0000	00/00/0000
Accident & Health	00/00/0000	00/00/0000
Variable Contract	00/00/0000	00/00/0000
Property	00/00/0000	00/00/0000
Casualty	00/00/0000	00/00/0000
Other	00/00/0000	00/00/0000

6. No regulatory action has been taken against the licensee.

7. Following is the current licensing record for the above named:

    A. 1. Not currently licensed as a broker.

    B. 2. Authorized member of the following firm(s):
            I.D.# _____ Firm Name: _____

    C. 3. Individual operating under the trade name(s):
            Name: _____

    D. 4. Individual has (not) met the prelicensing requirements of this state.

E. 5. Individual has (not) met the continuing education requirements of this state.

8. In testimony whereof, I _____, hereto set my hand at _____[City]_____, _____[State]_____ this ___[Date]___ day of ___[Month]___, 19__.

_____
Director of Insurance

Standard Letter of Clearance

INSTRUCTIONS FOR COMPLETING THE CLEARANCE

Area 1

Should contain the name of the state, the name of the department, commission, division, section, unit, etc., issuing the clearance and the address of the issuer of the clearance.

Area 2

Should contain the date the clearance is issued and a page number.

Area 3

Should contain the name and address of the person or entity to which the clearance is sent.

Area 4

Should identify the document and contain the identification number (social security number or tax identification number, if possible), name and address of the individual or entity whom the clearance is for.

Area 5

This area should contain:

A. The name of the state issuing the clearance.
B. The manner by which the individual qualified for licensure. Possibilities would include:

   1. Passing the department's written examination;
   2. Being licensed prior to qualification law;
   3. By certification from the State of [name of state];
   4. Exemption from examination which is not required for limited license;
   5. Holding a temporary license pending completion of examination;
   6. Holding a [CLU] [CPCU] designation;
   7. An optional plan approved by the state.

C. The line(s) of insurance for which the individual has qualified and the date of qualification for each. The general lines of insurance should be:

   1. Life
   2. Accident and Health
   3. Variable Contract
   4. Property
   5. Casualty

Types of Limited Licenses should be categorized under one of these general lines, and the Clearance would, for example, read as follows:

Life — Limited to Group Credit on 00/00/0000.
Casualty — Limited to Crop-Hail on 00/00/0000.

Area 6

Should either state "No regulatory action has been taken against the licensee" or "Regulatory action has been taken against the licensee."

Area 7

This area should include:

A. The date that the most recent license(s) held by the individual were canceled.
B. If an individual held both an agent and broker license, both should be listed with the various types of insurance directly below each. If either is not applicable to the individual or the state does not issue either, it should be noted by the word "NONE."

If the individual held a limited license, it should be so identified.

C. States which have prelicensing requirements should state either "Individual has met the prelicensing requirements of this state" or "Individual has not met the prelicensing requirements of this state." States which do not have prelicensing requirements or where such requirements are not applicable to the individual should state "Prelicensing requirements not applicable."

D. States which have continuing education requirements should state either "Individual has met the continuing education requirements of this state" or "Individual has not met the continuing education requirements of this state." States which do not have continuing education requirements or where such requirements are not applicable to the individual should state "Continuing education requirements not applicable."

Area 8

This area is self-explanatory.

1.2 Agents Continuing Education Regulation

Page 268, add the following to the Table of Enactments and Related State Laws Governing Continuing Education:

See also:

Alabama Code § 27-8A-1 et seq.
North Carolina Admin. Code tit. 11 ch. 6A § .0801 et seq.
North Dakota Admin. Code § 45-02-24.

Ohio Ins. Regs 3901-5-01

1.4 Producer Licensing Model Act

On January 27, 2000, the NAIC adopted the Producer Licensing Model Act in an attempt to achieve nationwide uniformity in licensing. The Act permits agents licensed in one or more states to receive licenses from other states via reciprocal agreements. The Act is particularly important considering the federal mandate that states adopt uniform licensing in order to deal with the growth in the financial services industry.

Table of Contents

Section 1.	Purpose and Scope
Section 2.	Definitions
Section 3.	License Required
Section 4.	Exceptions to Licensing
Section 5.	Application for Examination
Section 6.	Application for License
Section 7.	License

Section 8.   Nonresident Licensing
Section 9.   Exemption From Examination
Section 10. Assumed Names
Section 11. Temporary Licensing
Section 12. License Denial, Non-Renewal or Revocation
Section 13. Commissions
Section 14. Appointments [OPTIONAL]
Section 15. Notification to Insurance Commissioner of Termination
Section 16. Reciprocity
Section 17. Reporting of Actions
Section 18. Regulations
Section 19. Severability
Section 20. Effective Date

Section 1. Purpose and Scope

This Act governs the qualifications and procedures for the licensing of insurance producers. It simplifies and organizes some statutory language to improve efficiency, permits the use of new technology and reduces costs associated with issuing and renewing insurance licenses.

This Act does not apply to excess and surplus lines agents and brokers licensed pursuant to Section [refer to state excess and surplus lines statutes] except as provided in Section 8 and Section 16C of this Act.

Drafting Note: *It is recommended that any statute or regulation inconsistent with this Act be repealed or amended.*

Drafting Note: *This Act also requires a report to the insurance commissioner of the termination of a producer by an insurer, whether with or without cause.*

Section 2. Definitions

A. "Business entity" means a corporation, association, partnership, limited liability company, limited liability partnership, or other legal entity.

B. "Home state" means the District of Columbia and any state or territory of the United States in which an insurance producer maintains his or her principal place of residence or principal place of business and is licensed to act as an insurance producer.

C. "Insurance" means any of the lines of authority in [insert reference to appropriate section of state law].

D. "Insurance producer" means a person required to be licensed under the laws of this state to sell, solicit or negotiate insurance.

E. "Insurer" means [insert reference to appropriate section of state law].

F. "License" means a document issued by this state's insurance commissioner authorizing a person to act as an insurance producer for the lines of authority specified in the document. The license itself does not create any authority, actual, apparent or inherent, in the holder to represent or commit an insurance carrier.

G. "Limited line credit insurance" includes credit life, credit disability, credit property, credit unemployment, involuntary unemployment, mortgage life, mortgage guaranty, mortgage disability, automobile dealer gap insurance, and any other form of insurance offered in connection with an extension of credit that is limited to partially or wholly extinguishing that credit obligation that the insurance commissioner determines should be designated a form of limited line credit insurance.

H. "Limited line credit insurance producer" means a person who sells, solicits or negotiates one or more forms of limited line credit insurance coverage to individuals through a master, corporate, group or individual policy.

I. "Negotiate" means the act of conferring directly with or offering advice directly to a purchaser or prospective purchaser of a particular contract of insurance concerning any of the substantive benefits, terms or conditions of the contract, provided that the person engaged in that act either sells insurance or obtains insurance from insurers for purchasers.

J. "Person" means an individual or a business entity.

K. "Sell" means to exchange a contract of insurance by any means, for money or its equivalent, on behalf of an insurance company.

L. "Solicit" means attempting to sell insurance or asking or urging a person to apply for a particular kind of insurance from a particular company.

M. "Terminate" means the cancellation of the relationship between an insurance producer and the insurer or the termination of a producer's authority to transact insurance.

N. "Uniform Business Entity Application" means the current version of the NAIC Uniform Business Entity Application for resident and nonresident business entities.

O. "Uniform Application" means the current version of the NAIC Uniform Application for resident and nonresident producer licensing.

Section 3. License Required

A person shall not sell, solicit or negotiate insurance in this state for any class or classes of insurance unless the person is licensed for that line of authority in accordance with this Act.

Section 4. Exceptions to Licensing

A. Nothing in this Act shall be construed to require an insurer to obtain an insurance producer license. In this section, the term "insurer" does not include an insurer's officers, directors, employees, subsidiaries or affiliates.

B. A license as an insurance producer shall not be required of the following:

(1) An officer, director or employee of an insurer or of an insurance producer, provided that the officer, director or employee does not receive any commission on policies written or sold to insure risks residing, located or to be performed in this state and:

    (a) The officer, director or employee's activities are executive, administrative, managerial, clerical or a combination of these, and are only indirectly related to the sale, solicitation or negotiation of insurance; or

    (b) The officer, director or employee's function relates to underwriting, loss control, inspection or the processing, adjusting, investigating or settling of a claim on a contract of insurance; or

    (c) The officer, director or employee is acting in the capacity of a special agent or agency supervisor assisting insurance producers where the person's activities are limited to providing technical advice and assistance to licensed insurance producers and do not include the sale, solicitation or negotiation of insurance;

(2) A person who secures and furnishes information for the purpose of group life insurance, group property and casualty insurance, group annuities, group or blanket accident and health insurance; or for the purpose of enrolling individuals under plans; issuing certificates under plans or otherwise assisting in administering plans; or performs administrative services related to mass marketed property and casualty insurance; where no commission is paid to the person for the service;

(3) An employer or association or its officers, directors, employees, or the trustees of an employee trust plan, to

the extent that the employers, officers, employees, director or trustees are engaged in the administration or operation of a program of employee benefits for the employer's or association's own employees or the employees of its subsidiaries or affiliates, which program involves the use of insurance issued by an insurer, as long as the employers, associations, officers, directors, employees or trustees are not in any manner compensated, directly or indirectly, by the company issuing the contracts;

(4) Employees of insurers or organizations employed by insurers who are engaging in the inspection, rating or classification of risks, or in the supervision of the training of insurance producers and who are not individually engaged in the sale, solicitation or negotiation of insurance;

(5) A person whose activities in this state are limited to advertising without the intent to solicit insurance in this state through communications in printed publications or other forms of electronic mass media whose distribution is not limited to residents of the state, provided that the person does not sell, solicit or negotiate insurance that would insure risks residing, located or to be performed in this state;

(6) A person who is not a resident of this state who sells, solicits or negotiates a contract of insurance for commercial property and casualty risks to an insured with risks located in more than one state insured under that contract, provided that that person is otherwise licensed as an insurance producer to sell, solicit or negotiate that insurance in the state where the insured maintains its principal place of business and the contract of insurance insures risks located in that state;

(7) A salaried full-time employee who counsels or advises his or her employer relative to the insurance interests of the employer or of the subsidiaries or business affiliates of the employer provided that the employee

does not sell or solicit insurance or receive a commission; or

(8) Employees of an insurer or of an insurance producer who respond to requests from existing policyholders on existing policies provided that those employees are not directly compensated based on the volume of premiums that may result from these services and provided those employees do not otherwise sell, solicit or negotiate insurance.

Drafting Note: *Persons who provide general insurance advice in connection with providing other professional services such as legal services, trust services, tax and accounting services, financial planning and investment advisory services are not deemed to be soliciting the sale of insurance under this Act. Sections 3 and 4 of this Act are intended to address all persons meeting the definition of "insurance producer" as defined in Title III, Section 336, of Public Law No. 106-102 (the "Gramm-Leach-Bliley Act").*

Section 5. Application for Examination

A. A resident individual applying for an insurance producer license shall pass a written examination unless exempt pursuant to Section 9. The examination shall test the knowledge of the individual concerning the lines of authority for which application is made, the duties and responsibilities of an insurance producer and the insurance laws and regulations of this state. Examinations required by this section shall be developed and conducted under rules and regulations prescribed by the insurance commissioner.

B. The insurance commissioner may make arrangements, including contracting with an outside testing service, for administering examinations and collecting the nonrefundable fee set forth in [insert appropriate reference to state law or regulation].

C. Each individual applying for an examination shall remit a nonrefundable fee as prescribed by the insurance commissioner as set forth in [insert appropriate reference to state law or regulation].

D. An individual who fails to appear for the examination as scheduled or fails to pass the examination, shall reapply for an examination and remit all required fees and forms before being rescheduled for another examination.

Drafting Note: *A state may wish to prescribe by regulation limitations on the frequency of application for examination in addition to other prelicensing requirements.*

Section 6. Application for License

A. A person applying for a resident insurance producer license shall make application to the insurance commissioner on the Uniform Application and declare under penalty of refusal, suspension or revocation of the license that the statements made in the application are true, correct and complete to the best of the individual's knowledge and belief. Before approving the application, the insurance commissioner shall find that the individual:

(1) Is at least eighteen (18) years of age;

(2) Has not committed any act that is a ground for denial, suspension or revocation set forth in Section 12;

(3) Has completed a prelicensing course of study for the lines of authority for which the person has applied;

Drafting Note: *Paragraph (3) would apply only to those states that have prelicensing education requirements.*

(4) Has paid the fees set forth in [insert appropriate reference to state law or regulation]; and

(5) Has successfully passed the examinations for the lines of authority for which the person has applied.

B. A business entity acting as an insurance producer is required to obtain an insurance producer license. Application shall be made using the Uniform Business Entity Application. Before approving the application, the insurance commissioner shall find that:

(1) The business entity has paid the fees set forth in [insert appropriate reference to state law or regulation]; and

(2) The business entity has designated a licensed producer responsible for the business entity's compliance with the insurance laws, rules and regulations of this state.

Drafting Note: *Subsection B is optional and would apply only to those states that have a business entity license requirement.*

C. The insurance commissioner may require any documents reasonably necessary to verify the information contained in an application.

D. Each insurer that sells, solicits or negotiates any form of limited line credit insurance shall provide to each individual whose duties will include selling, soliciting or negotiating limited line credit insurance a program of instruction that is approved by the insurance commissioner.

Section 7. License

A. Unless denied licensure pursuant to Section 12, persons who have met the requirements of Sections 5 and 6 shall be issued an insurance producer license. An insurance producer may receive qualification for a license in one or more of the following lines of authority:

(1) Life–insurance coverage on human lives including benefits of endowment and annuities, and may include benefits in the event of death or dismemberment by accident and benefits for disability income.

(2) Accident and health or sickness–insurance coverage

for sickness, bodily injury or accidental death and may include benefits for disability income.

(3) Property—insurance coverage for the direct or consequential loss or damage to property of every kind.

(4) Casualty—insurance coverage against legal liability, including that for death, injury or disability or damage to real or personal property.

(5) Variable life and variable annuity products—insurance coverage provided under variable life insurance contracts, variable annuities or any other life insurance or annuity product that reflects the investment experience of a separate account.

(6) Credit—limited line credit insurance.

(7) Any other line of insurance permitted under state laws or regulations.

B. An insurance producer license shall remain in effect unless revoked or suspended as long as the fee set forth in [insert appropriate reference to state law or regulation] is paid and education requirements for resident individual producers are met by the due date.

C. An individual insurance producer who allows his or her license to lapse may, within twelve (12) months from the due date of the renewal fee, reinstate the same license without the necessity of passing a written examination. However, a penalty in the amount of double the unpaid renewal fee shall be required for any renewal fee received after the due date.

D. A licensed insurance producer who is unable to comply with license renewal procedures due to military service or some other extenuating circumstance (e.g., a long-term medical disability) may request a waiver of those procedures. The producer may also request a waiver of any examination requirement or any other fine or sanction imposed for failure to comply with renewal procedures.

Drafting Note: *References to license "renewal" should be deleted in those states that do not require license renewal.*

E. The license shall contain the licensee's name, address, personal identification number, and the date of issuance, the lines of authority, the expiration date and any other information the insurance commissioner deems necessary.

F. Licensees shall inform the insurance commissioner by any means acceptable to the insurance commissioner of a change of address within thirty (30) days of the change. Failure to timely inform the insurance commissioner of a change in legal name or address shall result in a penalty pursuant to [insert appropriate reference to sate law].

Section 8. Nonresident Licensing

A. Unless denied licensure pursuant to Section 12, a nonresident person shall receive a nonresident producer license if:

(1) The person is currently licensed as a resident and in good standing in his or her home state;

(2) The person has submitted the proper request for licensure and has paid the fees required by [insert appropriate reference to state law or regulation];

(3) The person has submitted or transmitted to the insurance commissioner the application for licensure that the person submitted to his or her home state, or in lieu of the same, a completed Uniform Application; and

(4) The person's home state awards non-resident producer licenses to residents of this state on the same basis.

Drafting Note: *In accordance with Public Law No. 106-102 (the "Gramm-Leach-Bliley Act") states should not require any* *additional attachments to the Uniform Application or impose any other conditions on applicants that exceed the information requested within the Uniform Application.*

B. The insurance commissioner may verify the producer's licensing status through the Producer Database maintained by the National Association of Insurance Commissioners, its affiliates or subsidiaries.

C. A nonresident producer who moves from one state to another state or a resident producer who moves from this state to another state shall file a change of address and provide certification from the new resident state within thirty (30) days of the change of legal residence. No fee or license application is required.

D. Notwithstanding any other provision of this Act, a person licensed as a surplus lines producer in his or her home state shall receive a nonresident surplus lines producer license pursuant to Subsection A of this section. Except as to Subsection A, nothing in this section otherwise amends or supercedes any provision of [refer to state excess and surplus lines statutes].

E. Notwithstanding any other provision of this Act, a person licensed as a limited line credit insurance or other type of limited lines producer in his or her home state shall receive a nonresident limited lines producer license, pursuant to Subsection A of this section, granting the same scope of authority as granted under the license issued by the producer's home state.

Section 9. Exemption from Examination

A. An individual who applies for an insurance producer license in this state who was previously licensed for the same lines of authority in another state shall not be required to complete any prelicensing education or examination. This exemption is only available if the person is currently licensed in that state or if the application is received within ninety (90) days of the cancellation of the applicant's previous license and if the prior state issues a certification that, at the time of cancellation, the applicant was in good standing in that state or the state's Producer Database records, maintained by the National Association of Insurance Commissioners, its affiliates or subsidiaries, indicate that the producer is or was licensed in good standing for the line of authority requested.

B. A person licensed as an insurance producer in another state who moves to this state shall make application within ninety (90) days of establishing legal residence to become a resident licensee pursuant to Section 6. No prelicensing education or examination shall be required of that person to obtain any line of authority previously held in the prior state except where the insurance commissioner determines otherwise by regulation.

Section 10. Assumed Names

An insurance producer doing business under any name other than the producer's legal name is required to notify the insurance commissioner prior to using the assumed name.

Section 11. Temporary Licensing

A. The insurance commissioner may issue a temporary insurance producer license for a period not to exceed one hundred eighty (180) days without requiring an examination if the insurance commissioner deems that the temporary license is necessary for the servicing of an insurance business in the following cases:

(1) To the surviving spouse or court-appointed personal representative of a licensed insurance producer who dies or becomes mentally or physically disabled to allow adequate time for the sale of the insurance business owned by the producer or for the recovery or return of the producer to the business or to provide for the training and licensing of new personnel to operate the producer's business;

(2) To a member or employee of a business entity licensed as an insurance producer, upon the death or disability of an individual designated in the business entity application or the license;

(3) To the designee of a licensed insurance producer entering active service in the armed forces of the United States of America; or

(4) In any other circumstance where the insurance commissioner deems that the public interest will best be served by the issuance of this license.

B. The insurance commissioner may by order limit the authority of any temporary licensee in any way deemed necessary to protect insureds and the public. The insurance commissioner may require the temporary licensee to have a suitable sponsor who is a licensed producer or insurer and who assumes responsibility for all acts of the temporary licensee and may impose other similar requirements designed to protect insureds and the public. The insurance commissioner may by order revoke a temporary license if the interest of insureds or the public are endangered. A temporary license may not continue after the owner or the personal representative disposes of the business.

Section 12. License Denial, Nonrenewal or Revocation

A. The insurance commissioner may place on probation, suspend, revoke or refuse to issue or renew an insurance producer's license or may levy a civil penalty in accordance with [insert appropriate reference to state law] or any combination of actions, for any one or more of the following causes:

(1) Providing incorrect, misleading, incomplete or materially untrue information in the license application;

(2) Violating any insurance laws, or violating any regulation, subpoena or order of the insurance commissioner or of another state's insurance commissioner;

(3) Obtaining or attempting to obtain a license through misrepresentation or fraud;

(4) Improperly withholding, misappropriating or converting any monies or properties received in the course of doing insurance business;

(5) Intentionally misrepresenting the terms of an actual or proposed insurance contract or application for insurance;

(6) Having been convicted of a felony;

(7) Having admitted or been found to have committed any insurance unfair trade practice or fraud;

(8) Using fraudulent, coercive, or dishonest practices, or demonstrating incompetence, untrustworthiness or financial irresponsibility in the conduct of business in this state or elsewhere;

(9) Having an insurance producer license, or its equivalent, denied, suspended or revoked in any other state, province, district or territory;

(10) Forging another's name to an application for insurance or to any document related to an insurance transaction;

(11) Improperly using notes or any other reference material to complete an examination for an insurance license;

(12) Knowingly accepting insurance business from an individual who is not licensed;

(13) Failing to comply with an administrative or court order imposing a child support obligation; or

(14) Failing to pay state income tax or comply with any administrative or court order directing payment of state income tax.

Drafting Note: Paragraph (14) is for those states that have a state income tax.

B. In the event that the action by the insurance commissioner is to nonrenew or to deny an application for a license, the insurance commissioner shall notify the applicant or licensee and advise, in writing, the applicant or licensee of the reason for the denial or nonrenewal of the applicant's or licensee's license. The applicant or licensee may make written demand upon the insurance commissioner within [insert appropriate time period from state's administrative procedure act] for a hearing before the insurance commissioner to determine the reasonableness of the insurance commissioner's action. The hearing shall be held within [insert time period from state law] and shall be held pursuant to [insert appropriate reference to state law].

C. The license of a business entity may be suspended, revoked or refused if the insurance commissioner finds, after hearing, that an individual licensee's violation was known or should have been known by one or more of the partners, officers or managers acting on behalf of the partnership or corporation and the violation was neither reported to the insurance commissioner nor corrective action taken.

D. In addition to or in lieu of any applicable denial, suspension or revocation of a license, a person may, after hearing, be subject to a civil fine according to [insert appropriate reference to state law].

E. The insurance commissioner shall retain the authority to enforce the provisions of and impose any penalty or remedy authorized by this Act and Title [insert appropriate reference to state law] against any person who is under investigation for or charged with a violation of this Act or Title [insert appropriate reference to state law] even if the person's license or registration has been surrendered or has lapsed by operation of law.

Section 13. Commissions

A. An insurance company or insurance producer shall not pay a commission, service fee, brokerage or other valuable consideration to a person for selling, soliciting or negotiating insurance in this state if that person is required to be licensed under this Act and is not so licensed.

B. A person shall not accept a commission, service fee, brokerage or other valuable consideration for selling, soliciting or negotiating insurance in this state if that person is required to be licensed under this Act and is not so licensed.

C. Renewal or other deferred commissions may be paid to a person for selling, soliciting or negotiating insurance in this state if the person was required to be licensed under this Act at the time of the sale, solicitation or negotiation and was so licensed at that time.

D. An insurer or insurance producer may pay or assign commissions, service fees, brokerages or other valuable consideration to an insurance agency or to persons who do not sell, solicit or negotiate insurance in this state, unless the payment would violate [insert appropriate reference to state law, i.e. citation to anti-rebating statute, if applicable].

Section 14. Appointments [Optional]

A. An insurance producer shall not act as an agent of an insurer unless the insurance producer becomes an appointed agent of that insurer. An insurance producer who is not acting as an agent of an insurer is not required to become appointed.

B. To appoint a producer as its agent, the appointing insurer shall file, in a format approved by the insurance commissioner, a notice of appointment within fifteen (15) days from the date the agency contract is executed or the first insurance application is submitted. An insurer may also elect to appoint a producer to all or some insurers within the insurer's holding company system or group by the filing of a single appointment request.

Drafting Note: *The group appointment provision of Subsection B is only applicable in jurisdictions that have implemented an electronic appointment process.*

C. [Optional] Upon receipt of the notice of appointment, the insurance commissioner shall verify within a reasonable time not to exceed thirty (30) days that the insurance producer is eligible for appointment. If the insurance producer is determined to be ineligible for appointment, the insurance commissioner shall notify the insurer within five (5) days of its determination.

D. An insurer shall pay an appointment fee, in the amount and method of payment set forth in [insert appropriate reference to state law or regulation], for each insurance producer appointed by the insurer.

E. [Optional] An insurer shall remit, in a manner prescribed by the insurance commissioner, a renewal appointment fee in the amount set forth in [insert appropriate reference to state law or regulation].

Drafting Note: *This act designates as optional the section on appointments of producers by insurers. That designation recognizes that some states do not require the formal appointment of a producer before business can be conducted with an insurer or multiple insurers.*

Section 15. Notification to Insurance Commissioner of Termination

A. Termination for Cause. An insurer or authorized representative of the insurer that terminates the appointment, employment, contract or other insurance business relationship with a producer shall notify the insurance commissioner within thirty (30) days following the effective date of the termination, using a format prescribed by the insurance commissioner, if the reason for termination is one of the reasons set forth in Section 12 or the insurer has knowledge the producer was found by a court, government body, or self-regulatory organization authorized by law to have engaged in any of the activities in Section 12. Upon the written request of the insurance commissioner, the insurer shall provide additional information, documents, records or other data pertaining to the termination or activity of the producer.

B. Termination Without Cause. An insurer or authorized representative of the insurer that terminates the appointment, employment, or contract with a producer for any reason not set forth in Section 12, shall notify the insurance commissioner within thirty (30) days following the effective date of the termination, using a format prescribed by the insurance commissioner. Upon written request of the insurance commissioner, the insurer shall provide additional information, documents, records or other data pertaining to the termination.

Drafting Note: *Those states that do not require formal appointments may delete any reference to appointments in Subsections A and B above.*

C. Ongoing Notification Requirement. The insurer or the authorized representative of the insurer shall promptly notify the insurance commissioner in a format acceptable to the insurance commissioner if, upon further review or investigation, the insurer discovers additional information that would have been reportable to the insurance commissioner in accordance with Subsection A had the insurer then known of its existence.

D. Copy of Notification to be Provided to Producer.

 (1) Within fifteen (15) days after making the notification required by Subsections A, B and C, the insurer shall mail a copy of the notification to the producer at his or her last known address. If the producer is terminated for cause for any of the reasons listed in Section 12, the insurer shall provide a copy of the notification to the producer at his or her last known address by certified mail, return receipt requested, postage prepaid or by overnight delivery using a nationally recognized carrier.

(2) Within thirty (30) days after the producer has received the original or additional notification, the producer may file written comments concerning the substance of the notification with the insurance commissioner. The producer shall, by the same means, simultaneously send a copy of the comments to the reporting insurer, and the comments shall become a part of the insurance commissioner's file and accompany every copy of a report distributed or disclosed for any reason about the producer as permitted under Subsection F.

E. Immunities

(1) In the absence of actual malice, an insurer, the authorized representative of the insurer, a producer, the insurance commissioner, or an organization of which the insurance commissioner is a member and that compiles the information and makes it available to other insurance commissioners or regulatory or law enforcement agencies shall not be subject to civil liability, and a civil cause of action of any nature shall not arise against these entities or their respective agents or employees, as a result of any statement or information required by or provided pursuant to this section or any information relating to any statement that may be requested in writing by the insurance commissioner, from an insurer or producer; or a statement by a terminating insurer or producer to an insurer or producer limited solely and exclusively to whether a termination for cause under Subsection A was reported to the insurance commissioner, provided that the propriety of any termination for cause under Subsection A is certified in writing by an officer or authorized representative of the insurer or producer terminating the relationship.

(2) In any action brought against a person that may have immunity under Paragraph (1) for making any statement required by this section or providing any information relating to any statement that may be re-

quested by the insurance commissioner, the party bringing the action shall plead specifically in any allegation that Paragraph (1) does not apply because the person making the statement or providing the information did so with actual malice.

(3) Paragraph (1) or (2) shall not abrogate or modify any existing statutory or common law privileges or immunities.

F. Confidentiality

(1) Any documents, materials or other information in the control or possession of the department of insurance that is furnished by an insurer, producer or an employee or agent thereof acting on behalf of the insurer or producer, or obtained by the insurance commissioner in an investigation pursuant to this section shall be confidential by law and privileged, shall not be subject to [insert open records, freedom of information, sunshine or other appropriate phrase], shall not be subject to subpoena, and shall not be subject to discovery or admissible in evidence in any private civil action. However, the insurance commissioner is authorized to use the documents, materials or other information in the furtherance of any regulatory or legal action brought as a part of the insurance commissioner's duties.

(2) Neither the insurance commissioner nor any person who received documents, materials or other information while acting under the authority of the insurance commissioner shall be permitted or required to testify in any private civil action concerning any confidential documents, materials, or information subject to Paragraph (1).

(3) In order to assist in the performance of the insurance commissioner's duties under this Act, the insurance commissioner:

(a) May share documents, materials or other information, including the confidential and privileged documents, materials or information subject to Paragraph (1), with other state, federal, and international regulatory agencies, with the National Association of Insurance Commissioners, its affiliates or subsidiaries, and with state, federal, and international law enforcement authorities, provided that the recipient agrees to maintain the confidentiality and privileged status of the document, material or other information;

(b) May receive documents, materials or information, including otherwise confidential and privileged documents, materials or information, from the National Association of Insurance Commissioners, its affiliates or subsidiaries and from regulatory and law enforcement officials of other foreign or domestic jurisdictions, and shall maintain as confidential or privileged any document, material or information received with notice or the understanding that it is confidential or privileged under the laws of the jurisdiction that is the source of the document, material or information; and

(c) [OPTIONAL] May enter into agreements governing sharing and use of information consistent with this subsection.

Drafting Note: *The language in Paragraph 3(a) assumes the recipient has the authority to protect the applicable confidentiality or privilege, but does not address the verification of that authority, which would presumably occur in the context of a broader information sharing agreement.*

(4) No waiver of any applicable privilege or claim of confidentiality in the documents, materials, or information shall occur as a result of disclosure to the commissioner under this section or as a result of sharing as authorized in Paragraph (3).

(5) Nothing in this Act shall prohibit the insurance commissioner from releasing final, adjudicated actions including for cause terminations that are open to public inspection pursuant to [insert appropriate reference to state law] to a database or other clearinghouse service maintained by the National Association of Insurance Commissioners, its affiliates or subsidiaries of the National Association of Insurance Commissioners.

G. Penalties for Failing to Report. An insurer, the authorized representative of the insurer, or producer that fails to report as required under the provisions of this section or that is found to have reported with actual malice by a court of competent jurisdiction may, after notice and hearing, have its license or certificate of authority suspended or revoked and may be fined in accordance with [insert appropriate reference to state law].

Section 16. Reciprocity

A. The insurance commissioner shall not assess a greater fee for an insurance license or related service to a person not residing in this state based solely on the fact that the person does not reside in this state.

B. The insurance commissioner shall waive any license application requirements for a nonresident license applicant with a valid license from his or her home state, except the requirements imposed by Section 8 of this Act, if the applicant's home state awards nonresident licenses to residents of this state on the same basis.

C. A nonresident producer's satisfaction of his or her home state's continuing education requirements for licensed insurance producers shall constitute satisfaction of this state's continuing education requirements if the non-resident producer's home state recognizes the satisfaction of its continuing education requirements imposed upon producers from this state on the same basis.

Section 17. Reporting of Actions

A. A producer shall report to the insurance commissioner any administrative action taken against the producer in another jurisdiction or by another governmental agency in this state within thirty (30) days of the final disposition of the matter. This report shall include a copy of the order, consent to order or other relevant legal documents.

B. Within thirty (30) days of the initial pretrial hearing date, a producer shall report to the insurance commissioner any criminal prosecution of the producer taken in any jurisdiction. The report shall include a copy of the initial complaint filed, the order resulting from the hearing and any other relevant legal documents.

Section 18. Regulations

The insurance commissioner may, in accordance with [insert appropriate reference to state law], promulgate reasonable regulations as are necessary or proper to carry out the purposes of this Act.

Section 19. Severability

If any provisions of this Act, or the application of a provision to any person or circumstances, shall be held invalid, the remainder of the Act, and the application of the provision to persons or circumstances other than those to which it is held invalid, shall not be affected.

Section 20. Effective Date

This Act shall take effect [insert date].

Drafting Note: *A minimum of six months to one year implementation time for proper notice of changes, fees and procedures is recommended.*

Chapter 2

State Guide

2.1 State Insurance Commissioners

AL Comm. of Ins., 135 S. Union, Montgomery, AL 36130. 334/269-3550.

AK Dir. of Ins., P.O. Box 110805, Juneau, AK 99811-0805. 907/465-2515.

AZ Dir. of Ins., 2910 North 44th St., Ste. 210, Phoenix, AZ 85018-7256. 602/912-8400.

AR Ins. Comm., 1200 West Third St., Little Rock, AR 72201-1904. 501/371-2600.

CA Comm. of Ins., 300 Capitol Mall, Ste. 1500, Sacramento, CA 95814. 916/445-5544.

CO Comm. of Ins., 1560 Broadway, Ste. 850, Denver, CO 80202. 303/894-7499.

CT Comm. of Ins., P.O. Box 816, Hartford, CT 06142-0816. 860/297-3802.

DE Ins. Comm., P.O. Box 7007, 841 Silver Lake Blvd., Dover, DE 19903-1507. 302/739-4251.

DC Comm. of Ins., 441 4th St., N.W., 8th Floor N., Washington, DC 20001. 202/727-8000.

FL Ins. Comm., 200 E. Gaines St., Tallahassee, FL 32399-0300. 904/922-3100.

GA Ins. Comm., 2 ML King, Jr. Dr., Ste. 716, Atlanta, GA 30334. 404/656-2056.

HI Ins. Comm., P.O. Box 3614, Honolulu, HI 96811-3614. 808/586-2790.

ID Dir. of Ins., 700 W. State St., Third Fl., P.O. Box 83720, Boise, ID 83720-0043. 208/334-4250.

IL Dir. of Ins., 320 W. Washington St., Springfield, IL 62767. 217/782-4515.

IN Comm. of Ins., 311 W. Washington St., Ste. 300, Indianapolis, IN 46204-2787. 317/232-2385.

IA Comm. of Ins., Lucas State Office Bldg., 6th Fl., Des Moines, IA 50319. 515/281-5705.

KS Comm. of Ins., 420 S.W. 9th St., Topeka, KS 66612-1678. 913/296-3071.

KY Ins. Comm., P.O. Box 517, 215 W. Main St., Frankfort, KY 40602. 502/564-6027.

LA Comm. of Ins., P.O. Box 94214, Baton Rouge, LA 70804-9214. 504/342-5900.

ME Sup. of Ins., 34 State House Station, Augusta, ME 04333-0034. 207/624-8475.

MD Ins. Comm., 501 St. Paul Place, Baltimore, MD 21202-2272. 410/333-2521.

MA Comm. of Ins., 470 Atlantic Ave., 6th Fl., Boston, MA 02210. 617/521-7794.

MI Comm. of Ins., P.O. Box 30220, Lansing, MI 48909-7720. 517/373-9273.

MN Comm. of Commerce, 133 E. 7th St., St. Paul, MN 55101. 612/296-6848.

MS Comm. of Ins., P.O. Box 79, Jackson, MS 39205. 601/359-3569.

MO Dir. of Ins., P.O. Box 690, Jefferson City, MO 65102-0690. 573/751-4126.

MT Comm. of Ins., 126 N. Sanders, Mitchell Bldg., P.O. Box 4009, Helena, MT 59601-4009. 406/444-2040.

NE Dir. of Ins., Terminal Bldg., 941 O St., Ste. 400, Lincoln, NE 68508. 402/471-2201.

NV Comm. of Ins., Capitol Complex, Carson City, NV 89710. 702/687-4270.

NH Ins. Comm., 169 Manchester St., Concord, NH 03301-5151. 603/271-2261.

NJ Comm. of Ins., 20 W. State St., CN325, Trenton, NJ 08625. 609/292-5363.

NM Sup. of Ins., P.O. Drawer 1269, Santa Fe, NM 87504-1269. 505/827-4601.

NY Sup. of Ins., 160 W. Broadway, New York, NY 10013. 212/602-0429.

NC Comm. of Ins., P.O. Box 26387, Raleigh, NC 27611. 919/733-7349.

ND Comm. of Ins., 600 East Blvd., Bismarck, ND 58505-0320. 701/328-2440.

OH Dir. of Ins., 2100 Stella Court, Columbus, OH 43215-1067. 614/644-2658.

OK Ins. Comm., P.O. Box 53408, Oklahoma City, OK 73152-3408. 405/521-2828.

OR Ins. Comm., 350 Winter St., N.E., Salem, OR 97310. 503/378-4120.

PA Ins. Comm., 1326 Strawberry Sq., 13th Fl., Harrisburg, PA 17120. 717/783-0442.

RI Ins. Comm., 233 Richmond St., Ste. 233, Providence RI 02903-4233. 401/277-2223.

SC Ins. Comm., 1612 Marion St., P.O. Box 100105, Columbia, SC 29202-3105. 803/737-6160

SD Dir. of Ins., Dept. of Commerce and Regulation, 500 E. Capitol Ave., Pierre, SD 57501-3940. 605/773-3563.

TN Comm. of Ins., 500 James Robertson Pkwy., Nashville, TN 37243-0565. 615/741-2241.

TX Comm. of Ins., P.O. Box 149104, Austin, TX 78714-9104. 512/463-6169.

UT Comm. of Ins., State Office Bldg., Room 3110, Salt Lake City, UT 84114-1201. 801/538-3800.

VT Comm. of Ins., 89 Main St., Drawer 20, Montpelier, VT 05620-3101. 802/828-3301.

VA Comm. of Ins., P.O. Box 1157, Richmond, VA 23218. 804/371-9694.

WA Ins. Comm., P.O. Box 40255, Olympia, WA 98504-0255. 360/753-7300.

WV Ins. Comm., 2019 Washington St. East, P.O. Box 50540, Charleston, WV 25305-0540. 304/558-3354.

WI Comm. of Ins., P.O. Box 7873, Madison, WI 53707-7873. 608/266-3585

WY Ins. Comm., Herschler Bldg., 3 East, 122 W. 25th St., Cheyenne, WY 82002-0440. 307/777-7401.

2.2 Excerpts From Licensing Statutes (Alphabetical by State)

Colorado

Page 299, add at end of page:

The following provisions took effect January 1, 1995:

§ 10-2-101. Short title.... "Colorado Single Insurance Producer Licensing Act."

§ 10-2-102. Scope — applicability. This article governs the qualifications and procedures for licensing insurance producers. This article applies to any and all lines of insurance and types of insurers, including but not limited to life, sickness and accident, property, casualty, credit, or title operating on a stock, reciprocal, fraternal plan, mutual, or other legal organizational structure.

§ 10-2-105. Insurance producer — exemption from definition.... "[I]nsurance producer" does not include the following:

(a) A regularly salaried officer or employee of an insurance company...who is engaged in the performance of usual or customary executive, administrative, or clerical duties which do not include the negotiation or solicitation of insurance;

(b) Any...salaried employee in the office of an insurance producer and who devotes full time to clerical and administrative services, including the incidental taking of insurance applications and receipt of premiums...as long as the person does not receive any commission on such applications and the person's compensation is not varied by the volume of applications or premiums...

(c) Any person who, without earning a commission for such services, secures and furnishes information for the purpose of:

(I) Group life insurance, annuities, or group or blanket health coverage, or for the purpose of enrolling individuals under such plans; or

(II) Issuing certificates under group life insurance, annuities, or group or blanket health coverage, or otherwise assisting in administering such plans;

(d) Employers or their officers or employees, or the trustees of any employee trust plan, to the extent that [they] are engaged in the administration or operation of any program of employee benefits for their own employees or the employees of their subsidiaries or affiliates, which program involves the use of insurance issued by an insurance company; except that [they] shall not in any manner be compensated, directly or indirectly, by the company issuing the contracts;

(e) Employees of insurance companies or organizations employed by insurance companies who are engaging in the inspection, rating, or classification of risks or in the supervision of the training of insurance producers and who are not individually engaged in the solicitation or negotiation of policies or contracts for insurance; or

(f) Management associations, partnerships, or corporations whose operations do not entail solicitation of insurance from the public.

Prelicensure Education

§ 10-2-201. Prelicensure education — when required. (a) Except as otherwise provided in § 10-2-202, in addition to other requirements...an individual applicant for qualification in life, sickness and accident, or property and casualty lines shall be required to provide evidence to the commissioner that the individual applicant has satisfactorily completed an approved prelicensure education or training course...:

(I)...[A]t least fifty hours of an approved course or program for certification in life insurance;...[of which] at least three hours shall pertain specifically to insurance industry ethics;

(II)...[A]t least fifty hours of an approved course or program for certification in sickness and accident insurance;...[of which] at least three hours shall pertain specifically to insurance industry ethics;

(III)...[A]t least fifty hours of an approved course or program for certification in property or casualty insurance or both;...[of which] at least three hours shall pertain specifically to insurance industry ethics.

(b) An individual seeking an insurance producer license to include life, sickness and accident, property, or casualty lines or any combination thereof shall not be eligible to take the written examination provided for in section 10-2-402 until the pre-licensure education requirements...have been satisfied.

(2) The commissioner shall adopt all rules necessary to carry out the prelicensing education provisions...

(3) An individual seeking an insurance producer license shall pay to the commissioner, in addition to any other applicable fees or charges, a fee established by the commissioner...for operation of the prelicensing education program.

§ 10-2-202. Exemption from prelicensure education requirements.

(1) Prelicensure education ...shall not be required of an individual who is:

(a) Applying to reinstate a canceled or expired resident insurance producer license in this state when such license has been inactive for one year or less;

(b) Applying for temporary license authority under section 10-2-410;

(c) Applying for a resident insurance producer license...[if] previously licensed in his or her former resident state, and has completed or satisfied pre-licensure education as required by that state pertinent to the line or lines of insurance applied for in this state.

(d) Applying for a nonresident license...and has been licensed in his or her resident state for at least one year or has completed or satisfied pre-licensure education requirements in his or her home state pertinent to the line or lines of insurance applied for in this state.

Continuing Education

§ 10-2-301. Continuing education requirement — advisory committee.

(1) Producers...shall satis-factorily complete up to twenty-four hours of instruction...within twenty-four months after the date the producer's license is required to be renewed.... If a producer has more than one license...the required hours of instruction shall be completed within twenty-four months after the date the first such license is required to be renewed....An instructor...shall qualify for the same number of hours of continuing education as a person attending and successfully completing the course...but no instructor shall receive credit more than once...during the twenty-four-month period...

(2) Any producer who is subject to the requirements of this section shall furnish...written proof of compliance...The requirements of this section are mandatory for any person specified in subsection (3) (a) of this section, and if any such person holds more than one license..., such person shall be required to complete the hours of instruction required under this section only once....

(3) (a)...[T]his section shall apply to any resident or nonresident person licensed to solicit and sell...Life insurance and

annuity contracts, including variable life and annuity contracts; sickness, accident and health insurance; property and casualty insurance; and any other type of insurance for which the state requires an examination for licensure.

(b) This section shall not apply to any person holding a limited or restricted license which the commissioner determines to be exempt..., nor shall it apply to a nonresident who complies with the continuing education requirements of his or her state of residence, if the insurance commission of such state and the insurance division of this state have in effect a reciprocity agreement... ...

(5) Any person who fails to comply with the requirements of this section or is found...to have submitted a false or fraudulent certificate of compliance...shall have his or her license suspended until such person satisfactorily demonstrates to the commissioner that all of the requirements of this section, and any other applicable licensing requirement or other statute, has [sic] been met.

(6) (a) The commissioner shall be responsible for administering the continuing insurance education requirements...For persons licensed pursuant to section 10-11-116 (1) (c), C.R.S., compliance with the continuing legal education credits requirements of the Colorado supreme court shall be deemed to meet the requirements of this section.

(b) [Commissioner shall establish position of continuing education administrator either within the division of insurance or by contract with an outside service provider.]

(c) Each producer shall be responsible for paying...a reasonable biennial fee for the operation of the continuing insurance education program...

(7) (a) There is hereby established an advisory committee to the commissioner for the purpose of making recommendations ... pursuant to the provisions of this section....Members of the advisory committee shall serve on a voluntary basis and shall serve without compensation.

(b) [Provisions for review and termination of advisory committee]

Licensing and Appointment of Insurance Producers

§ 10-2-401. License required.

(1) No person shall act as or hold oneself out to be an insurance producer unless duly licensed... Every insurance producer who solicits or negotiates an application for insurance of any kind on behalf of an insurer shall be regarded as representing the insurer and not the in-

Colorado

sured or any beneficiary of the insured in any controversy between the insurer and such insured or beneficiary.

(2) No insurance producer shall make application for, procure, negotiate for, or place for others any policies for any line or lines of insurance for which he or she is not then qualified and licensed.

(3) (a) Any representative of a fraternal benefit society who solicits and negotiates insurance contracts is an insurance producer and is subject to the same licensing requirements…; except that a license is not required of any officer, employee, or secretary…who devotes substantially all of his or her time to activities other than…insurance contracts and who receives no commission or other compensation directly dependent upon the…insurance contracts….

(b) Any agent, representative, or member of a fraternal benefit society who in the preceding calendar year solicited and procured life insurance contracts on behalf of any society…not exceeding fifty thousand dollars or, in the case of any other kind of insurance,…on behalf of not more than twenty-five individuals, who received no commissions or other compensation therefor, and who does not reasonably expect to exceed soliciting or procuring insurance on behalf of more than twenty-five individuals in the current year, shall be exempt….

(4) No insurance producer license shall be granted or extended to any person…for the purpose of writing controlled business…. [Defined as] insurance procured or to be procured by or through such person upon:

(a) The person's own life, person, property, or risks, or those of his or her spouse; or

(b) The life, person, property, or risks of the person's employer or the person's own business.

(5) Such a license shall be deemed to have been…for the purpose of writing controlled business, if during any twelve-month period the aggregate amount of premiums on controlled business would exceed the aggregate amount of premiums on all other insurance business of the applicant or licensee.

§ 10-2-406. Licensing of agencies. (1) For the purposes set forth in section 10-2-701, an insurance agency shall be licensed as an insurance producer.

(2) (a) The insurance agency shall register the name of every natural person who…is acting as and is licensed as an insurance producer.

(b) A fee…in accordance with § 10-2-413, shall be paid for the registration of each insurance producer.

(3) The insurance agency shall, within ten days, notify the commissioner...of every change relative to [its] licensed individual insurance producers....

(4) The insurance agency shall, within ten days, notify the commissioner...of any change relative to the agency name, officers, directors, partners, or owners, to report a merger or that the agency has ceased doing business in this state.

(5) When an insurance agency ceases to do business in this state, the agency shall return the producer license to the commissioner within ten days after ceasing to do business.

(6) When an insurance agency changes its principal address to another state, the agency shall, within ten days, notify the commissioner and return the producer license for cancellation....

(7) (a) The insurance agency shall comply with § 10-2-404.

(b) A nonresident insurance agency shall also comply with...§ 10-2-501.

§ 10-2-408. License — contents — continuation due date - bond.

(1) The commissioner shall issue a perpetual insurance producer license to an applicant. ...

(4) Subject to continuation, each insurance producer license shall remain in effect unless revoked or suspended as long as the continuation fee...is paid and education requirements are met on or before the due date.

(5) The commissioner shall establish, by rule, the continuation due date and application procedures for continuation...

(6) Any...resident of the state... [who] holds a Colorado insurance producer license and is deemed by the commissioner to be competent and trustworthy may be licensed as a surplus line producer.... [T]he applicant shall file with the commissioner and thereafter...keep in force, evidence of a savings account, deposit, or certificate of deposit meeting the requirements of section 11-35-101,...or a bond in favor of the state...in the penal sum of fifteen hundred dollars, with authorized corporate sureties.... No such bond shall be terminated unless written notice thereof is filed with the commissioner at least thirty days prior to the specified date of termination.

§ 10-2-415. Appointment of insurance producer by insurer continuation exceptions.

(1) No insurance producer shall claim to be a representative or authorized or appointed agent of, or any other term implying a contractual relationship with, a particular insurer or accept applications on behalf of such insurer unless such insurance producer becomes a producer appointee, appointed...to act in the

capacity of an agent of that insurer.

(2) (a)...Each insurer shall keep on file with the commissioner a current list of insurance producers...[and] a list of new appointments of insurance producers...submitted...monthly or at such other intervals as the commissioner may prescribe....

(b) Subject to continuation or renewal, each insurance producer appointment shall remain in effect until:

(I) The insurance producer's license is discontinued or canceled...or revoked..

(II) Notice of termination of the appointment is filed with the commissioner by the insurer.

(3) Each active insurance producer appointment shall be subject to continuation or renewal effective October 1 of the [renewal] year.... A computer list of active insurance producer appointees shall be produced by the commissioner and furnished to the insurer along with a renewal invoice....

(4) Any appointment which is not continued on or before October 1 shall be deemed to have expired or discontinued effective on that date.

(5) The commissioner may, on or before October 31 of any year, continue or renew the appointments of an insurer who has failed to pay...by October 1 upon receipt of the...invoice together with the...fees due and...late penalty fee.

(6) Notwithstanding any provision of subsections (1) to (5)...:

(a) An insurance producer may show the benefits, rates, and features of insurance products of companies by which the producer has not been appointed.

(b) If an insurance producer who seeks to place a risk or policy which the company appointing the producer cannot accept..., the producer may place such risk in another company doing the same type of business without being appointed...; except that no insurer shall be required to accept a risk from a producer with whom the insurer does not have a contractual relationship. Nothing in this paragraph (b) shall be deemed to supersede any provision contained in a contract between a producer and a company.

§ 10-2-416. Termination of appointment — notice.

(1) Upon termination of the agent appoint-ment...the insurer shall notify the commissioner and the appointee of such termination within fifteen days. The commissioner may require the insurer to demonstrate that the insurer has made a reasonable effort to give such notice....

(2) In the event the termination is for any of the causes listed under § 10-2704, the insurer shall notify the commissioner of the reason and if the commissioner so requests, the insurer shall provide

any information...which may be used by the division...in any action taken pursuant to § 10-2-801.

(3) Any information...provided pursuant to this section shall be privileged, and there shall be no liability on the part of, nor shall a cause of action of any nature arise against, the division of insurance, the insurance company, or any authorized representative of either.

(4) In addition to any other penalty or liability...the failure or refusal of any insurer to comply with...subsection (1) or (2)...shall be cause for the assessment against the insurer of a civil penalty of one thousand dollars for each such failure or refusal.

Connecticut

Page 300, add at top of page:

Conn. Gen. Stat. § 38a.702, 704, 706, 707, 711, 712, 715, 716, and 717 have been amended effective January 1, 1996 and at that time will provide as follows:

Definitions...In sections 38a-703 to 38a-706, inclusive, 38a-769, 38a-774 and 38a775, unless the context or subject matter otherwise requires:

(1) "Insurance producer" or "producer" means any person, partnership, association or corporation, or any person, partnership, association or corporation acting under a trade name, or any member, stockholder, officer or employee of such an entity, holding a producer's license then in force in this state, and which, for compensation, aids in any manner or acts as a representative on behalf of an insured or client, and who solicits and negotiates coverage of insurance for the public without an agreement or contract with any specific insurance company, and not as an officer, traveling salaried employee or appointed agent of the insurance company, or a licensed producer holding an agent's appointment. A producer's license shall not be used as a substitute for an agent's appointment;

(2) "Insurance agent" means a person, partnership, association or corporation, or any person, partnership, association or corporation acting under a trade name, holding an insurance producer's license then in force in this state and a direct appointment in writing, by any insurance company authorized to transact business in this state, to solicit, negotiate or effect contracts of insurance or surety on behalf of such company or any member, stockholder, officer or agent of a partnership, association or corporation, or partnership, association or corporation acting under a trade name when that individual is engaged in soliciting, negotiating or effecting such contracts. "Insurance agent" shall not include persons acting as executive officers or traveling salaried employees of an insurance company authorized to transact business in this state.

§ 38a-704. Penalty for acting as insurance producer without license. Any person, partnership, association or corporation, or any person, partnership, association or corporation acting under a trade name, who acts within this state... as an insurance producer, as defined in subsection (1) of section 38a-702, unless such person holds an insurance producer license then in force from the commissioner authorizing him so to act, shall be fined not more than five hundred dollars or imprisoned not more than three months or both.

§ 38a-706. Sharing commission. Any licensed producer may share with any other licensed producer his commission on insurance business brought to him by such other licensed producer, provided such insurance business shall be of such character as such other licensed producer is licensed to transact.

§ 38a-707. Service fees chargeable by insurance producers limited. (a) No insurance producer shall have any right to compensation, other than commissions deductible from premiums on insurance policies or contracts, from any insured or prospective insured for or on account of the negotiation or procurement of, or other services in connection with, any contract of insurance made or negotiated in this state or for any other services on account of any such insurance policies or contracts, including, but not limited to, adjustment of claims arising therefrom, unless such right to compensation is based upon a written memorandum, signed by the party to be charged, and specifying or clearly defining the amount or extent of such compensation, provided such compensahon is in compliance with regulations adopted pursuant to subsection (b)...

(b) The insurance commissioner may, by regulation, establish a reasonable schedule of maxlmum fees which may be charged by insurance producers or he may regulate such fees on an individual basis.

(c) Nothing herein contained shall affect the right of any such producer to recover from the insured the amount of any premium or premiums for insurance effected by or through such producer.

§ 38a-711. Payment of commissions to unlicensed persons. No insurance company or producer shall pay, directly or indirectly, any commission or other valuable consideration...for servlces performed within this state as an insurance producer unless such person, partnership or corporation holds a license to act as an insurance producer in this state, provided the provisions of this section shall not prevent the payment of renewal or other deferred commissions to formerly licensed insurance agents, brokers or producers nor shall this section apply to persons acting as executive officers or traveling salaried employees of an insurance company authorized to transact business in this state. Any person, partnership or corporation which violates any provision of this section shall be fined not more than five hundred dollars.

§ 38a-712. Report of failure of producer to remit premiums and of checks returned for insufficient funds or otherwise dishonored. (a) Each insurance company authorized or permitted to do business in this state and each residual market mechanism established pursuant to section 38a-329 shall report to the insurance commissioner (1) any failure on the part of an insurance producer or excess line broker to remit premiums... within thirty days following the due date of the account of the producer with the company, its state agent or managing general agent or (2) whenever a check issued by such producer to the company or residual market mechanism is returned for insufficient funds or otherwise dishonored and remains outstanding fifteen days following receipt of such return.

(b) If, upon investigation of a report concerning a failure to remit premiums, the commissioner determines that a producer has received premiums directly or indirectly from insureds and has failed to remit them to the proper company, its state agent or managing general agent, he may, following a hearing as specified in section 38a-774, suspend or revoke the license of the producer. Upon receipt of a report concerning a dishonored check, the commissioner shall notify the producer issuing such check of the report. If an arrangement for payment of such funds is not made to the satisfaction of the commissioner by the producer within fifteen days of receipt of such notice, the license of the producer shall be automatically suspended. The commissioner may institute procedures for the restoration of the licensee's insurance accounts to best protect the interests of all parties concerned.

(c) The commissioner may adopt such reasonable regulations as he deems necessary for the implementation of this section...

§ 38a-715. Payment by insured to producer as payment to company. Any payment made by or on behalf of an insured to any producer for policies of insurance which have been issued to such producer for delivery to the insured or issued directly to the insured on the order of such producer shall, in controversies between the insured and the company, be deemed to have been paid to the company.

§ 38a-717. Payment of commissions to producers. An insurance company or producer may pay compensation to a licensed producer, for or on account of such producer's solicitation or negotiation of contracts for insurance or suretyship which such company is authorized to write. No insurance company or producer authorized to do business in this state, shall pay compensation to any person, partnership, association or corporation of another state, to effect contracts of insurance as to which a producer's license is required..., unless such person, partnership, association or corporation of such other state has a producer's license in this state.

Georgia

Page 316, add following 33-23-10, Examination of applicants:

33-23-12. Limited licenses. (a) Except as provided in subsection (b) of this Code section for credit insurance licenses, the Commissioner may provide by rule or regulation for licenses of agents or subagents which are limited in scope to specific lines or sublines of insurance as defined in this title, and such limited license may be issued without requiring the applicant to hold an agent's license.

(b) (1) Licenses shall be issued to individual persons for the purpose of writing credit insurance as provided in this subsection. Applicants must be sponsored by an insurer authorized to write credit insurance in this state, and the applicant must certify that he or she has read and understands the provisions of this title and regulations promulgated pursuant to this title which are pertinent to credit insurance in this state.

(2) No prelicensing education or prelicensing examination shall be required for issuance of such license, and the insurer shall certify that the licensee has completed a minimum of five hours of self-study in credit insurance subjects.

(3) The lines or sublines of insurance included in the scope of authority of credit insurance licenses issued under this Code section, whether issued as an agent or subagent license, shall include, but not be limited to, the following:

(A) Credit life and credit accident and sickness insurance;

(B) Credit casualty insurance;

(C) Credit property insurance;

(D) Credit unemployment insurance;

(E) Accidental death and dismemberment insurance;

(F) Nonfiling or nonrecording insurance;

(G) Vendors' single interest insurance; and

(H) Any other lines or sublines of insurance which may become accepted as credit insurance by the insurance and lending industries unless otherwise disapproved by the Commissioner.

Hawaii

Page 322, add at end of page:

§ 431:9-222.5 Workers' compensation claims adjusters; limited license. The commissioner may issue a limited license to an adjuster who only adjusts workers' compensation claims: provided that the adjuster:

(1) Is domiciled in the State of Hawaii, or in a state that permits residents of the State of Hawaii to act as adjusters in that other state;

(2) Has had experience, special education, or training in handling loss claims under workers' compensation insurance contracts of sufficiently reasonable duration and to enable an individual to fulfill the responsibilities of an adjuster;

(3) Has a passing grade on the workers' compensation examination pursuant to section 431:9-206; and

(4) Pays the applicable fees. An adjuster with a limited license issued under this [section] may extend the license biennially upon successfully passing a reexamination on workers' compensation.

§ 431:9-230 Reporting and accounting for premiums. (a) Every licensed general agent, subagent, solicitor, and adjuster shall have the responsibilities of a trustee for all premium and return premium funds received or collected under this article.

(b) The licensee, upon receipt of the funds, shall either:

(1) Remit the premiums (less commissions) and return premiums received or held by the licensee to the insurers or the persons entitled to such funds: or

(2) Maintain the funds at all times in a federally insured account with a bank, savings and loan association, or financial services loan company situated in Hawaii, separate from the licensee's own funds or funds held by the licensee in any other capacity, in an amount at least equal to the premiums (net of commissions) and return premiums received by such licensee and unpaid to the insurers or persons entitled to such funds. Return premiums shall be returned within thirty days, unless directed otherwise in writing by the person entitled to the funds.

The licensee shall not be required to maintain a separate bank account or other account for the funds of each insurer or person entitled to such funds, if and so long as the funds held for the insurer or person entitled to such funds are reasonably ascertainable from the books of account and records of the licensee. Only such additional funds as may be reasonably necessary to pay bank, savings and loan association, or financial services loan company charges may be commingled with the premium funds. In the event the bank, savings and loan association, or financial services loan company account is an interest earning account, such licensee may not retain the interest earned on such funds to the licensee's own use or benefit without the prior written consent of the insurers or person entitled to such funds. A premium trustee account shall be designated on the records of the bank, savings and loan association, or financial services loan company as a "trustee account established pursuant to section 431:9-230, Hawaii Revised Statutes", or words of similar import.

(c) Any such licensee who, not being lawfully entitled to such funds, diverts or appropriates such funds or any portion of them to the licensee's own use, shall be guilty of embezzlement and shall be punished as provided in the criminal statutes of this State.

§ 431:9-239 Reinstatement or relicensing. The commissioner shall not reinstate the license of or relicense any licensee or former licensee as to whom a license has been suspended, revoked, or extension refused, until:

(1) Any cause for the suspension, revocation, or refusal of such license is no longer existing;

(2) Any fine levied upon the licensee pursuant to section 431:9-238 and section 431:9-240 has been fully paid; and

(3) The commissioner is satisfied that such causes for the suspension, revocation, or refusal of such license will not reoccur in the future.

Indiana

Page 331, add at end of page:

Business Transacted With Producer-Controlled Property And Casualty Insurers
(Effective September 1994):

SECTION		SECTION	
27-1-35-1	Applicability.	27-1-35-11	Contract between controlling producer and controlled insurer.
27-1-35-2	"Accredited state" defined.		
27-1-35-3	"Captive insurer" defined.		
27-1-35-4	"Control" — "Controlled" defined.	27-1-35-12	Audit committee.
		27-1-35-13	Annual report on loss ratios and reserves.
27-1-35-5	"Controlled insurer" defined.		
27-1-35-6	"Controlling producer" defined.	27-1-35-14	Annual report on commissions.
27-1-35-7	"Licensed insurer" defined — "Insurer" defined.	27-1-35-15	Notice of relationship between producer and controlled insurer.
27-1-35-8	"Producer" defined.	27-1-35-16	Order to cease business.
27-1-35-9	Applicability — Amount of premiums.	27-1-35-17	Civil action — Intervention.
27-1-35-10	Nonapplicability of 27-1-35-11 through IC 27-1-35-14.	27-1-35-18	Sanctions.
		27-1-35-19	Other penalties — Rights.

§ 27-1-35-1. Applicability. This chapter applies to licensed insurers either domiciled in Indiana or domiciled in a state that is not an accredited state having in effect a substantially similar law. All provisions of the Insurance Holding Company System Regulation Act, to the extent the provisions are not superseded by this chapter, continue to apply to all parties within holding company systems subject to this chapter.

§ 27-1-35-2. "Accredited state" defined. ...[A] state in which the insurance department or regulatory agency has qualified as meeting the minimum financial regulatory standards promulgated...by the National Association of Insurance Commissioners (NAIC).

§ 27-1-35-5. "Controlled insurer" defined. ...[A] licensed insurer that is controlled, directly or indirectly, by a producer.

§ 27-1-35-6. "Controlling producer" defined. ...[A] producer that, directly or indirectly, controls an insurer.

§ 27-1-35-7. "Licensed insurer" defined. "Insurer" defined. "...[L]icensed insurer" or "insurer" means any person, firm, association, or corporation licensed to transact a property/casualty insurance business in Indiana. The following are not licensed insurers for the purposes of this chapter:

(1) All risk retention groups (as defined in the Superfund Amendments Reauthorization Act of 1986, Pub. L. No. 99-499, 100 Stat. 1613 (1986), the Risk Retention Act, 15 U.S.C. Section 3901 et seq. (1982 & Supp. 1986), and IC 27-7-10-11).

(2) All residual market pools and joint underwriting authorities or associations.

(3) All captive insurers.

§ 27-1-35-8. "Producer" defined. ...[A]n insurance broker or brokers or any other person, firm, association, or corporation, when, for any compensation, commission, or other thing of value, the person, firm, association, or corporation acts or aids in any manner in soliciting, negotiating, or procuring the making of any insurance contract on behalf of an insured other than the person, firm, association or corporation.

§ 27-1-35-11. Contract between controlling producer and controlled insurer. A controlled insurer shall not accept business from a controlling producer and a controlling producer shall not place business with a controlled insurer unless there is a written contract...specifying the responsibilities of each party, which contract has been approved by the board of directors of the controlled insurer and contains the following minimum provisions:

(1) The controlled insurer may terminate the contract for cause, upon written notice to the controlling producer. The controlled insurer shall suspend the authority of the controlling producer to write business during the pendency of any dispute regarding the cause for the termination.

(2) The controlling producer shall render accounts to the controlled insurer detailing all material transactions, including infor-

Indiana

mation necessary to support all commissions, charges, and other fees received by or owing to the controlling producer.

(3) The controlling producer shall remit all funds due under the terms of the contract to the controlled insurer on at least a monthly basis. The due date shall be fixed so that premiums or installments of premiums collected shall be remitted not later than ninety (90) days after the effective date of any policy placed with the controlled insurer under this contract.

(4) All funds collected for the controlled insurer's account shall be held by the controlling producer in a fiduciary capacity, in one (1) or more appropriately identified bank accounts in banks that are members of the Federal Reserve System, in accordance with the provisions of the insurance law as applicable. However, funds of a controlling producer not required to be licensed in Indiana shall be maintained in compliance with the requirements of the controlling producer's domiciliary jurisdiction.

(5) The controlling producer shall maintain separately identifiable records of business written for the controlled insurer.

(6) The contract shall not be assigned in whole or in part by the controlling producer.

(7) The controlled insurer shall provide the controlling producer with the controlled insurer's underwriting standards, rules, and procedures, manuals setting forth the rates to be charged, and the conditions for the acceptance or rejection of risks. The controlling producer shall adhere to the standards, rules, procedures, rates, and conditions. The standards, rules, procedures, rates, and conditions shall be the same as those applicable to comparable business placed with the controlled insurer by a producer other than the controlling producer.

(8) The rates and terms of the controlling producer's commissions, charges, or other fees, and the purposes for those charges or fees. The rates of the commissions, charges, and other fees shall be no greater than those applicable to comparable business placed with the controlled insurer by producers other than controlling producers. For purposes of this subdivision and subdivision (7), examples of "comparable business" include the same lines of insurance, same kinds of insurance, same kinds of risks, similar policy limits, and similar quality of business.

(9) If the contract provides that the controlling producer, on insurance business placed with the insurer, is to be compensated contingent upon the insurer's profits on that business, then such compensation shall not be determined and paid until at least five

(5) years after the premiums on liability insurance are earned and at least one (1) year after the premiums are earned on any other insurance. The commissions may not be paid until the adequacy of the controlled insurer's reserves on remaining claims has been independently verified under § 13 [IC 27-1-35-13] of this chapter.

(10) A limit on the controlling producer's writings in relation to the controlled insurer's surplus and total writings. The insurer may establish a different limit for each line or sub-line of business. The controlled insurer shall notify the controlling producer when the applicable limit is approached and shall not accept business from the controlling producer if the limit is reached. The controlling producer shall not place business with the controlled insurer if the controlling producer has been notified by the controlled insurer that the limit has been reached.

(11) The controlling producer may negotiate but shall not bind reinsurance on behalf of the controlled insurer on business the controlling producer places with the controlled insurer, except that the controlling producer may bind facultative reinsurance contracts under obligatory facultative agreements if the contract with the controlled insurer contains underwriting guidelines, including for both reinsurance assumed and ceded a list of reinsurers with which such automatic agreements are in effect, the coverages and amounts or percentages that may be reinsured, and commission schedules.

§ 27-1-35-15. Notice of relationship between producer and controlled insurer. A producer, before the effective date of the policy, shall deliver written notice to the prospective insured disclosing the relationship between the producer and the controlled insurer, except that, if the business is placed through a subproducer who is not a controlling producer, the controlling producer shall retain in the controlling producer's records a signed commitment from the subproducer that the subproducer is aware of the relationship between the insurer and the producer and that the subproducer has or will notify the insured.

Louisiana

Page 346, add at end of page:

PART XXV-A. PRELICENSE AND CONTINUING EDUCATIONAL PROGRAMS

Section
1194. Louisiana Consortium of Insurance and Financial Services; creation.
1194.1. Purpose.
1194.2. Board of directors.
1194.3. Advisory committee.

Section
1194.4. Powers and duties of the consortium.
1194.5. Powers and duties of the advisory committee.
1194 6. Plan of operation.
1194.7. Funds.

§ 1194. Louisiana Consortium of Insurance and Financial Services; creation. There is hereby created a public nonprofit unincorporated legal entity known as the "Louisiana Consortium of Insurance and Financial Services". The consortium shall be domiciled at Louisiana State University and Agricultural and Mechanical College at Shreveport. The consortium shall perform its functions under a plan of operation established under R.S. 22:1194.6 and shall exercise its powers through a board of directors with the advice and consent of an advisory committee.

§ 1194.1. Purpose. The purpose of the consortium shall be to promote the development of academic courses in insurance and financial services, to encourage the establishment of a subspecialty degree program in insurance and financial services, and to develop, promote, and administer continuing education courses and professional development for the insurance industry.

§ 1194.2 Board of directors. A. The board of directors of the consortium shall consist of eleven persons serving terms as established in the plan of operation. The board shall be composed of five members representing the insurance industry and selected by the Financial Security Study

Foundation of Louisiana, Incorporated, two persons selected by the commissioner of insurance, one member of the Senate Committee on Insurance selected by the president of the Senate, one member of the House Committee on Insurance selected by the speaker of the House of Representatives, and two members representing Louisiana State University at Shreveport selected by the chancellor. Legislative members shall serve as ex officio members only.

B. Members of the board shall serve without compensation but may be reimbursed for expenses incurred as members of the board of directors. Legislative members shall receive such per diem and expenses as provided for legislators during attendance of committee meetings.

C. The powers and duties of the board of directors shall be:

(1) To develop, promote, and administer the Louisiana Insurance and Financial Education Consortium.

(2) To provide direction and guidance to the advisory committee.

(3) To report periodically to the commissioner of insurance.

§ 1194.4. Powers and duties of the consortium. The consortium shall:

(1) Provide direction, oversight, and information to consortium members.

(2) Increase the quality of standards for insurance and financial services practice and education in the state of Louisiana.

(3) Develop and offer to consortium members academic courses and curricula and continuing professional education in insurance and financial services.

(4) Develop means and mechanisms for increasing the public awareness of the issues and concerns of the insurance and financial services industry.

(5) Develop and provide means for delivering credit and noncredit instruction from qualified insurance professors to consortium members.

§ 1194.5. Powers and duties of the advisory committee. The advisory committee shall:

(1) Under the supervision and guidance of the board of directors, develop and implement policies, practices, and procedures for the daily operation of the consortium.

(2) Plan and implement strategies for the accomplishment of the purpose of the consortium.

(3) Report periodically to the board of directors.

§ 1194.6. Plan of operation. A. (1) The consortium shall submit to the commissioner a plan of operation and any amendments thereto necessary or suitable to assure the fair, reasonable, and equitable administration of the

Louisiana

consortium. The plan of operation and any amendments thereto shall become effective either upon the commissioner's written approval or thirty days after submission if he has not disapproved it.

(2) If the consortium fails to submit a suitable plan of operation within one hundred twenty days following September 30, 1995, or if at any time thereafter the consortium fails to submit suitable amendments to the plan, the commissioner shall, after notice and hearing, adopt and promulgate such reasonable rules as are necessary or advisable to effectuate the provisions of this Part. The rules shall continue in force until modified by the commissioner or superseded by a plan submitted by the consortium and approved by the commissioner.

B. The plan of operation shall:

(1) Establish the procedure for the election of officers of the board of directors for the consortium.

(2) Establish procedures whereby all the powers and duties of the consortium and the advisory committee under R.S. 22:1194.2 and 1194.3 will be performed.

(3) Establish the amount and method of reimbursing the members under R.S. 22:1194.2 and 1194.3.

(4) Establish regular places and times for meetings of the board of directors.

(5) Establish procedures for records to be kept of all financial transactions of the consortium, its agents, and the board of directors.

(6) Establish additional provisions necessary or proper for the execution of the powers and duties of the consortium....

C. The books and records of the consortium shall be subject to audit by the legislative auditor.

Page 347, add at beginning of page:

(Excerpts from Maine Rev. Stat. Ann. title 24-A § 1401 *et. seq.*)

§ 1411. License required

1. Producer. A person may not act as or purport to be an insurance producer or limited insurance producer or engage in producer activities with respect to insurance risks resident, located or to be performed in this State or elsewhere for any kind or kinds of insurance unless licensed for such a kind or kinds in accordance with this chapter.
2. Consultant; adjuster. A person may not act as or purport to be a consultant with respect to insurance risks resident, located or to be performed in this State or elsewhere unless licensed as a consultant under this chapter. A person may not act as or purport to be an adjuster unless licensed as an adjuster under this chapter, except as provided in section 1475.
3. Insurance business. A person may not for a fee or commission engage in the business of offering any advice, counsel, opinion or similar service with respect to the benefits, advantages or disadvantages under any policy of insurance that is issued in this State unless that person is:
A. Engaged or employed as an attorney licensed in this State to practice law;
B. A licensed insurance producer offering advice concerning a kind of insurance for which the insurance producer is licensed to transact business and does not receive a separate fee for rendering such advice other than commissions or fees for the sale of an insurance or annuity policy;
C. An actuary or a certified public accountant engaged or employed in a consulting capacity, performing duties incidental to that position;
D. A licensed adjuster acting within the scope of the license; or
E. A licensed insurance consultant acting within the scope of the license.
4. Liability. A licensee is personally liable under any insurance contract made by or through the licensee that is outside the scope of the license authority. An insurance contract issued on an application solicited, received, or for-

warded by an unlicensed person and otherwise valid is not thereby rendered invalid.

§ 1417. Suspension; revocation; refusal of license

1. Suspension. Notwithstanding Title 5, chapter 375, subchapter VI, the superintendent may, after notice and opportunity for hearing, deny, revoke, suspend, or limit the permissible activities under any license issued under this chapter, including agency licenses, or any surplus lines broker license if the superintendent finds that, as to the applicant or licensee, any of the following causes exist:

A. For any cause for which issuance of the license could have been refused had it then existed and been known to the superintendent;

B. For a violation or noncompliance with any applicable provision of this Title or for willful violation of any rule or order of the superintendent;

C. For obtaining or attempting to obtain any license through misrepresentation, failure to disclose a material fact required to be disclosed in the application or fraud;

D. For misappropriation or conversion of money belonging to others to the applicant's or licensee's own use or for illegal withholding of money or failure under the license to remit money received in the conduct of business belonging to policyholders, insurers, beneficiaries or others;

E. For material misrepresentation of the teems of any existing or proposed insurance contract;

F. For willful over insurance of property located in this State;

G. For holding at the same time licenses as a resident insurance producer in this State and any other state; or

H. If in the conduct of the licensee's affairs under the license, the licensee has used fraudulent, coercive, or dishonest practices, or has been shown to be incompetent, untrustworthy, financially irresponsible or a source of injury and loss to the public.

2. Agency suspension. The superintendent may deny, suspend, revoke or limit the permissible activities under an agency license if cause exists to deny, suspend, revoke or limit the permissible activities under a person's license who is affiliated to the agency.

3. Voluntary surrender. The superintendent may, after notice and opportunity for a hearing under this section. deem the license suspended or revoked of a previously licensed person who voluntarily surrendered an insurance license.

4. Exceptional circumstances. The superintendent may revoke or suspend any license issued under this chapter, pursuant to Title 5, section 10004, without

proceeding in conformity with chapter 3 or Title 5, chapter 375, subchapter IV or VI, when:

A. The decision to take that action is based solely upon a conviction in court of any offense under Title 5, section 5301, subsection 2, or a conviction in the courts of any other state or country of an offense under Title 5, section 5301, had the offense occurred in this State. Any revocation, suspension or denial of license under this paragraph must be in accordance with Title 5, sections 5302 to 5304;

B. The license has been issued upon the basis of a reciprocal agreement with another government and the action in this State is based upon evidence, in the form of a certified copy, that the authority issuing the license that provided the basis for reciprocal licensing in this State has revoked or suspended the licensee's license;

C. The health or physical safety of a person or persons is in immediate jeopardy at the time of the superintendent's action and, acting in accordance with chapter 3 or Title 5, chapter 375, subchapter IV or VI, the superintendent would fail to adequately respond to a known risk, provided that the revocation, suspension or refusal to renew does not continue for more than 30 days;

D. The licensee has failed after being notified twice by regular mail at the licensee's last known address to pay any money due the superintendent; or

E. The licensee has failed after being notified twice by regular mail at the licensee's last known address to comply within 60 days with continuing education requirements pursuant to section 1482.

§ 1441-A. Appointment of insurance producers or agencies

1. Appointment. Each insurer, health maintenance organization, fraternal benefit society, nonprofit hospital or medical service organization, viatical settlement provider or risk retention group appointing an insurance producer or agency in this State shall appoint the producer or agency in writing, specifying the kinds of insurance or annuity business to be transacted by the insurance producer or agency for the insurer, health maintenance organization, fraternal benefit society, nonprofit hospital or medical service organization, viatical settlement provider or risk retention group, and shall pay the appointment fee at the rate specified in section 601. The insurer, health maintenance organization, fraternal benefit society, nonprofit hospital or medical service organization, viatical settlement provider or risk retention group may forward new appointment fees to the superin-

tendent on a quarterly basis. The insurer, health maintenance organization, fraternal benefit society, nonprofit hospital or medical service organization, viatical settlement provider or risk retention group need not file the appointments with the superintendent but shall maintain the appointments in the insurer's office. Upon request of the superintendent, the insurer, health maintenance organization, fraternal benefit society, nonprofit hospital or medical service organization, viatical settlement provider or risk retention group shall provide copies of appointments to the superintendent within 14 days unless the request is part of an examination pursuant to section 221. The insurer, health maintenance organization, fraternal benefit society, nonprofit hospital or medical service organization, viatical settlement provider or risk retention group shall designate and maintain a list of each insurance producer within an appointed agency that represents the insurer, health maintenance organization, fraternal benefit society, nonprofit hospital or medical service organization, viatical settlement provider or risk retention group. The fee for designation of an insurance producer within an agency is the same as for an appointment. The insurer, health maintenance organization, fraternal benefit society, nonprofit hospital or medical service organization, viatical settlement provider or risk retention group shall pay the full appointment fee without regard to the effective date of the appointment. An insurance producer who qualifies to be licensed to sell variable annuity contracts pursuant to section 1411 must be separately appointed as to variable annuities and the insurer, health maintenance organization, fraternal benefit society, nonprofit hospital or medical service organization, viatical settlement provider or risk retention group shall pay a separate appointment fee for the appointment.

§ 1441-B. Termination of producer or agency appointment.

1. Termination. Subject to the producer's or agency's contract obligations and rights, if any, an insurer, health maintenance organization, fraternal benefit society, nonprofit hospital or medical service organization, viatical settlement provider, risk retention group, agency, or producer may terminate a producer's or agency's appointment at any time. If the insurer, health maintenance organization, fraternal benefit society, nonprofit hospital or medical service organization, viatical settlement provider or risk retention group intends to terminate the producer's or agency's authority to represent

the insurer, health maintenance organization fraternal benefit society, nonprofit hospital or medical service organization, viatical settlement provider or risk retention group for any kind of business, the insurer, health maintenance organization, fraternal benefit society, nonprofit hospital or medical service organization, viatical settlement provider or risk retention group shall provide 90 days' advance written notice of the termination or modification to the producer or agency. A notice is not required when:

A. The producer or agency is subject to suspension or revocation of license under section 1417;
B. The producer or agency fails to pay money due the insurer, health maintenance organization, fraternal benefit society, nonprofit hospital or medical service organization, viatical settlement provider or risk retention group;
C. There is a sale or merger of the agency;
D. There is an insolvency or bankruptcy of the agency;
E. The producer or agency holds a limited license;
F. The producer or agency is an employee of an insurer, health maintenance organization, fraternal benefit society, nonprofit hospital or medical service organization, viatical settlement provider or risk retention group or when the producer or agency by contractual agreement represents only one insurer, health maintenance organization, fraternal benefit society, nonprofit hospital or medical service organization, viatical settlement provider or risk retention group or a group of affiliated insurers and the property rights in the renewals are owned by the insurer, health maintenance organization, fraternal benefit society, nonprofit hospital or medical service organization, viatical settlement provider or risk retention group or a group of affiliated insurers. An insurer, health maintenance organization, fraternal benefit society, nonprofit hospital or medical service organization, viatical settlement provider or risk retention group may not cancel or renew policies as a result of the termination of the producer's or agency's contract under this paragraph;
G. The producer has died or been adjudicated as incompetent if the producer is a natural person;
H. The agency or producer has dissolved if the agency or producer is a corporation;
I. A date mutually agreed upon by an insurer, health maintenance organization, fraternal benefit society, nonprofit hospital or medical service organization, viatical settlement provider or risk retention group and the agency or producer has been reached;

J. An insurer, health maintenance organization, fraternal benefit society, nonprofit hospital or medical service organization, viatical settlement provider or risk retention group and the agency or producer have mutually agreed upon other terms; or
K. All insurers' licenses or appointments terminate or expire.

2. Notice. Notice of cancellation of an appointment must be maintained in the insurer's office and must be forwarded to the superintendent within 14 days of a request from the superintendent.
3. Rights of insureds. The termination of an appointment under this section does not affect the rights of insureds.

Montana

Page 374, add at the beginning of page:

§ 33-17-211. General qualifications — application for license.

(1) An individual applying for a license shall apply on a form specified by the commissioner and declare under penalty of refusal, suspension, or revocation of the license that statements made in the application are true, correct, and complete to the best of the individual's knowledge and belief. Before approving the application, the commissioner shall verify that the individual:

(a) is 18 years of age or older;

(b) has not committed an act that is a ground for refusal, suspension, or revocation as set forth in 33-17-1001;

(c) has paid the license fees stated in 33-2-708;

(d) has successfully passed the examinations for each kind of insurance for which the individual has applied within 12 months of application;

(e) is a resident of this state or of another state that grants similar privileges to residents of this state. Licenses issued based upon Montana state residency terminate if the licensee relocates to another state;

(f) is competent, trustworthy, and of good reputation;

(g) has experience or training or otherwise is qualified in the kind or kinds of insurance for which the applicant applies to be licensed and is reasonably familiar with the provisions of this code which govern the applicant's operations as an insurance producer; and

(h) if applying for a license as to life or disability insurance:

(i) is not a funeral director, undertaker, or mortician operating in this or any other state;

(ii) is not an officer, employee, or representative of a funeral director, undertaker, or mortician operating in this or any other state; or

(iii) does not hold an interest in or benefit from a business of a funeral director, undertaker, or mortician operating in this or any other state.

(2) A person acting as an insurance producer shall obtain a license. A person shall apply for a license on a form specified by the commissioner. Before approving the application, the commissioner shall verify that:

(a) the person meets the requirements listed in subsection (1);

(b) the person has paid the licensing fees stated in 33-2-708 for each individual licensed in conjunction with the person's license. A licensed person shall promptly notify the commissioner of each change relating to an individual listed in the license.

(c) the person has designated a licensed officer responsible for compliance by the person with the insurance laws and rules of this state;

(d) each member and employee of a partnership and each officer, director, stockholder, or employee of a corporation who is acting as an insurance producer in this state has obtained a license;

(e) (i) if the person is a partnership or corporation, the transaction of insurance business is within the purposes stated in the partnership agreement or the articles of incorporation; and

(ii) if the person is a corporation, the secretary of state has issued a certificate of existence or authorization under 35-1-1312 or filed articles of incorporation under 35-1-220.

(3) The commissioner may license as a resident insurance producer an association of licensed Montana insurance producers, whether or not incorporated, formed and existing substantially for purposes other than insurance. The license must be used solely for the purpose of enabling the association to place, as a resident insurance producer, insurance of the properties, interests, and risks of the state of Montana and of other public agencies, bodies, and institutions and to receive the customary commission for the placement. The president and secretary of the association shall apply for the license in the name of the association, and the commissioner shall issue the license to the association in its name alone. The fee for the license is the same as that required by 33-2-708 for the license of an insurance producer. The commissioner may, after a hearing with notice to the association, revoke the license if the commissioner finds that continuation of the license is not in the public interest or that a ground listed in 33-17-1001 exists.

(4) An insurance producer using an assumed business name shall register the name with the commissioner before using it.

Nevada

Page 383, add at end of existing text:

§ 683A.270. Renewal and expiration of license.

(1) Each license issued under this code continues in force until it expires or is suspended, revoked or otherwise terminated, subject to payment of the applicable fee for renewal and a fee of $15 for deposit in the insurance recovery account created by NRS 679B.305 to the commissioner at his office in Carsor City, Nevada, on or before the last day of the month in which the license is renewable. The fees must be accompanied by a written request for renewal of the license. The request must be made and signed:

(a) By the licensee in the case of a broker's, nonresident broker's, surplus lines broker's, agent's or managing general agent's license.

(b) By the employing agent or broker in the case of a solicitor's license.

(c) By the employing title insurer or agent in the case of an escrow officer.

(2) Any license referred to in subsection 1 which is not continued on or before the last day specified for its renewal shall be deemed to have expired at midnight on that day. The commissioner may accept a request for renewal received by him within 30 days thereafter if it is accompanied by a renewal fee of 150 percent of the fee otherwise required and the fee of $15 for deposit in the insurance recovery account created by NRS 679B.305.

(3) If the commissioner has reason to believe that any licensed agent, broker or solicitor has for any cause raised a reasonable question as to the competence of the licensee or of any natural person designated to exercise the license powers of a firm or corporate licensee, the commissioner may require, as a condition to continuation of the license, that the licensee or natural person take and pass to the commissioner's satisfaction a written examination as required under this chapter of natural persons who intend to apply for a similar license.

(4) The commissioner may by regulation require the successful completion of a reasonable number of appropriate courses of

study as a condition to continuation of any license to which this section applies.

(5) The license of a managing general agent for a particular insurer or underwriter's department must be terminated by the commissioner upon written request by that insurer or department.

(6) This section does not apply to temporary licenses issued under NRS 683A.300.

§ 683A.290. Termination of appointment of agent; termination of employment of solicitor.

(1) Subject to an agent's contract rights, if any, an insurer may terminate the agent's appointment, resident or nonresident, at any time. The insurer shall promptly give written notice of any termination for cause, the effective date thereof and the reason for termination to the commissioner, on forms prescribed by the commissioner, and to the agent if reasonably possible. The commissioner may require of the insurer reasonable proof that the insurer has also given such a notice to the agent if reasonably possible. Any information or document so disclosed or furnished to the commissioner shall be deemed a qualifiedly privileged communication and is not admissible as evidence in any action or proceeding unless so permitted by the insurer in writing.

(2) An agent or broker terminating the employment and license of a solicitor shall promptly give written notice of termination and such proof as required pursuant to subsection 1 to the commissioner, together with all information related to the reasons for termination. Such information shall be deemed a privileged communication unless the privilege is waived in writing by the agent or broker.

(3) No agreement between an insurer and agent, or between an employing agent or broker and a licensed solicitor, affects the commissioner's termination of the appointment or license if so requested by the insurer or by the agent or broker, as the case may be.

Utah

Page 440, add at beginning of page:

§ 31A-23-215. Organization licensees — Reports — Suspension, revocation, or limitation of license.

(1) Every two years, on a date specified by rule, each organization licensed as an agent, managing general agent, broker, or consultant shall report to the commissioner, in a form the commissioner establishes by rule, all natural person agents, brokers, or consultants acting in those capacities for the organization.

(2) Organizations licensed under this chapter shall report to the commissioner promptly, in the detail and form prescribed by rule, every change in the list of natural person agents, managing general agents, brokers, or consultants authorized to act in those capacities for the organization.

(3) (a) Organizations licensed under this chapter shall report to the commissioner the cause of termination of a designated licensee's appointment. The information provided the commissioner shall remain confidential.

(b) An organization is immune from civil action, civil penalty, or damages if the organization complies in good faith with Subsection (3) in reporting to the commissioner the cause of termination of licensees' appointments. Notwithstanding any other provision in this section, an organization is not immune from any action or resulting penalty imposed on the reporting organization as a result of proceedings brought by or on behalf of the department if the action is based on evidence other than the report submitted in compliance with Subsection (3).

(4) Organizations licensed under this chapter may act in the capacities for which they are licensed only through natural persons who are licensed under this chapter to act in the same manner.

(5) Organizations licensed under this chapter shall designate and report promptly to the commissioner the name of at least one natural person who has authority to act on behalf of the organization in all matters pertaining to compliance with this title and orders of the commissioner.

(6) When a license is held by an organization, both the organization itself and any persons named on the license shall, for purposes of this section, be considered to be the holders of the license. If a person named on the organization license commits any act or fails to perform any duty that is a ground for suspending, revoking, or limiting the organization license, the commissioner may suspend, revoke, or limit the license of that person or of the organization, or both.

§ 31A-23-216. Termination of license.

(1) A license issued under this chapter remains in force until:

(a) revoked, suspended, or limited under Subsection (2);

(b) lapsed under Subsection (3);

(c) surrendered to and accepted by the commissioner; or

(d) the licensee dies or is adjudicated incompetent as defined under Title 75, Chapter 5, Part 3 or 4.

(2) (a) After an adjudicative proceeding under Title 63, Chapter 46b, Administrative Procedures Act, the commissioner may revoke, suspend, or limit in whole or in part the license of any agent, broker, surplus lines broker, or consultant who is found:

(i) to be unqualified;

(ii) to have violated an insurance statute, valid rule under Subsection 31A-2-201(3), or a valid order under Subsection 31A-2-201(4); or

(iii) if the licensee's methods and practices in the conduct of business endanger the legitimate interests of customers and the public.

(b) Every order suspending a license issued under this chapter shall specify the period for which the suspension is effective, but in no event may the period exceed 12 months.

(3) Any license issued under this chapter shall lapse if the licensee fails to pay when due a fee under Section 31A-3-103. The commissioner shall by rule prescribe the license renewal and reinstatement procedures, in accordance with Title 63, Chapter 46a, Utah Administrative Rulemaking Act.

(4) A licensee under this chapter whose license is suspended, revoked, or lapsed, but who continues to act as a licensee, is subject to the penalties for acting as a licensee without a license.

(5) Any person licensed in this state shall immediately report to the commissioner:

(a) a suspension or revocation of that person's license in any other state, District of Columbia, or territory of the United States;

(b) the imposition of a disciplinary sanction imposed on that person by any other state, District of Columbia, or territory of the United States; and

(c) a judgment or injunction entered against that person on the basis of conduct involving fraud, deceit, misrepresentation, or violation of an insurance law or rule.

(6) An order revoking a license under Subsection (2) may specify a time, not to exceed five years, within which the former licensee may not apply for a new license. If no time is specified, the former licensee may not apply for a new license for five years without express approval by the commissioner.

(7) Any person whose license is suspended or revoked under Subsection (2) shall, when the suspension ends or a new license is issued, pay all fees that would have been payable if the license had not been suspended or revoked, unless the commissioner by order waives the payment of the interim fees. If a new license is issued more than three years after the revocation of a similar license, this subsection applies only to the fees that would have accrued during the three years immediately following the revocation.

Index to Supplement Material

References are to section numbers. For a full discussion of the topics covered in this supplement, be sure to consult the main volume as well.

Accounting §1.4, §4.4, §4.8, §6.7, §6.8
Actual cash value vs. replacement cost §5.5, §6.6
Advice of agent or broker §5.3, §6.5
Age Discrimination in Employment Act §4.7
Agency contracts §4.1
Agent of record §5.12
Agent's duties to insurer §4.5
Agreements to procure insurance §6.3
Alternate employer endorsement §6.6
Annuity §6.2, §6.7
Apparent authority §1.4, §4.5, §5.7, §6.4, §6.7, §6.8
Application for coverage §1.4, §5.2, §5.3, §6.4, §6.8
    Filling out application §5.3
    Forwarding the application §5.4
Assignment of claims §5.12
Attorneys' fees as damages §6.1
Auto liability §5.5
Authority to bind insurer §1.4, §3.5, §6.3, §6.4, §6.8

Bad faith §5.2, §5.6, §5.12
    Agent's lack of liability for insurer's bad faith §5.2
    Wrongful denial of claim §5.12
Binders and certificates of insurance §5.7 *See also* Authority to bind insurer
Breach of agreement §6.3
Breach of contract §1.4, §4.4, §4.5, §4.8, §5.2, §5.8, §5.9, §5.10, §6.1, §6.3, §6.6
Brokers:
    Advice to insured §6.5
    Agent of insurer §6.4, §6.8
    Agent of the insured §6.1
    Authority to bind insurer §1.4, §6.8, §7.2
    Duties to insured §6.2
    Failure to cancel policy §6.8
    Knowledge of loss §5.12, §6.8
    Negligence not imputed to insurer §6.8
    Presumed diligent §5.6
Building code §6.5
Business interruption §5.5, §6.2, §6.5, §6.6

Cancellation:
    For nonpayment §1.4, §6.3, §6.7, §7.3
    Failure to cancel §6.8
    Prior to loss §6.7
Cash value vs. replacement cost
    See Actual cash value vs. replacement cost
Certificates of insurance §5.7
    See also Authority to bind
Changing health insurers §6.9
Claims adjuster (insurer's agent) §5.12
Claims handling §5.12, §6.8
Claims-made policies §6.8
Client lists §4.8
COBRA §6.9
Collecting and transmitting premiums §3.3, §5.9, §6.7, §6.8
    No coverage under E&O policies §4.9
Commissions §3.5, §4.1, §4.4
Constructive termination §4.6
Conversion §4.9, §5.9, §6.2, §6.7
Covenants not to compete §4.8

Deceptive Trade Practices Act §5.2, §5.5, §7.1, §7.4
Deduction of premium from paycheck §6.2
Defamation §4.7
Defaults §5.11
Delay
    In notice §5.12

In payment §6.8
In processing application §5.4
Delivery of policy §6.8
Designated beneficiaries §5.3, §6.2
Directors and officers liability §5.12, §6.8
Disability benefits §7.1
Dual agencies §2.6, §6.9
Duty to advise §5.2
Duty of good faith and fair dealing §5.12
Duty to defend §4.9, §5.5

E&O — Exclusions §4.9, §6.7
Economic duress §5.12
Emotional distress §5.12
Employee as insured §6.9
Employer's collection of premiums §2.6, §6.9
Employers liability §6.1
ERISA §2.6, §3.5, §5.2, §5.3, §6.6, §6.9, §7.1, §7.3
Excess coverage §2.3, §3.3, §5.12, §6.3
Experience rating premium endorsement §4.9
Extraterritorial coverage §6.3
Extreme and outrageous conduct §5.12

Failure to disclose material information §5.2
Failure to forward premiums §6.7

Index

Fair Housing Act §4.7
Fidelity bonds and E&O coverage §4.9
Fiduciary duties §5.6, §5.9, §6.1, §6.2, §6.9
Fraud §1.4, §5.6, §6.2, §6.7, §7.3

Gaps in coverage §6.8
General agent §2.1, §5.7, §6.8
Group insurance §5.3, §5.6, §6.2, §6.3, §6.9

Health insurance §2.6, §4.5, §5.3, §5.9, §6.3, §6.4, §6.9

Increasing limits §5.5
Innocent misrepresentation §7.1
Insolvency §4.9, §5.6
Issuing the policy §5.8
Insurance requirement in loan document §5.5
Insurance requirement in lease §5.2, §5.5, §6.6

Knowledge of existing claim §5.5

Lapse and nonrenewal §5.7
Licensing qualifications §3.3, §3.5
Life insurance §4.5, §5.3, §5.4, §5.9, §6.3, §6.9
Liquor liability coverage §3.5, §4.5, §6.8
Loss of goods in transit §5.5

Marketing brochures §7.1
Marketing practices §5.6
Misappropriation of funds §1.4, §3.3, §4.5
Misrepresentation §5.6, §5.8, §6.8, §7.1
Misrepresentation on application §5.2, §5.3, §6.4, §7.1, §7.2, §7.3
Misrepresenting employee status §6.9

Negligence §4.5, §6.3
Nonadmitted company §3.3, §5.6, §6.8
Nonresident insurance agent license §3.3
Notice of claim §4.9, §5.5, §5.12, §6.8
Notice of nonrenewal or cancellation §5.2, §5.7
Notice of termination §4.6
Notice to broker §6.1, §6.8
Notifying insureds of termination §4.6

Obtaining coverage that was ordered §5.5, §6.2
Oral modification of binder §5.7
Overpayment §6.7

Payroll deductions §2.6, §6.9
Placing coverage (duty of care) §5.2, §5.5, §6.6
Policy limits §2.1, §6.5, §6.8, §7.1

Post-termination obligations
    §4.8
Power of attorney §5.10
Preexisting conditions §5.3,
    §6.8
Premium financing §3.3, §5.10,
    §6.7
Procure the requested coverage
    §5.2, §6.6
Product liability §5.12
Psychiatric benefits §5.2, §7.1

Ratification of broker's acts
    §6.1, §6.7
"Reasonable consumer" doctrine
    §5.2, §6.1
Rebating premiums §3.3
Release of claim against insurer
    §6.6
Renewal by broker §6.1, §6.7
Replevin §4.8
Restriction on branch offices
    §4.7
Restriction on writing new
    business §4.6
Retroactive coverage §5.5, §6.9
    Preexisting claims §4.5

Servicing rights §4.6
Soliciting agents §2.3
Solvent insurers §5.6
Sprinkler system §6.5

Statutory authority §6.8
Subagents §2.4, §4.4
Surplus lines §5.6

Taking applications for coverage
    §1.4, §5.2, §6.4, §6.8
Termination of agency §4.6,
    §4.7, §5.6
    Broker's duties §6.2
    Constructive termination
    §4.6
    Post-termination obligations
    §4.8
    Terminations for cause §4.7
Third-party administrator §5.9
Tortious interference with
    contract §4.7, §4.8
Trade secrets §4.8
Transmitting premiums §5.9
Treble damages (fraud and
    misrepresentation) §7.1

Unauthorized insurer §5.12
Underinsured motorist coverage
    §5.2, §6.6
Unfair trade practices §4.6, §7.4

Wind damage §6.8
Wrongful denial of claim §5.12
Wrongful discharge §5.2, §6.1
Wrongful termination of agency
    §4.6, §4.7